CW01661950

Word Aware 2 – Access your online resources

Word Aware 2 is accompanied by a number of printable online materials, designed to ensure this resource best supports your professional needs.

Activate your accompanying online resources

- Go to www.routledge.com/cw/speechmark then click on the cover of this book
- Click the 'Sign in or Request Access' button and follow the instructions, in order to access your accompanying online resources

Word Aware 2

Teaching vocabulary in the Early Years

Stephen Parsons & Anna Branagan

Routledge
Taylor & Francis Group
LONDON AND NEW YORK

Please note that, for simplicity, throughout this book 'he' is used to refer to children and 'parents' to refer to parents, guardians and carers.

First published 2016 by Speechmark Publishing Ltd.

Published 2017 by Routledge
2 Park Square, Milton Park, Abingdon, Oxon OX14 4RN
711 Third Avenue, New York, NY 10017, USA

Routledge is an imprint of the Taylor & Francis Group, an informa business

British Library Cataloguing in Publication Data

A catalogue record for this book is available from the British Library

ISBN 9781909301672 (pbk)

Contents

Acknowledgements

This book is based on ideas that have been developed specifically over the past five years but are based in working practice that dates back over 20 years. Along the way, numerous people on training courses and in classrooms have been involved in discussions. We would like to thank everyone who has shared our interest in vocabulary but in particular: Claire Berry, Emma Caddick and Maggie Burlington for their contribution to the editing of the book.

Many thanks to Rod Boucher for his songs. They are true earworms.

A special thank you goes to the staff and students at Sebright Language Impairment Unit. Working together all those years ago cemented a passion for language and child development that continues undiminished.

Once again, we owe a great deal to Kevin Foster and Steve Branagan for their encouragement, support and patience.

Stephen Parsons and Anna Branagan
January 2016

Chapter 1
Introduction

Chapter 1
Introduction

The vocabulary gap

A pre-school child who comes from a family where language is appreciated will be exposed to a far greater range of vocabulary than his peer who has had relatively little language directed at them. In language-rich environments a child will have access to challenging vocabulary through books being read to him and wide-ranging daily interactions (Hart & Risley, 1995). The peer who has not benefited from this rich pre-school language experience will start school with a more limited vocabulary. The child who knows fewer words will also learn words at a slower rate, so this gap will continue to grow throughout childhood (Biemiller, 2004).

Vocabulary impacts

Spoken vocabulary is important in its own right but it also has a major impact on other areas of learning (Cunningham & Stanovich, 1997). A young child who does not understand early concepts such as **big** and **empty**, when his peers do, will miss out on crucial learning about the world around him. An eloquent child, who can talk with precision about his experiences, will develop more abstract thinking than a peer who is limited to pointing or simply labelling items. Thus a weakness in early vocabulary will impact on later mathematical and scientific understanding.

The young child with limited vocabulary will also struggle to comprehend the stories that are read to him and, even when he does learn to read, he may not fully understand the meaning because too many of the words will be unknown. In addition, he will be unable to use sophisticated language when writing, and may instead be limited to repetitious vocabulary (Beck *et al*, 2008). Thus limited early vocabulary impacts on later literacy development or, to summarise it another way: 'Literacy floats on a sea of talk' (based on Britton, 1970).

The gap between a child with an enriched vocabulary experience and his peer who has fewer word-learning opportunities start out as a vocabulary gap but, over time, it becomes a gulf in overall academic achievement.

Vocabulary and the curriculum

Practitioners frequently report that many children start school without the necessary vocabulary to access the curriculum. At school entry, many children only have basic everyday words and lack the more advanced vocabulary expected within the curriculum. For children who can access it, the curriculum gives them many word-learning opportunities. But for those without the necessary foundation vocabulary, it is overwhelming.

As the curriculum advances, the hands-on, play-based opportunities of Early Years disappear and learning becomes increasingly language-based. Without a mastery of Early Years vocabulary, the more abstract, language-based curriculum of the primary or elementary classroom is beyond reach and this pattern continues as the curriculum becomes more vocabulary-heavy. Thus the limited vocabulary in the pre-school years continues to have an impact right through schooling.

Closing the gap

A child with less pre-school vocabulary experience starts school with fewer words and learns words at a slower rate than his peers. This gap continues to grow as children who know more words also learn new words more quickly (Biemiller, 2004). If children from linguistically deprived backgrounds are to keep pace, early intervention is crucial.

In many schools there will be a significant proportion of children who lack the vocabulary required to access the curriculum, and so a whole class intervention is warranted. This approach is known to be successful (Wasik & Bond, 2001). Even in schools where the number of children with poor vocabulary is limited, whole class approaches can still be used to promote the word-learning of all children.

The sheer number of words that children are required to learn makes closing the gap a daunting task. Even the most word-focused Early Years experience will not achieve this. Therefore, a whole school approach is required that starts in Early Years but extends right through the school.

A general enriched language environment will undoubtedly contribute to word learning because it exposes children to a wide range of language experiences, including vocabulary. However, for children who are missing key concepts in particular, this will not be enough.

Children with English as an additional language or English language learners

A strong basis in the home language is essential for children to develop English proficiency, so parents should be urged to speak to their children in the language they are most comfortable with. A rich first language experience will equip children better to learn the school language, including vocabulary.

Speaking a language other than English does not in itself cause vocabulary learning difficulties. As with their monolingual peers, children with English as an additional language (EAL) or English language learners (ELL) will also have a range of pre-school vocabulary experiences and innate word-learning abilities. This presents practitioners with complexities as, frequently, children will be learning words at school which they do not know in their home language. Therefore, an inclusive and adaptable approach to word learning is necessary so that the needs of all word learners can be met. Working with families is a crucial part of this approach, but with EAL or ELL students, it is essential to work closely with families so that children have increased word-learning opportunities across all languages.

Working with vocabulary learning in Early Years

Many children will start school with a limited number of spoken words. Closing this gap is an ambitious target and evidence suggests that Early Years interventions alone will not be enough (Marulis & Neuman, 2010). However, by starting early, children are given a greater chance to have the crucial words in place before the impacts of their poor vocabulary can be seen on literacy and conceptual understanding. The Early Years curriculum provides ample opportunities for teaching the fundamental concepts that underpin later learning. So it is essential that the whole school approach to vocabulary teaching starts when children enter educational provisions.

Word Aware in Early Years

If you are familiar with the first *Word Aware* book (Parsons & Branagan, 2014), this book is an extension of it, based on the same principles but adapted to the needs of the younger age group.

If you are not familiar with the previous publication, in essence, both *Word Aware* books are about working together as a school, in conjunction with parents, to provide a structured process for teaching vocabulary within a word-rich learning environment. This process uses a wide range of explicit and implicit methods which, in combination, build the power of the approach.

The two *Word Aware* books complement each another because they allow practitioners to apply the approach with children aged from 3 to 12 years. There is some necessary overlap but this book also emphasises elements such as early verbal concepts which are most relevant in the pre-school years.

Word Aware applies theory to a practical and structured approach that can be used across all parts of the curriculum. It can be used effectively by individual practitioners. However, Word Aware will have the most long-term effect on word learning if it is adopted by the whole school, so that everyone involved develops a common understanding and applies a consistent approach.

This resource has been developed from classroom practice in conjunction with wide-ranging reading. We aim to build on these techniques for vocabulary teaching and, in particular, to investigate their effectiveness. We would appreciate hearing about your experiences and we can be contacted at www.thinkingtalking.co.uk.

Key principles of effective vocabulary teaching in Early Years

1 Build a strong foundation

2 Make words a priority

3 Maintain a sustained effort

4 Use a range of methods

5 Go with the child (at the right rate)

6 Use multiple exposures

7 Teach words in context

8 Teach strategies

The Word Aware principles have been developed by reviewing the literature and applying these concepts in the classroom. By working with children and practitioners over a period of time, the principles have been refined so that, while having a basis in theory, they also make sense in the classroom. The eight principles, which are described overleaf, form the basis of the approach that is outlined in this book.

The overarching principle is that all children will benefit if they are exposed to enriched vocabulary within an environment where the spoken and the written word are appreciated. By creating a Word Aware environment, children will:

- be exposed to a large number of words at an accessible level
- experience the explicit teaching of useful words
- learn strategies for independent word learning
- have opportunities to enjoy words.

Principle 1: Build a strong foundation

- Recognise that poor vocabulary impacts on learning
- Target vocabulary early as this reduces impacts

A child who starts school without the necessary vocabulary required to access learning will encounter difficulties which will be amplified unless an effort is made to close the gap. Not being able to understand early verbal concepts such as **later** and **next** will impact on later mathematical understanding, as these concepts are fundamental in shaping thinking about time and space, respectively. Likewise, not being able to understand **different** and **heavy** will impact on children's later scientific understanding, as these relate to scientific experiment and weight, respectively.

It is well established that children who have early difficulties with oral language, and in particular vocabulary, are most at risk of reading difficulties. Even if they do master phonics and can decode, they later struggle with reading comprehension because they do not understand the words they encounter.

By starting an effective vocabulary intervention at an early age, children have greater opportunities to build a strong foundation in spoken language, thus reducing any negative impacts of their weaker vocabulary skills.

Principle 2: Make words a priority

- Build a word-enriched environment
- Promote language in general
- Have fun with words

A word-enriched Early Years environment will expose children to wide and varied vocabulary and thus give them opportunities for incidental word learning. Building a word-enriched environment is not about one major event; rather, it involves many small actions by everyone in the team. For example, selecting books or poetry for their use of vocabulary, highlighting the use of words in texts and other media, and commending students for their use of vocabulary will all contribute. Words can be given a higher profile by running whole class or whole school events, such as 'word of the week' awards.

One caveat is that the enriched vocabulary that children are exposed to still needs to be at an accessible level. Children need to be enthralled by words rather than overwhelmed by them.

Language is one of the core areas of development in Early Years and the settings can do a range of activities to promote language. The cornerstone is adult–child interaction.

Having fun with words (by playing vocabulary games) motivates word learners as well as giving them opportunities to learn new words and reinforce known words. Most word games require the player to use phonological (speech sound) and semantic (meaning) skills. These are the same skills that are needed for word learning. Therefore, having fun with words is important and should be a key component of any vocabulary intervention (Stahl & Nagy, 2005).

Principle 3: Maintain a sustained effort

- A whole school approach is needed
- Teach vocabulary across all ages

It is estimated that the average child learns 2000–3000 words per year, every year throughout their schooling (Clark, 1993). This equates to six to eight words per day on average. While many of these words will be learned without specific teaching, the sheer enormity of the task underlines that this process must be continued across a number of years.

In addition, some children start school with a limited vocabulary. A reasonable target for them might be to develop their vocabulary so that it progresses from the 20th to the 50th centile over three years, thus moving from below average to average. To meet this target, the child's rate of learning needs to increase from seven to ten words per day, and to be sustained at this level for three years (Stahl & Nagy, 2005). No matter how effective they are, one teacher in one year will not be enough to make a difference. Instead, a sustained day-on-day, year-on-year, whole school approach is required.

While the specific techniques will change as children move through the school, there needs to be a consistent commitment to the principles and their application.

Principle 4: Use a range of methods

- Sensory experiences are important in Early Years
- Adapt over time to maintain interest

The multisensory experiences available in Early Years should be fully utilised so that children can use the hands-on opportunities to gain an in-depth understanding of words, and in particular concepts. Where possible, go for a high impact. So, for example, when teaching **big**, find things that really are **big**; when teaching interesting words from text, make them sound wonderfully enticing by emphasising their sounds, eg **whoosh**.

As children develop over time, they will be able to access more language to support their learning and so the style of presentation will change. However, by building in songs, signs, pictures and games, all word learners will continue to be engaged.

Principle 5: Go with the child (at the right rate)

- Select words at the right level
- Ensure time for in-depth teaching
- Teach concepts one at a time

Selecting the right vocabulary is one of the most powerful tasks that a practitioner can undertake. It is important to select words that are at the right level and equate to Vygotsky's 'zone of proximal development' (Robson, 2006). Selecting words that are beyond the grasp of a child may lead to superficial knowledge and the child being unable to apply the word meaningfully to their understanding of the world. While reinforcing existing words is important, selecting words that are too well known is an inefficient use of time.

Similarly, the rate of vocabulary learning is also important. With so many words to learn, and within the general tempo of the curriculum, there are inevitable time pressures. Despite this, it is important to allocate enough time to teach useful words to an appropriate depth (Stahl & Nagy, 2005; Beck *et al*, 2008). In-depth teaching allows children to experience several meaningful exposures of the word and to link the new word to existing knowledge, thus avoiding superficial learning.

Principle 6: Use multiple exposures

- Children need to hear or read a word many times
- They need opportunities to link new knowledge to what they already know

Young children have well-developed word-learning abilities and may form a tentative understanding after a few exposures (Rice *et al*, 1990). Research indicates that a child needs 12 instructional encounters to fully know the word (Stahl & Nagy, 2005). Exposures should be in a variety of contexts so that the child has the opportunity to build full comprehension (Block & Mangieri, 2006). Rather than learning definitions, children should hear the new word in real sentences which are related to situations that they are familiar with. For young children, this is about adults using the target word while engaging with the child. High quality adult–child interaction is the key to word learning.

Word knowledge develops over time and, initially, a child will have only a vague understanding of a new word. However, as he hears the word in a variety of contexts, he will add new information and develop a richer and more complete understanding. Exposures to the word may come from adults in school and at home. Opportunities to use the word will further reinforce word knowledge as well as add to the word knowledge of other children in the class.

Selecting words that will be encountered in other contexts, such as in books, at home, through other media or in other subject areas, will give the child opportunities to further develop his understanding of the word naturally. For instance, if **discover** is introduced at nursery or kindergarten, the child may also encounter it in conversation in various parts of the setting, both inside and outside, as well as at home or on a DVD. However, if a specific term such as **Jolly Roger** had been taught during a pirate topic, the child is far less likely to encounter the word again and, therefore, will not have natural opportunities to expand his learning of the word. Of course, exposures can be increased by reading books to children that contain the target word or sending home 'talking homework' tasks that require parents and children to talk about the targeted word.

Principle 7: Teach words in context

- Teach the words in practical, 'hands-on' contexts
- Follow the child's lead
- Use the word in a variety of sentences

Children learn the meaning of words by linking the language they hear to the context around them. For instance, if a young child has a toy **bunny**, he can use his senses to explore the object. He touches its soft fur, he looks at its pink eyes and maybe even tastes its ear. When his parent labels the toy **bunny**, the child will, over time, link the word **bunny** to the toy. By learning all about **bunny** in a physical context, the child can establish its meaning.

The parent will also use a range of linguistic (language) contexts such as 'He's a soft **bunny**', 'The **bunny** is jumping' and 'You're cuddling **bunny**'. By using a range of different sentences, the word **bunny** is also placed in a linguistic context and the child will learn that it is a noun. The physical and linguistic contexts have both added to the development of a full understanding of the word. This is a natural process that children are predisposed to.

In the classroom, children's natural word learning can be enhanced by giving them opportunities to explore new words in their physical context. This is well-established Early Years practice. Hands-on experience will give children an understanding of the world, but it is adults' use of language that will build their vocabulary. Adults should therefore engage children in meaningful ongoing conversations that follow what the children are interested in at that time. Vocabulary can then be added to this, but the high-quality interaction needs to be in place first.

Principle 8: Teach strategies

- Children need to develop their own strategies
- Strategies become more important as children get older, but they can be started in Early Years

The most advanced Early Years word learners are the same children who frequently ask what words mean, whereas children with more limited vocabularies are less likely to enquire about the meaning of words. By establishing a supportive classroom culture, as well as specifically teaching simple strategies to identify and ask about words' meanings, the foundation for later developing strategies is established.

Having strategies to decipher the meaning of new words in both spoken and written form becomes increasingly important for older children, but establishing children's awareness and skills at an early age will set them on the right path.

The Word Aware approach

The Word Aware approach for Early Years has been developed to guide practitioners in implementing the principles of word learning. It is based on the same theory that informs the first *Word Aware* book (Parsons & Branagan, 2014) but it has been adapted to meet the needs of younger children and the practitioners who work with them. It is easy to understand, flexible, quick to implement, and can be applied across a wide range of ability levels.

The Word Aware approach consists of four strands:

	**Make words count**	Provide an environment in which children are surrounded by spoken and written words and are inspired to learn them.
	**Teaching vocabulary**	Introduce new words from the curriculum as well as teach words sourced from books. This includes teaching concepts which are particularly important in Early Years.
	**Fun with words**	Enjoy, celebrate and reinforce vocabulary.
	**Word detective**	Teach strategies to enhance children's independent word learning.

Each strand is explained more fully later in this book, but first here is a brief outline.

1 'Make words count' is about providing an enriched word-learning environment. Children need to know that spoken and written words are important. They need to be exposed to many words through many different methods and to be encouraged to use an extended vocabulary.

2 'Teaching vocabulary' is based on the 'select, teach, activate and review' process outlined by Blachowicz & Fisher (2010). Here it has been applied to teaching curriculum vocabulary, early verbal concepts and the rich vocabulary that is found in children's literature.

3 'Fun with words' completes the approach. Playing with words and having fun instils enjoyment and subsequent motivation. Word games are, of course, in themselves instructional and can be used to reinforce new vocabulary as well as word-learning skills.

4 The 'word detective' strand teaches children how to learn new words. In the pre-school years, this is very simple but it forms the basis for skills that become increasingly important as children develop.

Each of the four strands is in itself useful but, together, they form a powerful approach to vocabulary learning. If all four strands are used, within a word-rich environment, children will be taught vocabulary in a methodical manner, master independent strategies for learning unknown words and have fun.
As a result, they will become competent and motivated word learners.

Chapter 2

Make Words Count: Developing a Word Enriched Environment

Wow !

Chapter 2

Make Words Count: Developing a Word Enriched Environment

Introduction

A rich word-learning environment is a powerful component of any vocabulary intervention. Such an environment will expose children to a diverse, but accessible, range of vocabulary and facilitate their natural word learning (Chiat, 2000). A carefully structured word-learning environment has the power to motivate word learners as well as provide a multitude of natural word-learning opportunities.

This book focuses on vocabulary and so a word-learning environment will be particularly emphasised. In Early Years, any environment that promotes language in general will implicitly promote vocabulary. As vocabulary is such a key component of language, it is a particularly artificial discrimination to make with this age group.

It is estimated that each child needs to learn seven words per day throughout their schooling if they are to reach the average of knowing 30,000 words by adulthood (Clark, 1993). It is not practical or possible to reach this target by direct teaching alone. Direct teaching plays a part, as explained in Chapter 3, but enriching the word-learning environment remains crucial.

Most Early Years settings will already have many features of an enriched word-learning environment in place, so the first step to moving forwards is to reflect on current practice. Enriching the word-learning environment is not about one major change; rather, it is about creating a culture in which practitioners can reflect and make small changes that suit the children in their class.

Developing an enriched word-learning environment

Before you start making changes, audit what you are doing already. A comprehensive audit tool is available at:

- http://webarchive.nationalarchives.gov.uk/20130401151715
- www.education.gov.uk/publications/eOrderingDownload/DCSF-00854-2008.pdf

The crucial aspect is, as a staff team, to think of your Early Years setting from a child's perspective.

Start by listening. What words do you hear adults use? What words do you hear children use? What conversations do you hear between children and adults? Are they shared conversations or do adults dominate? Are there some children who do lots of talking and others who do little?

Then think about where children talk. Are there areas where children do lots of talking and are there other areas where they are quiet? Think about outside areas as well as the more obvious indoors. What makes some areas so chat-friendly and others not? What changes can be made?

Once you have reflected on current practice, consider each one of the following key principles to 'make words count'.

1 Promote language
2 Expose children to a rich and wide, but appropriately demanding, vocabulary
3 Make sure children know that both spoken and written words are important
4 Facilitate word learning beyond the classroom
5 Make word learning fun

Are there actions you do already that promote these principles? Using the ideas listed below, can you add anything else to an action plan? Once you have completed an audit, develop an action plan that involves all members of staff working together.

Key principles and activities to make words count

1 Promote language

(a) Adapt the environment

The physical environment will affect how children interact with each other and with adults. Lively and interesting indoor and outdoor areas will give children topics to talk about as well as providing inviting places to stop and talk to adults and to one another. The Early Years environment should be varied and promote sensory experiences. It does not require expensive equipment but rather imagination.
For instance, use large cardboard boxes and fabric to make play dens. This can create contained spaces where children feel safe and can be together. Make spaces that are delineated, creating contained spaces, both inside and outside. Transparent or translucent fabrics can be used so children feel that they are hidden but adults can keep an eye on them. Fabrics and cushions can create soft cosy places for quiet times. The addition of soft materials also naturally absorbs noise: a quiet environment makes listening less challenging. Jarman (2013) also recommends seeing spaces from a child's point of view. Take photographs from an adult's point of view and compare these with a child's point of view. How inviting are the spaces to children? Places may look surprisingly different from a child's perspective.

(b) Adult–child interaction

The most important element of any word-learning environment is the adult–child interaction. Adults have the capacity to make every activity a language-learning activity. A good place to start is listening and watching children, and giving them space to talk. Spending a few moments one-to-one, following the child's lead and commenting on what they are focused on, rather than asking questions, will promote language development. Vocabulary can specifically be added to this high-quality interaction by the adults using appropriately challenging words, as well as reinforcing the children's use of words. Developing this interaction style takes practice and reflection but will pay dividends. There are further details at: www.keenacummins.co.uk/verve_child_interaction.html

(c) Peer interaction

Peer interaction is often overlooked and is also under-researched, but in Early Years the majority of children's interactions will be with their peers. The adults' direct role in peer interaction is limited, but practitioners can model language and start children off interacting with each other. Attracting a group of children to one activity, modelling related terminology and then stepping back is an informal but effective way of promoting higher quality peer-to-peer language.

(d) Support play

Some children create their own opportunities for interactive and creative play while others need some support. Look at practical ways of enabling children to develop interactive play. For instance, add a mechanic's workshop or petrol station to the bike riding area (Gross, 2013). This can encourage children to interact and not just ride around. Similarly, pit-stops can be added to the car mat or stations on train tracks.

Set up the home corner in different themes and then introduce new words to use in that scenario. This can be done by discussing words to use or whisper words (see page 47) to encourage children to use a particular word. Play-scripts may also be used to develop language, play skills and vocabulary learning. See the end of this chapter for more details (pages 24–5).

Microphones can really encourage children to talk as well as sing. Add these to role play areas for children to use. Join in with children's play, modelling their use; for instance, take turns at interviewing.

Make a pretend television by drawing the perimeter of the set, cutting out the screen and then laminating it. Hold this in front of two children. They can then either host a show or one can interview the other.

(e) Stories

Stories are a great way of sharing and developing language. Enjoy books but also encourage children to make up stories. Write down or record their stories, then add illustrations and make them into a 'book'. There is more about specifically using books as a source of vocabulary in Chapter 3.

(f) Use open questions

Comments are preferable to questions but the occasional question can have an impact. Open questions prompt thinking. 'I wonder what will happen if …?' invites comments whereas closed questions can seem threatening. Try not to overwhelm children with too many or overly complex questions.

(g) Involve children who have limited language

Children who have English as an additional language (English language learners), or children who have delayed language development, need to be able to be involved as much as possible. Encourage non-verbal involvement and model ways of participating without language as well as giving space for and praising verbal contributions.

(h) Provide a clear structure to the day

Make the day as predictable as possible. Use a visual timetable to help children know what is going to happen across the day. We all want to know when we next have access to food or drink or when we are going home. Children may be more confident when they understand more about what will happen in their day. For young children, photographs may be the easiest to understand but clear colourful symbols can also be effective.

2 *Expose children to a rich and wide, but appropriately demanding, vocabulary*

- The most important feature of any word-rich Early Years environment is the language that adults use. All adults in the classroom should take great care in using appropriately challenging vocabulary. Use a wide range of words, but ensure they are still at the right level. Inspire rather than overwhelm.
- Engage children in extended conversations so that thinking along with vocabulary can be developed.
- Use statements rather than questions so that children hear words in sentences. Children learn much more from hearing words in context rather than being repeatedly questioned about their knowledge.
- Early Years books are a wonderful source of interesting and varied vocabulary, so select books that are well written. Re-reading stories enhances children's understanding and provides extra opportunities for discussion about words.
- Audio books can boost exposure to the spoken word and do not require specific adult attention.
- By giving children access to topic-related books (both fiction and non-fiction), they will encounter a network of new words repeatedly, thus building stronger understanding.

3 *Make sure children know that both spoken and written words are important*

Give the spoken and the written word a profile in the classroom by:

- Jointly appreciating authors' use of vocabulary. When sharing books with children, jointly discuss the words that you both like.
- Highlighting interesting words in books. Encourage children to join in saying words that have a lovely sound (eg **swoosh**, **whoosh**, **wheee**) or express something disgusting (eg **yeuch!**). Act out words that involve movement, for example, **tramp**, **scuttle**, **nip** (Fearley, 2002; Ormerod & Gardiner, 2007). Practise talking in the described manner, for example, **whisper**, **shout**, **yell**, **whine**, **scream**.
- Prominently labelling vocabulary on regular displays. Use symbols attached to the word to aid understanding. Displays crucially act as reminders for all adults to be using rich vocabulary and so, to avoid becoming wallpaper, they need to be interactive. Attaching 'talking tins' or similar robust recordable devices to displays is one way of achieving this.
- Using symbols

house car swim

Symbols are an integral part of enabling young children to access the written word. Communicate in Print (www.widgit.com) or Boardmaker® (www.mayer-johnson.com) can be useful for this. Photographs can also be useful.

- Reinforce interesting words used by children by repeating them and adding words. The repetition of a word enables other children to hear the word again and is a natural way of praising a child's vocabulary. For example:

  Child: 'Look it is **shimmering**!'
  Adult: 'Oh, yes, it does **shimmer** in the light.'

- Highlighting key words before doing a task. For instance, before a cooking activity, verbs such as **pouring, kneading, stirring** and **whisking** may be introduced.

pouring

kneading

stirring

- Promote words by:
  - Dressing up as a favourite word. There is a slide show of children dressed up in fantastic costumes at www.debrafrasier.com/pages/books/msa.html#_costumes and a selection of costumes at www.pinterest.com/debrafrasier/vocabulary-parade-author-debra-frasier/.

    Examples include: **clean** and **bubblegum** (involving lots of pink balloons), **dull, slime, bite, brain, ocean**. There are also suggestions for hat parades, for example, **headstrong, aeroplane, flame** and **rescued**.

    Download a leaflet on setting up a vocabulary parade from www.debrafrasier.com/cla_sup_downloads/msa_parade.pdf
  - Building a 'tree of words'. Children and adults think of words to write on paper leaves. Add a picture if you can, then fix these to a large display of a tree trunk and branches that is displayed in a prominent location. The tree comes to life as more leaves are added. Words can be added in any language.

    (Source: inspired by https://uk.pinterest.com/pin/553309504189049217/)
  - Holding a 'Word Challenge Day'. Send all of the children home with a 'Word Challenge' on the same day. It could be a 'word walk' in which children are required to identify items that can be described by a particular word (eg **smooth** or **speckled**) on their walk home from school, or everybody goes home and plays 'I Spy' using an adjective (eg 'I spy something **red**'). Select ideas from Chapter 5 Fun with Words.
  - If you are part of a larger school, hold vocabulary assemblies where each class nominates their favourite word and prizes are given to the most interesting word.
  - Add vocabulary to any event. It might be the newsletter, sports day or permanent displays and artwork. Whatever you do, show that, in your setting, you make words count.

4 Facilitate word learning beyond the classroom

Vocabulary is not just for use in the classroom; it needs to be used everywhere so that children have the maximum opportunities to learn. Make a particular effort to link up with parents and carers. There are many ways of doing this (see Chapter 8 Involving Families), but it really is worth the effort to engage them. When planning how to build a word-rich environment, build in family involvement as an integral component rather than as an afterthought.

Use school outings and activities as well. Before going on a trip or engaging in a novel activity, think of the vocabulary that may be encountered. Do not just list nouns; also think of the verbs and adjectives.

For example, before going to the farm, think of related words such as **feed**, **groom**, **gobble**, **care**, **stroke** and **gentle**. Use symbols as well as the spoken word to help children remember the words in context.

When walking or travelling somewhere as a group, give children vocabulary-related tasks. Examples include: look for things that belong to a category (such as **transport** or **animals**) or share an attribute (such as made of **metal**, is **green**, is **tiny** or **grows**).

5 Make word learning fun

Fun is a key element of the Word Aware approach and is expanded in Chapter 5 Fun with Words. By building in opportunities to have fun with words, children will reinforce vocabulary, develop their word-learning skills and be motivated to learn. Fun activities can be played as a planned part of another activity or to fill in a spare few minutes, or they can be timetabled as a stand-alone slot.

Encourage word play. Many children naturally go through a phase of playing with words, especially with rhyme. Encourage and reinforce this whenever you can. Children with word learning difficulties may need extra support to access some vocabulary games but will benefit from them too.

Developing play and language via play-scripts

Play is how children explore and make sense of the world. Play-scripts are a well-tested way of extending social interaction and adding language (including vocabulary) to children's play.

Gather a small group of children together and use play people to act out a short scenario, eg 'at the doctor's'. Start by setting the location and allocating a role to each play person. The adult talks from each play person's perspective, describing who they are, for example 'I'm the doctor and I'm in my room at the surgery. I'm mum and I'm in the doctor's waiting room …'

The adult then acts out the play-script below using the play people, taking all of the roles. This is not as difficult as it sounds because the script is very simple. One of the key features of a play-script is that the story has no narration. Nobody says 'The girl goes upstairs.' Instead, the play person describes themselves what they are doing, eg: 'Here I go up. Stomp, stomp, stomp.' Label noises as much as possible. Children enjoy joining in with sound effects. The lack of narration keeps the language simple and accessible and emphasises the social interaction.

The doctor's surgery

Mum: I'm Mum and I'm in the waiting room.

Katy: I'm Katy and I'm in the waiting room.

Receptionist: I'm the receptionist and I'm in my office.

Doctor: I'm the doctor and I'm in my room.

Katy: I'm bored and my ear hurts.

Mum: We won't have to wait long. Have a look at this magazine.

Katy: I don't want to.

Receptionist: Katy Smith to see the doctor, room one.

Mum: Come on let's go.

[Mum knocks on the door. Knock, knock.]

Doctor: Hello, come in. What's the matter?

Mum: Katy's ear is hurting.

Doctor: Which ear is it?

Katy: It's this one. Ow! It hurts all the time.

Doctor: Let me have a look inside your ear. Oh yes, that looks very red. You need some medicine. Do you want banana medicine or strawberry medicine?

Katy: Strawberry please!

Doctor: Here you go, here is your prescription.

Mum: Thanks doctor.

The story can include a few of the new words you have introduced as part of your topic, eg **prescription**, so it is a useful opportunity for the new words to be heard and used in context.

Once the adult has introduced the play-script, the children can then practise the script, taking one part each, but start by keeping one role for an adult. If children forget what to say, wait. Wait for longer than you may feel inclined to. It is often amazing what children come up with when you wait. If children are stuck then prompt them in character using the role the adult has retained. For example, if the doctor has forgotten what to say, the adult playing the part of Mum can say 'Her ear is hurting. Please can you look at her ears?' Encourage children to use a few of their own words or actions spontaneously rather than copy what the adults say.

The next step is to set up a doctor's surgery in the home corner. Act out the play-script again but, rather than using play people, the children take on the roles themselves. Once the play-script has been acted, let the children play as they wish in the home corner but note and reinforce any elements that the children incorporate in their play.

Use the same play-script over several sessions. The more the children become familiar with it, the more confident they will be and the more they can explore it, improvising as they go.

Play-scripts can also be used to make books more accessible. Select any children's book. Edit out the narration, leaving just the dialogue. After simplifying the language, make sure that you have retained some useful vocabulary. Then use the process above. The story can be told simply with play people or you can get creative and add props to make the story come alive. For example, use cotton wool for a snowstorm and a piece of brown card made into a cone for the cave in the story *We're Going on a Bear Hunt* (Rosen, 1995).

Chapter 3
Direct Teaching of Vocabulary

Chapter 3
Direct Teaching of Vocabulary

Introduction

A child's understanding of a curriculum area and his vocabulary are intertwined. For instance, if a child is learning about mini-beasts but does not know the word **insect**, his ability to both fully understand that particular curriculum area and express his knowledge is severely limited. Vocabulary is also particularly closely related to conceptual understanding and, specifically, teaching verbal concepts will develop children's language, curriculum access and understanding of the world.

A vocabulary-rich curriculum is undoubtedly an important first step in promoting word learning because it exposes children to a wide range of words. Word learning can be further enhanced by introducing new words in a structured and specific manner, such as the 'STAR' process described below. The combined effect of general exposure and specific teaching will accelerate and deepen word learning for all learners, but specifically will be useful for children who need extra support with this skill.

The direct teaching process

STAR stands for:

- Select
- Teach
- Activate
- Review

- **Select** the most useful vocabulary.
- **Teach** the selected vocabulary in a structured manner.
- **Activate** the meaning by using the words in context.
- **Review** the taught words to ensure they are retained.

(Source: adapted from Blachowicz & Fisher, 2010)

By following each step in the STAR process, practitioners will promote children's natural word learning. In the **select** phase, words at the right level are chosen. In the **teach** phase, the new words are highlighted to children before meaning is expanded in a natural way in the **activate** phase. By building **review** activities into the process, the word continues to be heard and so deepens in meaning rather than being forgotten.

Once practitioners are familiar with the approach, it is quick and easy to deliver with minimal planning and preparation. It can be applied to any curriculum as well as to both topic-related vocabulary and vocabulary that is encountered in shared texts.

Selecting vocabulary

Selecting the right level of words to teach is an important first step. Words should be new to most of the children but common enough to be encountered again. Selecting the right words will ensure that words are naturally heard again and children have the opportunities to develop their understanding over a period of time. If the right words are chosen, they will be encountered again with very little planning or extra effort by the practitioner.

Use the guide below to identify 'Goldilocks' words that are 'not too easy, not too hard, but just right' for your children (Stahl & Nagy, 2005). 'Goldilocks' words are the focus of direct teaching, so it is worth spending time ensuring that they are particularly useful. There is no national standard for the words that are expected to be known by a particular age; rather, the words known by children will vary according to their experiences. For instance, children in rural areas will know different words from children in cities.

In our experience, most practitioners find this a straightforward task once they understand the process. While learning this process, we recommend that extra time is spent reflecting on decisions as well as cross-checking with colleagues who also know the children.

 **Anchor words**	 **Goldilocks words**	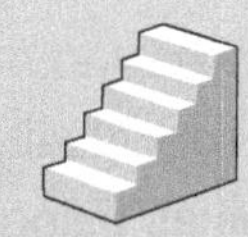 **Step on words**
Children have a thorough understanding of these words. Everyday spoken language for a child of this age. Used at home and in daily interactions.	**Really useful words** Likely to be encountered again. Average **older child*** has a **good** level of knowledge of the word. Words that are very topic-specific but core to the topic.	Less likely to be encountered again. Average **older child*** does not have much knowledge of the word. Words that are particularly topic-specific and not core to the topic.
If a child needs work on 'anchor' words, provide additional small group teaching or differentiated activities.	'Goldilocks' words are the words that are taught to the whole group. Select one word per teaching session.	'Step on' words that are needed for comprehension can be briefly explained but are not the main focus of teaching.

* An older child is defined as a child 2–3 years older than the children in your current class.
(Source: Stahl & Nagy, 2005; Blachowicz & Fisher, 2010)

Appropriate 'Goldilocks' words may come from:

- the topic
- shared books.

Teaching vocabulary that is sourced from the topic or shared books will ensure that children are taught a balanced range of useful words.

Selecting topic-related words

Topic-related words are useful to teach because they are connected thematically and thus more readily form a network. Also, during the topic, words will be encountered more frequently, so children will have more opportunities to expand their understanding of them.

Start by finding a source of curriculum-related words. Guidance may be provided by schemes of work or practitioners may generate their own curriculum vocabulary, drawing on a range of sources. Young children need to be exposed to a wide range of words. However, there is only enough time to select a few words that can be specifically taught, so ensure that your 'Goldilocks' words really are at the right level of difficulty, as well as being the most useful.

It is still important that children are exposed to a rich curriculum so, when talking about dinosaurs, continue to use words such as **stegosaurus**. However, a word such as **hunt** may be a better choice for in-depth teaching because it will have far more opportunities to be naturally developed over time as it is encountered at other times, for example in stories such as *We're Going on a Bear* ***Hunt*** (Rosen, 1995) and on occasions such as Easter egg **hunts**. After a period of natural encounters with a selected word, children will develop a robust understanding of it. However, if a rare word is selected, the children will not have the opportunity to hear it again and their understanding will not develop to the same level.

When brainstorming curriculum words, it is naturally easier to think of nouns, but it is important to represent all parts of speech, particularly verbs and adjectives. In addition, nouns are easier to learn without teaching so it may be wise to prioritise verbs and adjectives for direct teaching. We have used Twinkl (www.twinkl.co.uk) as a source of topic words to start the thinking process. This website frequently provides nouns so, where possible, verbs and adjectives will need to be added. Further examples are given at the end of this chapter (see pages 50–61). There is also a blank planning sheet in the Appendix.

Some Early Years topics (such as **pirates** – see page 31) are a vehicle for general learning rather than a curriculum area that children require specific knowledge of. Therefore, for this type of topic select vocabulary that is most useful for children to learn. Related verbs and adjectives (eg **dangerous**) may be more useful than the concrete nouns (eg **treasure map**). 'Goldilocks' words are also most likely to be applicable to more topics and more situations. For instance, **escape** is far more useful than **pieces of eight**. Even though the latter really enlivens the topic and will capture the imagination, **escape** is a word that can be applied across numerous topics and settings. So it is more useful and, over time, children will develop a full understanding of its meaning.

Examples of topic-based vocabulary

Topic: **Pirates**			
	Anchor words	**Goldilocks words** 'Not too easy and not too hard, but just right'	**Step on words**
Nouns	sword ship pirate	parrot treasure hook captain island adventure	palm tree eye patch Jolly Roger flag treasure map compass pieces of eight booty
Verbs	fight swim climb	sail discover sink capture escape explore	rove ransack smuggle
Adjectives	scary old	dangerous adventurous precious brave	lawless infamous bloodthirsty

Selecting words from shared books

Shared reading books are another important source of words because the vocabulary used in them is far richer than is commonly used in spoken language. For example, words such as **clambered** and **shrieked** bring children's literature to life but are relatively uncommon in spoken language. By selecting these types of words for direct teaching, children's current spoken language is being developed as well as building the foundation for their future literacy development.

The purpose is to use the shared books as a source of useful words rather than selecting words that are needed to understand the story. It is important to keep in mind that the shared books are being used as a source of vocabulary. If words are encountered that need to be understood for the story, these can be explained. However, unless they are a 'Goldilocks' word, they should not be selected for direct teaching.

Select one 'Goldilocks' word per book. 'Step on' words can be disregarded unless they are essential for understanding the text. The selected word may only be encountered once in the book and might not be central to the book's theme. But if it is particularly useful and widely applicable, it can still be a good 'Goldilocks' candidate.

Again, the process of selecting 'Goldilocks' words is usually straightforward for practitioners who are familiar with their children. When starting out, it is useful to spend time becoming familiar with the process and comparing judgements with those of a colleague. Rather than agonising over the choice of words, practitioners are advised to select words which clearly fit the 'Goldilocks' criteria:

- really **useful words**
- likely to be **encountered again** in reading or oral language
- average **older child** has a **good** level of **knowledge** of the word.

Examples of books

Practitioners are advised to choose one 'Goldilocks' word at a time from any story. In the following examples, several words have been chosen and put into categories, by part of speech (noun, verb, adjective, adverb and preposition). It is not necessary to categorise words like this but ensure that children are exposed to different parts of speech over a period of time.

Examples of 'Goldilocks' words from a range of books

Please note that there are large variations between settings and ages within Early Years, so these are examples only. Practitioners will need to select and categorise words according to their children's profiles.

Book: *Room on the Broom* (Donaldson & Scheffler, 2001)	
	Goldilocks words
Nouns	feast beast
Verbs	searched grinned clambered shrieked tumbling squelched
Adjectives	sticky
Other	wildly

Book: *The Kissing Hand* (Penn, 1993)	
	Goldilocks words
Nouns	No Goldilocks nouns selected from the text.
Verbs	nuzzled scamper
Adjectives	cosy silky
Other	gently

Book: *Possum Magic* (Fox, 1991)	
	Goldilocks words
Nouns	piece
Verbs	shrink
Adjectives	deep invisible squashed precious safe
Other	later over

There are additional examples of Goldilocks words selected from a range of books at the end of this chapter (see pages 62–67).

Finalising planning

The obvious question is 'How many "Goldilocks" words should be taught at one time?' There is no direct answer but starting with one topic word, one text-based word and one concept (see Chapter 4) each week will allow practitioners and children to adjust to the methods. The number may be increased but practitioners should be mindful not to overwhelm children with too many words as learning may then become superficial.

Shared books and topic sources will yield far more words than can be taught, so the next step is to sift through and identify words that are really the most useful. Prioritise words that are applicable across a range of situations and curriculum areas and which are also useful in life.

> There will only ever be a limited number of words that can be explicitly taught. Make sure that they really are useful.

The vocabulary teaching process

After selecting the vocabulary to be taught, the next part of the STAR process is 'teach'. This quick process sketches a brief outline of the word which is further embellished by natural exposure to the word in different contexts until, over time, the word is fully established.

The introductory 'teach' sequence should cover the following features which are then described further.

Summary of teaching sequence

	**Symbol:** use a picture or symbol that represents the word.
	**Phonology (sound):** • clap syllables • say word to partner.
	**Semantics (meaning):** Use a combination of: • sensory experiences • simple vocabulary to define the word • relating the word to what they know • telling a story.
	**Action:** gesture or sign where possible.
	**Word Aware song:** use a song to reinforce the word.
	**Word Wall:** the word and picture go on the Word Wall to remind adults to use the words in context.

Symbol

Draw or find a symbol or picture that represents the target word. Resources are available either online or in specific symbol software such as Communicate in Print (www.widgit.com) or Boardmaker® (www.mayer-johnson.com). Finding suitable symbols occasionally requires the use of imaginative search terms.

A symbol or an image acts as a focus and introduces the idea that a new word is about to be taught. It also provides visual support which is helpful for children with less developed language or who speak English as an additional language (English language learners).

Phonology (speech sounds)

- Syllables: instruct the class to clap out the syllables of the word as they say the word.
- Say the word to a partner: instruct the children to say the word to another child.

Clapping the syllables and saying the word out loud helps to emphasise the word's phonology (speech sounds) and establish a strong foundation that meaning can then be attached to. Many young children's speech sound systems are still developing, so highlighting the phonological features of a word is important. As well as emphasising the phonology of the word, clapping and saying the word out loud sends the signal to all children that this new word is what they need to focus on.

Semantics (meaning)

Before the lesson, practitioners should ensure that they all share the same understanding of a word. This may sound surprising for Early Years words, but it is important that the language children hear in the initial stages of learning a word is precise and consistent. With homonyms, agree which meaning will be the focus of the lesson. For example, if the target word is 'light', it needs to be clear whether this relates to weight or the opposite of dark.

Meaning can be added in several different ways, so use whichever method is most suited to the target word and the children. Keep the process as simple as possible and ensure that all language is simple and in short sentences.

- *Use sensory experiences that make an impact to convey the meaning.*

For example, when teaching **delicious**, taste **delicious** cakes. Experience **empty** by looking inside **empty** containers or rooms. Learn about **growing** by planting seeds and watching them **growing**. This does take some planning and thought, but being interested is an important first step in word learning. Try to start with the most high-impact sensory experience first and then add language.

- *Use simple vocabulary to define the new word.*

Always make sure that word meanings are described using 'anchor' words (everyday words for a child of that age). Look up the word even if it is very familiar to ensure that all aspects of its meaning are conveyed. The *Cobuild English Dictionary* (Collins, 2006) gives simple, straightforward definitions aimed at children with English as an additional language (English language learners). As a result, the definitions are clear and accessible for all learners. However, the definition does not help for some words. For words such as **sticky** and **gentle**, it is not possible to find simpler terms to define them. If there are no simpler terms, sensory experiences are the better option.

- *Relate the word to what they know.*

Link the new word to words the children already know by making links with real-life experiences. For example, when teaching **shrieking**, remind the children of the time they were squirted with water from the hosepipe: 'Remember the **shrieking**?' When introducing **gently**, instruct the children to reflect on the guinea pig and how he must be stroked **gently**.

- *Tell a story.*

Tell a story which highlights the meaning of a word. The story needs to be as interesting and engaging as possible. Stories based on the truth but then modified to add drama are often effective. For example, when teaching **capturing**, talk about a time when rabbits escaped from the cage or the cat got away and had to be **captured**.

Action

Use an action to represent the word. It can be a sign or a simple gesture. Be creative. This is a very powerful tool that helps children remember and make links between words. For example, move your hand up for **grow**, rub your tummy and say 'mmm' for **delicious**, mime a flashing light for a **lighthouse**, or 'talk' with your hand for **mumble**. The action is quick and easily repeated. Say the word at the same time as you say the action and encourage the children to do likewise.

Word Aware songs

The words for the songs are in the Appendix and are also downloadable from **www.routledge.com/cw/speechmark.** These can be either photocopied or printed and used as prompts. The songs can also be downloaded to sing along to or viewed on the Word Aware Youtube channel. The repetition of the target word within these songs helps the children to strengthen their understanding of the word's speech sounds and hence aids memory. Here are two examples:

Clap That Word!	
	Hey, hey ______
	Clap that word ______ Clap that word ______ Clap that word ______
	That's it ______

Jump Up High	
	Start down low ______, ______
	Move up more ______, ______
	A little bit more ______, ______
	Standing straight ______, ______
	Jump up high ______, ______
	Aaaaaahhhhhh!

Word Wall

The picture or symbol is placed on the Word Wall and in a place where it is likely to be used. This will remind adults to use it, so that the children hear it an increased number of times and, most importantly, link it to their experiences. It is not essential to have a symbol as well as the written word because it is targeted at adults rather than children. However, the pictures make it more engaging and act as a memory prompt.

Example of teaching vocabulary process

Growing

Symbol

growing

Phonology (sound)

'Everyone clap **growing**.' (Clap twice to indicate two syllables.) '**Grow – ing**.' 'Now everyone say the word **growing**.'

Semantics (meaning)

- **Simple definition: '****Growing** means to get bigger.'
- **Telling a story:** 'My friend had a baby. She was so little. I went back a few weeks later and the baby had been **growing**! She was much bigger. I went to see the baby when she was one year old. Wow! How much **growing** she had done! She was getting bigger and she was walking. I went to see her later and she was still **growing**! She had changed.' (Use hands to indicate size.)
- **Relate the word to what they know:** 'The plants in the garden are **growing** bigger. Look at the vine there. It has really been **growing** and **growing**.' (Use hands to indicate size.)

Action

Move your hand upwards to indicate **growing**.

Song

Everyone sings the Word Aware song: 'The word for today is **growing, growing, growing**. The word for today is **growing, growing, growing**.'

Word Wall

A **growing** picture with the word underneath is stuck on the Word Wall and next to the plants, to remind adults to use the words in context.

Activating words that have been taught

In the previous steps, the child has been introduced to the new word and been guided through developing the beginning of an understanding of it. This starts the word-learning process but to really develop a complete understanding of the word, children need to have meaningful encounters with the word in natural contexts. This is achieved in the 'activate' phase. By hearing the word used by different speakers in different ways over a period of time, children will develop a deep and fully nuanced understanding of the word. Once they 'own' the word they can apply it in a range of unique and meaningful ways, but to achieve full ownership takes time.

Adults should engage with children in activities that are of interest to the children and, as opportunities arise, add comments that include the new word. Children develop their understanding of the world through play, so play activities are ideally suited to activating new words. A range of different play opportunities will allow the new words to be heard and applied in different ways, so the child's understanding will be expanded. For instance: in the 'teach' phase, the word **search** was explored using a story about lost socks and a simple definition was given: 'looking carefully for something you need.' During the 'activate' stage, the adults use the word **search** when a child needs to find a specific toy in the toy box. This will allow the new word **search** to be linked into a context the child is familiar with.

The interaction and language used are particularly important and while it may appear straightforward, it requires much skill. The basis of the interaction is to follow the children's lead and focus on what they are engaged with. This sounds easy but it is a skill that needs developing over time. Video feedback is one way of improving practitioners' skill in this area.
(For more information go to: www.keenacummins.co.uk/verve_child_interaction.html)

Comments are much less demanding than questions and they guide children in how to use the new word. By hearing the new word in a range of phrases and sentences, they will learn so much more than from repetitive questioning. A sentence such as 'It's **dark** when I turn off the lights' is far more meaningful and gives the child far more information than 'Is it **light** or **dark**?' If you want children to use their new vocabulary in sentences, make sure they hear the new word in sentences.

With a little imagination a wide range of words can be added to any play situation. For example, if children are playing with cars on a ramp you can talk about **bumpy**, **both** and **following** as well as the more obvious **fast**, **chase** and **big**. Remembering which words to focus on, and when, is often an obstacle. Thus placing words on the wall or around the environment (see overleaf) are particularly useful techniques for reminding adults when to use the new words.

For homonyms (words with more than one meaning), it is important that all practitioners continue to focus on the same meaning as was introduced in the 'teach' phase. For instance, if **watch** (as a synonym of 'look') was introduced then **watch** (as in timepiece) should not be emphasised because this may cause confusion.

Avoid overloading children with too much language. Speak in short simple sentences, particularly when using concepts, and do not include too many new words in any one session.

Verb tenses (eg **hear**, **hearing**, **heard**) have the potential to cause some confusion, particularly with children whose understanding of these grammatical forms is still developing. However, it is still preferable for children to hear meaningful sentences of varying tense rather than practitioners being limited to one tense which reduces the opportunities to use the word.

Families are particularly important at the 'activate' stage; by including them in the process, children hear the new words more and, crucially, in different contexts. Words are taken from the school context and applied more broadly. There are further details about how to involve families in Chapter 8.

Some ideas are given below for activate activities that will promote children's understanding of the targeted words. Of course, there are many other ways but, in all of them, it is the adults' use of language which is key. While many of these routines can be applied to most words, some will require a little planning. To ensure that the input is coordinated and the whole team are using the same words, we advise building the activate stage into curriculum planning.

Examples of activate activities

Words on Word Wall

Establish a Word Wall in a place where members of staff will see it. Regularly update it, and refer back to it, so that it is kept fresh and all members of staff know which words to use with children throughout the day and across activities. If practitioners are aware of which words to use, they can be applied in all sorts of naturally occurring opportunities. To learn a word, children need to hear it a number of times, so it is essential that all staff members work together and use the same words.

Examples

- On one day, one practitioner might lead the children in a **creep** about the play area while another encourages them to **creep** up on an unsuspecting adult.
- On another day, one colleague may encourage **stomping** in the garden while another **stomps** in the dressing-up corner.
- On a third day, one team member instructs the children to look **grumpy** as they go to play and another colleague uses **grumpy** when talking about the morning routine.
- Use the words in different ways such as: 'The dinosaur is **hunting** for the eggs'; 'I've lost the scissors. I need to **hunt** for them.'
- Relate the words to what the children are doing and focusing on, such as when a child is experiencing messy play, use the word **touch**.

Words around the environment

Place the written word and its symbol around the setting, both indoors and outdoors, in areas where the new word may be applied. This will remind adults to use the new words in these contexts. To encourage generalisation, place the symbol in more than one area or move the symbols around each week. This is more straightforward for verbs and adjectives but look for ways of including concrete nouns.

Examples

- Pictures of **lips**, **hips** and **freckles** on a mirror in the home corner.
- **Hunt** and **sharp** next to the play dinosaurs.
- **Search** alongside the sand tray.
- **Calm** where the children line up.

'I need to hear' stickers

Print out sticky labels with 'A word I need to hear today ...' on them. Write the new word on the stickers and give them to some or all of the children. The phrase 'A word I need to hear today ...' reminds staff members and families to use the word in sentences rather than asking questions.

Example

> A word I need
> to hear today ...
> *search*

Emotions

Emotion words are best activated when applied to children while they are experiencing it. Describe what the child is feeling and the situation that has prompted the feeling.

Examples

- 'You didn't think that was about to happen! You were very **surprised**.'
- 'I can see you look **worried**. You want to know where your mum is. You don't know where she is.'
- 'We will be going to the seaside tomorrow. We are all very **excited**. We all enjoy the seaside and thinking about going.'

Treasure hunts

Go on treasure hunts around the setting, looking for objects that exemplify the word. This works well for adjectives. It may require placing extra objects that meet the criteria within the children's reach. Collect all of the objects back together and talk about, compare and touch them. If possible, keep them all together; if not, take photographs for display.

Examples

- 'Find things with **specks** on them.'
- 'What can you see that is **stripy**?'
- 'Let's find some things that are **colourful**.'
- 'Everyone needs to find something that can **flap**.'

Equipment to explore

Put out equipment on a table or in an area of the room. This works well if the equipment that was used in teaching is made available plus a few other items. This helps support children to generalise the new word. Allow the children to explore the objects.

Examples

- Put out boxes containing interesting objects for **discover** or **surprise**. Some of these might have been used in the 'teach' sequence and others will be new.
- Put out some play food, dolls and the symbol for **gobble** or **feast**.

Topic tables

Set up play equipment that relates to the topic and add target words to encourage adults to use them in play. Do not overload children with lots of words. Pick two or three but change them so that different words are used on different days.

Examples

- **Captain**, **treasure** or **adventure** next to the pirate ship.
- **Beetle**, **delicate** or **examine** next to mini-beasts.
- **Live**, **enormous** or **chimney** next to dolls' houses.

Sorting activity

This will require more direct adult involvement but it works well for adjectives and concepts. In small groups, lead the children in sorting the objects into groups. Language is particularly important here, so remember not to use opposites until both are well established. Instead use <u>no</u> or <u>not</u> to indicate the opposite.

Examples

- Present a range of animals and other items. Encourage the children to sort them by **creatures** and <u>not</u> **creatures**.
- Sort items that **shimmer** and things that do <u>not</u> **shimmer**.

Books

Books can be used to identify words to teach. They can also be used to activate words from the topic as children learn more about the new word. Read books to the children that include the new words. Highlight the new word and expand on it in a discussion.

Examples

- Baby bear is in bed **pretending** to be an aeroplane in *Peace at Last* (Murphy, 2007).
- The Queen loses her **favourite** hat in *The Queen's Hat* (Antony, 2014).

Word walk

Go on a walk in the local area looking for objects that exemplify the new word. Collect the objects or take photographs that can then be shared with other people. Parents can join you on such walks so that they may also repeat it on the way home.

Examples

- Go to a vegetable garden and look at what is **growing**.
- In the spring, find trees in **blossom**.
- Walk around the local neighbourhood talking about buildings with **chimneys**.

A monkey can ...

This is useful for verbs. Give each child a small toy and introduce the verb that has previously been taught. Say that your toy (monkey) is really good at the verb and he is going to teach all of the other toys how to do that action as well. All children copy the action and are encouraged to talk about their toy doing the action.

Example

The monkey is good at **swinging** and he is going to teach all of the others about **swinging**. Monkey **swings** like this. You do it too. Monkey is **swinging** in the trees. Elephant is **swinging** on a rope. Giraffe is **swinging** on the swings. Dog is **swinging** up and down.

Reviewing words that have been taught

Reviewing words is essential to establishing them in children's long-term memories. There are a variety of ways of reviewing words including Word Bag and associated activities, review games and parent activities. Working in Early Years settings is often very busy but having some way of keeping track of when words are reviewed is useful to ensure that all words are covered.

Word Bag

Make or find an attractive Word Bag. Put objects that represent words from previous weeks in a bag and talk about them as you take them out. It will take imagination to think of objects that represent each word but it is worth the effort because words that are not reviewed are more likely to be forgotten.

Keep the same target words in the bag for several weeks. However, change the objects occasionally to avoid rote learning. For example:

- **furry** is represented by a teddy bear and then changed to a cushion
- **delicious** is a banana, then a cake
- **precious** is a jewel, then something special to the teacher
- **creep** is a spider, then a cat
- **ocean** is a shell, then a fish
- **growing** is a child's and an adult's sock together and then a toy baby
- **gobble** is a spoon, then a toy ice-cream.

It is more difficult to find objects to represent verbs and emotions. You could take pictures of children acting out the verb or emotion and put those in the bag. It is much more meaningful to have photos of the children showing the verb rather than commercial images.

Some of the concrete nouns from the topic can be hard to represent with objects but do try to be creative before you resort to a picture. For example, a piece of play dough can be used to represent a **planet**; place a piece of fabric over a stick for a **tent**; a **chimney** can be built out of building bricks (with optional cotton wool smoke).

Remove a few objects from the bag each day and talk about them in a variety of different ways rather than just labelling. Accompany each Word Bag activity with the associated action, sign or gesture. Some more examples are given below.

Word Bag activity	Examples
Label Name the word as it is removed from the Word Bag.	'This teddy is **furry**.'
Which one? Present several objects and ask children to identify which one represents the word.	'Which one is **sweet**: a sausage, a cake or a piece of bread?'
Forced choices Ask the children to choose which one the word applies to. (Try to avoid opposite concepts, eg avoid 'Is an elephant light or **heavy**?' Instead, ask 'Which is **heavy** – a mouse or an elephant?')	'Who would **stomp**? A giant or a cat?' 'What would be **precious**? A bit of mud or a gold ring?'
What else? What else can you think of that is __________ ?	'The banana is **delicious**. What else is **delicious**?'
What can you see? What can you see in the classroom that is __________ ?	'What can you see in the classroom that is **growing**?'
Apply the word to a real event Talk about a familiar event using the reviewed word.	'On Tuesday, at the party, we had a wonderful **feast** with lots and lots to eat.'
Has that happened to you? Link the word back to children's own world knowledge by asking them whether they have ever experienced the word.	'In school we touched the chicks **gently**. What other things have you had to touch **gently**?'

(continues)

Word Bag activity	Examples
That sounds funny Play with the sounds of particularly attractive-sounding words. Repeat it, emphasising the sounds. Ask the children to repeat it also.	'Listen to the sound of the word. **Squelch. Squelch. Squ-e-l-ch**. It sounds funny! Now you say it slowly.'
You do it This is particularly useful for verbs. Encourage children to act out the action in their own way.	'Let's pretend we are all pirates and we are in a boat that is **sinking**. We are going down and **sinking**.'
When will you use it? Ask the children to consider when they will use the word both at school and in other contexts.	'**Squashed** is a great word. When do you think you might use it in school? When might you use it at home?' 'When might you use the word **caravan**?'

Review games and activities

In addition to the Word Bag activities, there is a range of review games and activities which will ensure that children encounter the words and build their knowledge of the words.

The following games will get you started but you can add your own as well. The challenge of working with young children is that because they do not have well-developed language skills, any chosen games need to use simple language. Some of these games are also included in Chapter 5 Fun with Words.

Teach a new word to Teddy

Introduce a soft toy or puppet and tell the children that he needs help learning a new word. Ask them to tell the soft toy what they know about the word. Once the children have made their contributions, the toy then summarises it back to them, thus providing a solid definition.

Let's all do it

This game is best if it compares the verb to a similar but familiar verb. Encourage all of the children to copy the action and then to choose which action to do. For example, 'Let's start walking and now let's **stomp**. **Stomp, stomp, stomp**. Shahad, shall we **stomp** or walk?'

Act it out

This is an extension of the above activity. Make up two or more short stories that include the word. Act them out. Ask the children to copy you and then encourage them to choose a story to retell.

For example, 'We built a very, very big tower, but when Florence put on one more brick, the tower came **crashing** down. I was trying to put the curtains up, but they slipped and the curtains came **crashing** down. Let's act them out. Now it's your turn to tell the stories.'

I heard a good word

Listen out for any of the words to be reviewed. Highlight this at an opportune moment. For example, 'I heard Jamila use a good word. I heard Jamila in the garden say she was **searching** for something. Jamila, tell me about what you were **searching** for.'

Whisper words

Introduce the idea of 'whisper words'. When walking around adults, identify review words that the children could use in their particular activity and then whisper them to the children. For instance, if the children are doing a craft activity, **fuzzy** could be whispered or, in the home corner, **snuggle** could be suggested. Later, encourage the children to talk about their play incorporating the whispered word.

When I play I will say

Choose one of the review words and ask the children to identify when they could use it.

Songs and action

Repeat any of the songs with a review word. Include the action. The songs are a fun way to highlight words but do not add much to the meaning. Build on this by adding another review game as well. There are song sheets in the Appendix and they can be downloaded to sing along to from **www.routledge.com/cw/speechmark** and also on the Word Aware Youtube.

Pass the object

Pass an object around and talk about its attributes and functions. Ask: 'What can it do? What is special about it? Where do you find it?' Repeat the children's contributions and add further information as required, thus building up a complete definition.

True or false?

Make up obvious 'true or false' questions. The false options can be as silly as you like. For example, for **mechanic**, 'Does a **mechanic** fix cars? Does a **mechanic** fix cows? Does a **mechanic** repair motorbikes? If you were ill, would you go to see a **mechanic**?' Extend this by asking 'Why or why not?'

Verb video

Filming the children doing the actions is a particularly motivating way to review the words. Review the video as a class. Describe what you see and encourage the children to describe as well. For example, 'I can see Dwayne **pretending** to be a doctor. Next we have Shanade **pretending** to be a dinosaur! Tell me what you see next.'

Memory game or Kim's Game

This is useful for nouns. Place an object which represents your review word on a tray with several other objects. Name them all. Then, out of the children's view, remove the review word object. Encourage the children to inspect the tray and name which object is missing.

Picture dictionary

Take lots of photographs of the children with objects that show new words they have learned. Or take pictures of children doing the action. Make the photos into a book. This can be reviewed as a group or left in the book corner for children to read as they wish.

Topic picture

Look at a picture that relates to a previous topic. Take turns giving clues about what you see. For example, for **seagull**, 'At the seaside, I saw something that was flying and making a loud noise. I saw a … Now it's your turn.'

Symbols in play sets

Place written words accompanied by their symbols in with sets of equipment. When the equipment is taken out, adults will again be reminded of some of the key words. Rather than making new words and symbols, words that were introduced to the class in previous terms can be recycled.

Help me find it

This is suitable for nouns. Pretend to have lost one of the objects you want to review and that you cannot remember what it is called. Describe the object until the children guess. Find the object, name it and, as a class, describe it together. Jointly decide a way in which you will remember it for next time.

Verb story

Select three or four verbs that have previously been taught. Make up a story. Encourage the children to retell and extend the story. For example, for **leaping**, **hearing**, **investigating** and **hatching**: 'One rainy day Sam was playing outside, **leaping** over puddles when he **heard** an interesting sound coming from under a bush. He went to **investigate** and found some baby ducks **hatching**. Now it's your turn to tell me the story. Also you can think about what happened next.'

Games and activities for families

Parents and families are particularly important to word learning because children develop a deeper and richer understanding of words if they hear them spoken by different people in a range of places.

Make sure that parents know that they need to use the words in context rather than test their child's knowledge of the word. 'Comments rather than questions' is a useful message to convey to parents.

There is more on how to involve parents in Chapter 8, but there are some specific ideas below.

Fridge words

Once words have been introduced, send home the words on the 'Fridge Words' sheet in the Appendix (page 244). This alerts parents to the words to use at home. Support parents to use the target words rather than ask the children about what the words mean.

Objects from home

Ask children to bring objects from home that exemplify the word. This can work well for adjectives or concepts.

For example: soft toys to talk about **furry**, a stone to show **flat**, a toy butterfly to exemplify **delicate**.

On the way home

Encourage parents to talk about the new word with their child on the journey home. For example, to look for objects that are **sparkly**, to **trudge** along or to feel **bones** on each other.

'I need to hear' stickers

Add the word that needs reviewing to stickers which read 'I need to hear …' Encourage parents and other family members to use the word when talking to their child.

A word I need to hear today …

search

Further examples of vocabulary planning

Note: there is a wide variaton in children's vocabulary at this age due to children's experiences, so these are examples only and practitioners will need to tailor them to their children.

Topic: **Mini-beasts**			
	 **Anchor words**	 **Goldilocks words** 'Not too easy and not too hard, but just right'	 **Step on words**
Nouns	caterpillar spider butterfly bee snail ladybird worm fly	dragonfly wasp centipede beetle	tarantula
Verbs	wiggle move look fly	flap squirm land (verb) search identify examine	scuttle
Adjectives	careful	tiny delicate	monstrous

Topic: **All about me – emotions**

	 **Anchor words**	 **Goldilocks words** 'Not too easy and not too hard, but just right'	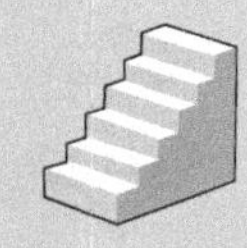 **Step on words**
Nouns	No nouns or verbs for this topic		
Verbs			
Adjectives	happy cross sad	astonished worried excited surprised embarrassed confused nervous	perplexed crazed bemused

Topic: **All about me – body parts**			
	 **Anchor words**	 **Goldilocks words** 'Not too easy and not too hard, but just right'	 **Step on words**
Nouns	arm back foot hand legs hair finger toe mouth face eyes nose ear tongue	hips shoulder freckles skin bones heart lips	lungs shin calf
Verbs	run jump	leap breathe	digest
Adjectives	big little	round long short	extended

Topic: **Houses and homes**

	Anchor words	**Goldilocks words** 'Not too easy and not too hard, but just right'	**Step on words**
Nouns	bathroom bedroom bricks door garage garden gate kitchen living room lounge stairs roof window	bungalow caravan castle chimney cottage farmhouse flat tent tiles	detached semi-detached terraced house windmill
Verbs	build	move (house) live	inhabit
Adjectives	big little old new	enormous tiny comfortable	Georgian

Note: this topic will vary considerably based on the children's experiences.

Topic: **Family**			
	Anchor words	**Goldilocks words** 'Not too easy and not too hard, but just right'	**Step on words**
Nouns	mum dad baby family grandad parents sister brother cousins granny/nan uncle aunt	son daughter niece nephew grandchild celebration	relatives relationship descendants
Verbs	cuddle love visit	caring	developing
Adjectives	nice	alike	similar

Topic: **Senses**

	Anchor words	Goldilocks words 'Not too easy and not too hard, but just right'	Step on words
Nouns	eyes nose mouth	taste buds	capillaries
Verbs	listen smell hear see	touch taste	savour
Adjectives	nice	bright hard soft smooth light dark sweet sour lumpy	dim

Topic: **Space**			
	 **Anchor words**	 **Goldilocks words** 'Not too easy and not too hard, but just right'	 **Step on words**
Nouns	moon rocket sun stars	astronaut planet Earth	comet asteroids Mercury Venus Mars Jupiter Saturn Uranus Neptune Pluto galaxy space shuttle vacuum
Verbs	fly look	explore discover travel	orbit rotate
Adjectives	exciting	dark bumpy far	intergalactic

Topic: **Spring**			
	Anchor words	**Goldilocks words** 'Not too easy and not too hard, but just right'	**Step on words**
Nouns	butterfly rain lamb flowers garden babies	buds chick tadpoles duckling blossom spring	frog spawn offspring
Verbs	jump fly	hatch grow plant capture wriggle	decompose developing
Adjectives	beautiful	young	bountiful perfumed newborn

Topic: **Beach**

	Anchor words	**Goldilocks words** 'Not too easy and not too hard, but just right'	**Step on words**
Nouns	T-shirt sandals ice-cream van ice lollies ice-cream sun lotion beach sandcastle crab rock shorts sunglasses beach ball bucket spade boat sea sun shells fish bat ball	kite pier pebbles lifeguard yacht seagull starfish lighthouse waves	deck chair Frisbee inflatable ring Punch and Judy ship-in-a-bottle windbreak beach huts life belt rock pool
Verbs	swim splash fly play	save search paddle	frolic
Adjectives	hot cold	bumpy smooth deep shallow	sweltering

Topic: **Plants and growth**			
	Anchor words	**Goldilocks words** 'Not too easy and not too hard, but just right'	**Step on words**
Nouns	flower leaf/leaves fruit rain water sun	bean root seed soil stem watering can vegetable	pollen
Verbs	dig	plant grow pick collect	harvest tend
Adjectives	beautiful dirty hungry	colourful	deciduous

Topic: **Dinosaurs**			
	Anchor words	**Goldilocks words** 'Not too easy and not too hard, but just right'	**Step on words**
Nouns	dinosaur	fossil scales	apatosaurus triceratops velociraptor brachiosaurus pterodactyl stegosaurus plesiosaur iguanodon tyrannosaurus rex
Verbs	fly chase catch	hunt stomp	contest
Adjectives	scary	dangerous sharp enormous fierce	scaly extinct carnivorous

Topic: **People who help us**

	Anchor words	**Goldilocks words** 'Not too easy and not too hard, but just right'	**Step on words**
Nouns	fire fighter nurse builder bus driver doctor teacher policeman policewoman postman postwoman	mechanic caretaker librarian vet taxi driver dentist job	paramedic secretary manager
Verbs	help drive	care fix deliver	direct detect
Adjectives	scary	brave helpful kind	responsible

Further examples from books

Book: *Peace at Last* (Murphy, 2007)	
	Goldilocks words
Nouns	drip
Verbs	None selected from this book
Adjectives	uncomfortable exhausted
Other	late

Book: *Mr Gumpy's Outing* (Burningham, 2001)	
	Goldilocks words
Nouns	None selected from this book
Verbs	squabble tease tip
Adjectives	None selected from this book
Other	–

Book: *The Gruffalo* (Donaldson & Scheffler, 1999)	
	Goldilocks words
Nouns	feast
Verbs	stroll flee
Adjectives	amazing dark
Other	–

Book: *We're Going on a Bear Hunt* (Rosen, 1995)	
	Goldilocks words
Nouns	None selected from this book
Verbs	hunt tiptoe trip
Adjectives	long dark wavy narrow furry
Other	through over under

Book: *Farmer Duck* (Waddell & Oxenbury, 1995)	
	Goldilocks words
Nouns	None selected from this book
Verbs	fetch answer squeeze waddle creak
Adjectives	lazy
Other	–

Book: *The Tiger Who Came to Tea* (Kerr, 1968)	
	Goldilocks words
Nouns	None selected from this book
Verbs	None selected from this book
Adjectives	furry stripy
Other	all suddenly nothing

Book: *Handa's Surprise* (Browne, 1995)	
	Goldilocks words
Nouns	surprise
Verbs	None selected from this book
Adjectives	delicious soft
Other	–

Book: *Hairy Maclary from Donaldson's Dairy* (Dodd, 2002)	
	Goldilocks words
Nouns	surprise
Verbs	snoop wail cover
Adjectives	skinny low
Other	–

Book: *Commotion in the Ocean* (Andreae, 2010)	
	Goldilocks words
Nouns	creatures
Verbs	pretend scamper bury jiggle grin snip waddle slither snuggle
Adjectives	sneaky gorgeous glowing massive
Other	beneath incredibly

Book: *Owl Babies* (Waddell & Benson, 1994)	
	Goldilocks words
Nouns	None selected from this book
Verbs	hunt lose fuss
Adjectives	dark brave silent
Other	night

Book: *Amy and Louis* (Gleeson, 2006)	
	Goldilocks words
Nouns	creatures ocean
Verbs	stare call
Adjectives	None selected from this book
Other	–

Book: *Corduroy* (Freeman, 2014)	
	Goldilocks words
Nouns	None selected from this book
Verbs	search wander reach gasp admire yank topple dash
Adjectives	comfortable enormous amazing fuzzy
Other	carefully everywhere suddenly always

Book: *The Giving Tree* (Silverstein, 2010)	
	Goldilocks words
Nouns	shade
Verbs	gather sell rest sail
Adjectives	older
Other	–

Book: *Diary of a Wombat* (French & Whatley, 2006)	
	Goldilocks words
Nouns	response
Verbs	reach demand bash discover offer amaze energetic
Adjectives	flat delicious
Other	curiously

Direct teaching (STAR) summary

Select

Pick a Goldilocks word: a word that is really useful and will be encountered again.

Choose words from:

- topic

- shared books.

Teach

Teach the Goldilocks word to the whole group.

Symbol
- Present a symbol that represents the word

Sound
- Clap syllables
- Say to partner

Meaning
Choose a combination of:
- sensory experiences
- simple vocabulary to define the word
- relate the word to what they know
- tell a story

Action

Song or rap

Word Wall (to remind adults)

Activate

Choose one or more of the following options.

- Words on the Word Wall
- Words around the environment
- 'I need to hear' stickers
- Emotions
- Treasure hunts
- Equipment to explore
- Topic tables
- Sorting activity
- Books
- Word walk
- A monkey can …

Review

Word Bag and activities

Games

Families

Chapter 4
Teaching Concepts

Chapter 4
Teaching Concepts

Introduction

Verbal concepts are the words that shape how we think about the world. They are particularly important in Early Years because, at this age, children are making sense of the world and verbal concepts give them the means to talk about, interact and expand their understanding. The concepts learned in Early Years form the foundation that later learning depends on, so they are more than 'just another word'. For example, if a child does not have time concepts such as **before** and **night**, he will be limited in how he thinks and talks about time. If a child does not have positional language such as **behind** or **through**, he will struggle to talk precisely about the location of objects.

Not surprisingly, Early Years concepts are highlighted in various curricula around the world. For example, in the UK, the Early Years Foundation Stage requires children to 'use everyday language to talk about size, weight, capacity, position, distance, time' (Foundation Years, 2016).

In the USA, the Common Core requires children to describe the relative positions of objects using terms such as **above**, **below**, **beside**, **in front of**, **behind** and **next to** to describe measurable attributes of objects, such as length or weight. Also to 'directly compare two objects with a measurable attribute in common, to see which object has "more of"/"less of" the attribute, and describe the difference. *For example, directly compare the heights of two children and describe one child as taller/shorter*' (Common Core, 2016).

In Australia, the Early Years Learning Framework requires children to 'demonstrate an increasing understanding of measurement and number using vocabulary to describe size, length, volume, capacity' (Australian Government, 2016).

The abstract nature of concepts makes them more challenging to teach and learn. However, because they are so fundamental, they do merit careful planning and methodical teaching.

The Early Years curriculum is loaded with a wide range of concepts, for instance:

- space (**next to**, **through**)
- size (**big**, **long**, **narrow**)
- quantity (**some**, **both**)
- movement (**slow**, **quick**)
- time (**after**, **early**).

In this resource, the process for teaching concepts has the same basic structure as topic-based and literacy-based word learning, which are outlined in Chapter 3. It follows the STAR sequence:

- Select
- Teach
- Activate
- Review

- **Select** the really useful vocabulary.
- **Teach** the selected vocabulary in a structured manner.
- **Activate** the meaning by using the words in context.
- **Review** the taught words to ensure they are retained.

(Source: adapted from Blachowicz & Fisher, 2010)

By following each step, practitioners will promote children's natural word learning. In the **select** phase, words at the right level are introduced. In the **teach** phase, the new words are highlighted to children, before meaning is expanded in a natural way in the **activate** phase. By building **review** activities into the process, the word continues to be heard and so deepens in meaning rather than being forgotten.

Select

Vocabulary is generally less prescribed in Early Years, so practitioners are required to select their own words to target. There is a list of relevant concepts on page 256. This list is created from various curricula, early language assessments and programmes such as the Early Years Foundation Stage (UK), the Common Core (USA), the Early Years Learning Framework (Australia), Living Language (Locke, 1985), Developing Language Concepts (Burrows, 2006), Pre-school CELF-2 (Wiig & Semel, 2006), Reynell Developmental Language Scales (Edwards *et al*, 2011), Pre-school Language Scale (Zimmerman *et al*, 2014) and Language Link (www.speechlink.info).

The concepts listed in the Appendix (page 256) are in three roughly developmental categories, although the order of teaching is left to individual discretion. Some of the concepts listed are 'anchor' words which the majority of children will know. These early developing concepts have been included because they will be useful for some children.

In some settings, it may be possible to assess individual children's concept knowledge. However, in most settings, practitioners will be required to make a judgement about which words to select, based on their working knowledge of the class members.

Practitioners may select concepts using a range of different methods. One possibility is to work through the concepts, selecting those which are most relevant to the children. An alternative is to choose concepts which relate to a particular topic or book that is being taught at the time. For instance:

- In the topic 'pirates', there will be **long** swords, **long** beards and **long** planks.

- During the 'house and home' topic, there will be many opportunities for **different**, such as **different** chairs, **different** doors and **different** houses.
- Sense-related concepts such as **heavy** and **rough** will be readily applicable during the 'senses' topic.
- The book *Owl Babies* (Waddell & Benson, 1994) highlights the concept **night**.
- The book *Possum Magic* (Fox, 1991) includes **late** and **over**.

Concepts that are not on the list on page 256 may still be taught but will require extra planning. There is also a blank planning sheet in the Appendix (page 255).

The rest of this chapter explains the activities that need to be included.

Teach

The underlying principles for teaching concepts are as follows.

Don't teach opposites at the same time

Traditionally, words that are opposites are often taught together. For instance, the words **in front** and **behind** are often introduced together. When opposites are taught together, the labels may be learned but may not be attached securely to the correct meaning and subsequently lead to confusion. Once confused, it may take considerable effort for a child to then work out which is which.

It is better to introduce one concept at a time and make sure that the first is established before introducing the other. If the opposite term needs to be used, it can be described with a negative, eg 'This is **in front** and this is not **in front**.'

This may sound a bit odd at first but classroom practice indicates that it works effectively.

Once the first concept has been established then the opposite term can be easily introduced because much of the conceptual learning has already been completed. However, take care not to introduce the second concept too quickly.

The **teach** sequence is divided into an **introduction**, a **Concept Cat story**, a **physical** or **personal** activity and an activity with **objects**.

In all of the activities, specific equipment is suggested. If you do not have the items readily to hand, use a suitable substitute.

Introduction

By working through the stages in the introductory sequence, the phonological (speech sound) components are supported by sign and gesture. This ensures that all children have a heightened awareness of the word before they attach meaning in the subsequent steps.

	**Use a sign or gesture.** Some staff members will be familiar with formal signing systems (eg Makaton) so, if you know the sign, use this. If you do not know a sign, a gesture can be just as effective.
	**Look at the symbol together.** At the top of each activity sheet there is a symbol for the concept, for your reference. Larger printable versions can also be downloaded from www.routledge.com/cw/speechmark
	**Say the word to your partner.** Instruct the children to say the word to a peer. It is important that they say the word as well as hear it.
	**Sing a Word Aware song including the word.** This reinforces the sounds of the word. The songs start on page 245 and sing-along versions can be be downloaded from www.routledge.com/ or the Word Aware channel on Youtube.

Concept Cat stories

Stories are an engaging and entertaining way of introducing ideas to children. These simple stories introduce each concept to the children, allowing them to build up meaning.

General principles of Concept Cat stories

The stories:

- Repeat the target word several times in meaningful contexts.
- Provide clear examples of the concept and what it is not. Negatives are used to highlight what the concept is not (eg this is cold and this is not cold) and opposites are avoided.
- Relate the concept to a range of objects. This extends the children's understanding. For example, the story about **loud** first introduces a **loud** drum, then **loud** stamping feet and then **loud** talking.
- Avoid using other concepts within the same story, where possible.
- Avoid other grammatical forms of the word. For example, the story about **tall** avoids using **taller** and **tallest** (superlatives and comparatives have specific stories on pages 159–62).

When telling the stories, remember to:

- Always use gesture to aid comprehension, eg shaking your head for negatives; gesturing or signs for the concepts.
- Emphasise the key concept and negative words (eg no, not).
- Use the symbol to support the understanding of the concept.
- Stick to the wording of the story.

By adding the following brief activities, children have the chance to experience the new concept, thus embedding their understanding.

Physical/personal activity

The children are given the opportunity to physically experience the concept so that they can develop an understanding of how it relates to them personally. This stage is about the children using their bodies without other objects. For instance, ask **all** of the children to stand up. Then tell one child to sit down. Then talk about not **all** children are standing up. Or encourage all of the children to be **noisy** by stamping their feet and then remaining not **noisy**.

Objects

This is slightly more abstract because it is less centred on the child but, at this stage, the children use objects to understand the concept. For instance, placing **rough** and not **rough** objects in a feely bag and sorting them accordingly or looking at a set of drawers and identifying a drawer that is **above** another one.

Activate

The purpose of the 'activate' phase is for the children to hear the word in their everyday environment. They are then able to build on this initial introduction until they have a full understanding of the concept.

A variety of activities are used, including:

- *Words around the environment.* The symbol is put in a place where the concept will be used. For example, **first** could be placed next to the door for lining up, and **wet** could be displayed in the water play area. This reminds adults to use the word.
- *Treasure hunts.* Go on a treasure hunt with the children, looking for items that exemplify the concepts. For example, looking on the **top** of cupboards or, in the outside play area, looking for **rough** things.
- *Equipment to explore.* Set out equipment for the children to explore. This could be the Concept Cat story items or other relevant equipment. For example, you may want to build an obstacle course for the children to climb **over** or put the symbol **above** next to a set of birds, butterflies or aeroplanes and take turns making objects go **above**.
- *Sorting activity.* This needs adult support to facilitate the understanding and use of the word. This is particularly useful for children who need a little more time to consolidate their learning, eg for **noisy**. Gather a range of silent, quiet and **noisy** items. Explore each one in turn and then categorise them into **noisy** and not **noisy**.
- *Word walk.* Go on a walk to look for objects and places that exemplify the concepts, eg to see buildings which are **old** and not **old**.

Review

Reviewing words helps to secure new learning in long-term memory, thus reducing the likelihood of them being forgotten. A choice of different activities is provided and we recommend that they are repeated occasionally. By using one activity, an object for the Word Bag, a concept book and a family activity, a robust system for reviewing words will be provided with relatively little effort.

Review activities

These comprise a selection of simple, quick activities.

- *Which one represents the word?* Set up situations that exemplify the word and then discuss, eg walk in different directions and ask the children to say when you are moving **forwards** or talk about the **front** of objects which have an obvious **front**, such as a microwave oven, a radio or a food packet.
- *Sorting activities.* For example, sort items into **thick** and not **thick**.
- *Choices.* For example, what time of day would be **light** or not **light**? Which place might be **light** – a cave or a beach?
- *What else can you see or think of that is ____________?* For example, talk about which animals might be **large**.
- *Talk about a familiar event using the reviewed word.* For example, talk about having a bath and needing to **dry** yourself or going to a cinema where it is **dark**.
- *Books.* Use books that contain the concept to highlight the word. For example, read *Goldilocks and the Three Bears* at story time. Ask the children to listen out for the word **hard**.

Word Bag

Place objects that exemplify the word in a suitable bag. For concepts, several objects are often needed to show them, eg put a **bendy** toy figure in the bag. For **next**, put a cup and a bottle in the bag. Mime the sequence of pouring and drinking and then retell the sequence using **next**.

Concept book

Make a paper or an electronic book of the concept. This could be the Concept Cat story in photos, or photos of children or toys showing the concept in the setting. For example, children making arches and going **through** them, toys hiding **under**, **old** things brought from home, children playing in the water for **wet**. As children are taught the concepts, they will engage in activities which can be photographed and collated in a book.

Family

Suggest simple activities for the family to do on the way home or at home. There is guidance for families about supporting concepts at home, given in two different formats, on the next two pages.

Information sheet for families

Word Aware

Helping your child to understand concepts

Your child has been learning some new concepts!

Concepts are words that shape how we think about the world. For instance, concepts such as 'early', 'night' or 'after' help us talk about time. Concepts are hard to learn but they are fundamental to learning, so worth spending time on.

Your child will be regularly learning new concepts through lots of fun activities. The more your child hears the new words in different situations, the better his or her understanding of the concept will be. You can help your child to learn the concept by carrying out the suggested activities. All of the activities are quick and easy to do. Often they can be done on the way home.

- Try to do the activity once or twice in the week it has been suggested.
- Children need to hear the new words in sentences, so make comments rather than ask questions.
- Stick to the exact word. If you are asked to do an activity about 'tall', stick to 'tall' – don't talk about 'tallest' or 'taller'.
- Do not use the opposite word. This can be very confusing for children. If 'tall' is the word being taught, say 'not tall' rather than 'short'.
- Do the activity in your home language. If a child understands the concept in their home language, this will help them with the word in English.

Information sheet for families

Helping your child to understand concepts

Stick to the exact word. If you are asked to do an activity about 'tall', stick to 'tall', don't talk about 'tallest' or 'taller'.

Do not use the opposite word. This can be very confusing for children. If 'tall' is the word being taught, say 'not tall' rather than 'short'.

Use comments rather than questions.

Concepts are words that help shape how we think about the world, eg 'new', 'straight', 'later', 'behind', 'hard.' They are important!

Try to do the activity once or twice in the week it has been suggested.

Do the activity in your home language.

Above

1 Teach

Use a sign or gesture for **above**.

Look at the symbol together.

Say the word **above** to your partner.

Sing a Word Aware song including the word **above**.

2 Teach

Equipment: a Concept Cat toy, four photos on the wall in a vertical line and a boy figure or doll (called 'Jake').

Concept Cat is a clever, clever cat. He looks here, he looks there, learning as he goes and, when he comes home, he tells us a story. Concept Cat is a clever, clever cat.

This story is all about **above**. Listen out for the word **above**.

Concept Cat and his friend Jake are looking at some photos.

Jake: That one's my favourite.

(Concept Cat points to the second picture from the bottom.)

Concept Cat: You mean this one?

Jake: No the one **above** it.

(Concept Cat points to the one below.)

Concept Cat: This one?

Jake: No, that's not **above**. Look, this one is **above** (points to the picture second from the top). I like the one **above** that as well.

Concept Cat: Yes I like that one and the one **above** too.

Concept Cat, what a clever, clever cat. He knows all about **above**.

3 Teach

A Tell children to hold up one hand. Then hold the other one **above** it.

B Look at a set of drawers. Identify a drawer in the middle and talk to children about the drawer **above**.

C Talk about what you can see that is **above** a certain point in the room, such as a window.

4 Activate

Put the symbol **above** on a wall and stick pictures **above** it.

5 Review

Activity: take a photo of children with their faces showing **above** a fence or play equipment.

Word Bag: put four building bricks in the bag. Make a tower. Point to one brick. Talk about which ones are **above** it.

Concept book: see page 76 for details.

Family: when putting things away, talk about things that go **above**.

After

1 **Teach**	 Use a <u>sign</u> or <u>gesture</u> for **after**.  Look at the <u>symbol</u> together.  <u>Say</u> the word **After** to your partner.  <u>Sing</u> a Word Aware song including the word **After**.
2 **Teach** 	**Equipment: Concept Cat toy, a doll ('Alice'), beanbag, hoop and ball.** Concept Cat is a clever, clever cat. He looks here, he looks there, learning as he goes and, when he comes home, he tells us a story. Concept Cat is a clever, clever cat. This story is all about **after**. Listen out for the word **after**. Concept Cat sees a beanbag. He wants a turn. Alice gets the beanbag and says, 'You need to go **after** me.' Alice plays with the beanbag. Then Concept Cat plays with the beanbag **after** Alice. Concept Cat sees the hoop. He wants to jump in the hoop. Alice says, 'You need to jump in the hoop **after** me.' Alice jumps in the hoop. Then Concept Cat jumps in the hoop **after** Alice. Concept Cat is a bit sad. He doesn't like going **after** Alice. He sees a ball. He says to Alice, 'I am going to kick the ball. You can kick the ball **after** me.' 'OK,' says Alice. Concept Cat kicks the ball. Then Alice kicks the ball **after**. Concept Cat played with the beanbag **after** Alice. Concept Cat jumped in the hoop **after** Alice. Alice kicked the ball **after** Concept Cat. Concept Cat, what a clever, clever cat. He knows all about **after**.
3 **Activate**	A Ask the children to stamp, clap and then nod. Talk about what you all did **after** you clapped. B Ask four children to line up. Discuss who lined up **after** whom, eg 'Maisy lined up first. Who was **after** Maisy?' Repeat the activity with different children. C Place the symbol **after** in the toilets or bathroom. Talk about **after** going to the toilet or bathroom, you need to wash your hands. D At key moments in the day, talk about what will happen **after** an event, eg '**After** snack time, we are going to have our story. Then **after** the story …'
4 **Review**	 **Activity:** look at the class visual timetable. Discuss what comes **after** each activity.  **Word Bag:** take three random items from the bag. Talk about which ones came **after**.  **Concept book:** see page 76 for details.  **Family:** discuss routines at home, eg what do you do **after** you have brushed your teeth?

All

1 **Teach**	 Use a <u>sign</u> or <u>gesture</u> for **all**.  Look at the <u>symbol</u> together.  <u>Say</u> the word **all** to your partner.  <u>Sing</u> a Word Aware song including the word **all**.
2 **Teach** 	**Equipment: Concept Cat toy and a drawer or tray with several knives, forks and spoons.** Concept Cat is a clever, clever cat. He looks here, he looks there, learning as he goes and, when he comes home, he tells us a story. Concept Cat is a clever, clever cat. This story is all about **all**. Listen out for the word **all**. Concept Cat was helping Mum. He needed to set the table. Mum said, 'Concept Cat, go and get **all** of the knives'. Concept Cat went into the kitchen and opened a drawer. Concept Cat thinks he got out **all** of the knives. (Leave some knives in the drawer.) Oh no! He did <u>not</u> get **all** of the knives. Mum said, 'Make sure that you have **all** of the knives.' (Concept Cat gets the last knife.) Now Concept Cat has **all** of the knives. Now Mum wants him to get **all** of the forks. (Concept Cat gets some of the forks.) Concept Cat has <u>not</u> got **all** of the forks. Mum says, 'You need **all** of the forks!' (Concept Cat gets the rest of the forks.) Now Concept Cat has got **all** of the forks. Now Mum wants him to get **all** of the spoons. (Concept Cat gets **all** of the spoons.) Concept Cat has got **all** of the knives, **all** of the forks and **all** of the spoons. Concept Cat, what a clever, clever cat. He knows all about **all**.
3 **Teach**	Ask **all** of the children to stand up. Then tell one child to sit down. Then talk about <u>not</u> **all** children standing up. Repeat the activity.
4 **Activate**	At snack time, talk about **all** of the milk/raisins/fruit/juice, eg 'I have **all** of the raisins. Look, **all** of the juice is now gone.'
5 **Review**	 **Activity:** read the book *The Tiger Who Came to Tea* (Kerr, 1968). Ask the children to listen out for the word **all**. Hold up the symbol for **all**. Remind the children about when they **all** stood up or when Concept Cat had got **all** of the forks. Can they put up their hands when they hear the word **all**?  **Word Bag:** put five of the same objects in the bag. Take out **all** five and place them on the table. Pick up four. Have you got them **all**? Show holding them **all**.  **Concept book:** see page 76 for details.  **Family:** when pouring a drink, or giving out fruit, talk about **all**.

Around

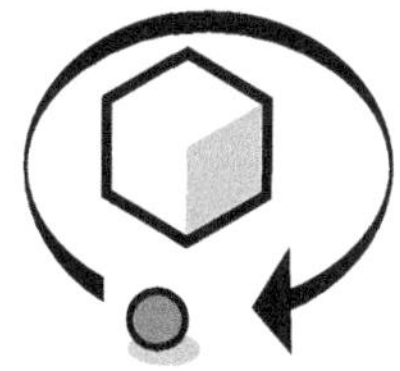

1 **Teach**	 Use a sign or gesture for **around**.  Look at the symbol together.  Say the word **around** to your partner.  Sing a Word Aware song including the word **around**.
2 **Teach** 	**Equipment: Concept Cat toy and a toy table and chair.** Concept Cat is a clever, clever cat. He looks here, he looks there, learning as he goes and, when he comes home, he tells us a story. Concept Cat is a clever, clever cat. This story is all about **around**. Listen out for the word **around**. Concept Cat is in the house. He wants to go outside to play but the furniture is in the way. (Concept Cat climbs on the table.) Dad tells him, 'Go **around** the table.' (Concept Cat crawls under the table.) Dad grumbles, 'That is not **around**. Go **around** the table.' Concept Cat goes **around** the table. Then he comes to the chair. Dad stops him and reminds Concept Cat, 'You need to go **around** the chair.' Concept Cat goes **around** the chair. He can even go **around** again and **around** the other way. Concept Cat, what a clever, clever cat. He knows all about **around**.
3 **Teach**	Line up the children by an item of furniture or a box. Instruct each one to go **around** the object, miming the action as you go. Then instruct some children to go **around** the furniture for a second time.
4 **Activate**	A In the bike-riding area, place some obstacles that children need to go **around**. B Go for a walk and, when you come to any obstacles, talk about going **around** them.
5 **Review**	 **Activity:** talk about how you move **around** the classroom using the word **around**.  **Word Bag:** put a tree and a toy person in the bag. Act out the person going **around**. Say, 'Look the person is going …'  **Concept book:** see page 76 for details.  **Family:** at home, talk about sitting **around** the table or walking **around** brother or sisters who are playing.

Back

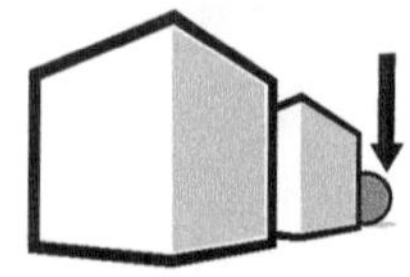

1 **Teach**	 Use a sign or gesture for **back**. 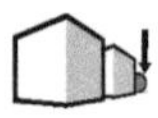 Look at the symbol together.  Say the word **back** to your partner.  Sing a Word Aware song including the word **back**.
2 **Teach** 	**Equipment: Concept Cat toy and three toy animals such as rabbit, elephant and monkey. Place the monkey at the back of the line of animals.** Concept Cat is a clever, clever cat. He looks here, he looks there, learning as he goes and, when he comes home, he tells us a story. Concept Cat is a clever, clever cat. This story is all about **back**. Listen out for the word **back**. Concept Cat is playing a game with his friends. Concept Cat closes his eyes and the others all get in a line. Concept Cat needs to guess who is at the **back** of the line. Who is at the **back**? Is Rabbit at the **back**? No Rabbit is not at the **back**. Is Elephant at the **back**? No Elephant is not at the **back**. Is Monkey at the **back**? Yes Monkey is at the **back** of the line. Concept Cat now stands at the **back** of Monkey. Concept Cat is at the **back**. Concept Cat, what a clever, clever cat. He knows all about **back**.
3 **Teach**	All of the children need to face in the same direction and remain in this orientation. Instruct them to rub their backs. This is their **back**. One adult moves so that she is at the **back** of the group. Children close their eyes and the adult who is at the **back** makes a noise. The noise is coming from the **back**.
4 **Activate**	When lining up, talk about who is at the **back**.
5 **Review**	 **Activity:** line up four children in front of the class. Talk about who is at the **back**. Change the order and direction and talk about it again.  **Word Bag:** place several small world people in the bag. Line them up all facing in one direction. Talk about which one is at the **back**.  **Concept book:** see page 76 for details.  **Family:** when the child is sitting on your lap, talk about you being at the **back** of them.

Backwards

1 **Teach**	 Use a <u>sign</u> or <u>gesture</u> for **backwards**.  Look at the <u>symbol</u> together.  <u>Say</u> the word **backwards** to your partner.  <u>Sing</u> a Word Aware song including the word **backwards**.
2 **Teach** 	**Equipment: Concept Cat toy and a toy monkey.** Concept Cat is a clever, clever cat. He looks here, he looks there, learning as he goes and, when he comes home, he tells us a story. Concept Cat is a clever, clever cat. This story is all about **backwards**. Listen out for the word **backwards**. Concept Cat and Monkey are having fun. Monkey says, 'I know! Let's see if we can do lots of things going **backwards**.' Concept Cat: 'Great! I love going **backwards**!' Monkey: 'Let's see if we can walk **backwards**.' (Both walk **backwards**.) Concept Cat: 'Let's run **backwards**.' (Monkey runs **backwards** and Concept Cat goes forwards.) Monkey: 'That is <u>not</u> **backwards**. Run **backwards**.' (Concept Cat runs **backwards**.) 'That's better. Now let's jump **backwards**.' Concept Cat: 'We are good at going **backwards**. We walked **backwards**, we ran **backwards** and we jumped **backwards**.' Concept Cat, what a clever, clever cat. He knows all about **backwards**.
3 **Teach**	In a clear space, encourage the children to walk **backwards**. Then jump **backwards**.
4 **Activate**	In the bike-riding area, designate a bell or horn that, when it sounds, means all of the riders need to change direction. Talk about when they are going **backwards** or <u>not</u> **backwards**.
5 **Review**	 **Activity:** say 'I've got a tree, some bubbles and a car. Which one can go **backwards**?'  **Word Bag:** put a toy man in the bag. Walk him **backwards** and then ask, 'How is he walking?'  **Concept book:** see page 76 for details.  **Family:** in a clear space, practise walking **backwards**.

Note: children need to confidently understand and use **first** and **after**, before you attempt to teach **before**.

Before

1 **Teach**	 Use a <u>sign</u> or <u>gesture</u> for **before**. 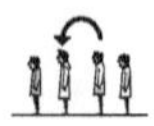 Look at the <u>symbol</u> together.  <u>Say</u> the word **before** to your partner.  <u>Sing</u> a Word Aware song including the word **before**.
2 **Teach** 	**Equipment: Concept Cat toy, a doll ('Mum'), a biscuit, an apple and a bin.** Concept Cat is a clever, clever cat. He looks here, he looks there, learning as he goes and, when he comes home, he tells us a story. Concept Cat is a clever, clever cat. This story is all about **before**. Listen out for the word **before**. Mum says, 'Concept Cat you must have an apple **before** you can have a biscuit.' Concept Cat takes the biscuit. Mum: '<u>No</u> Concept Cat. Eat the apple **before** the biscuit. Here, have some apple.' (Concept Cat eats the apple.) 'Now you can have a biscuit. You ate the apple **before** the biscuit.' Mum: 'Now put the apple core in the bin **before** you go out.' (Concept Cat goes out.) 'Concept Cat. You must put the apple core in the bin **before** you go out.' Concept Cat: 'I'll put the apple core in the bin **before** I go out.' Concept Cat, what a clever, clever cat. He knows all about **before**.
3 **Teach**	A Draw three pictures on the board: a tree, a house and a ball. Talk through the order in which you drew them. 'I drew the tree **before** I drew the house. I drew the house **before** I drew the ball.' B Put up a series of sequencing pictures. Talk about the order using **before**.
4 **Activate**	On the visual timetable, place the symbol for **before** next to the symbol for lunch/snack/going home time. Ask 'What do we have to do **before** we go to lunch?' (Wash hands, etc.)
5 **Review**	 **Activity:** ask **before** lunch did we have our story time? What did you do **before** lunch?  **Word Bag:** put a toy bed in the bag. Talk about what children do **before** they go to bed.  **Concept book:** see page 76 for details.  **Family:** talk about familiar routines. '**Before** bedtime you need to ...'

Behind

1 **Teach**	Use a <u>sign</u> or <u>gesture</u> for **behind**. Look at the <u>symbol</u> together. <u>Say</u> the word **behind** to your partner. <u>Sing</u> a Word Aware song including the word **behind**.
2 **Teach** 	**Equipment: Concept Cat toy plus another toy animal.** Concept Cat is a clever, clever cat. He looks here, he looks there, learning as he goes and, when he comes home, he tells us a story. Concept Cat is a clever, clever cat. This story is all about **behind**. Listen out for the word **behind**. Concept Cat wants to sneak up on his friend to surprise him from **behind**. (Approaches toy animal from the front.) 'That's no good, that's <u>not</u> **behind**.' (Approaches from the side.) 'That's no good. That's <u>not</u> **behind**.' (Approaches from above.) 'That's no good. That's <u>not</u> **behind**.' (Sneaks up from **behind**.) 'That's **behind**. Boo! Concept Cat sneaked up from **behind**. Now his friend is going to sneak up on Concept Cat from **behind**.' Concept Cat, what a clever, clever cat. He knows all about **behind**.
3 **Teach**	A Place a selection of items in front of you. Ask the children to close their eyes. Put an item **behind** your back. What is **behind** you? If they say an item that is front of you say, '<u>No</u>, that is <u>not</u> **behind** me.' B Ask one child to come to the front. Tell them to close their eyes. Choose another child to stand **behind** them. The first child has to ask 'Who is **behind** me?' The second child has to say, 'It's me!' The first child then guesses who 'me' is.
4 **Activate**	A Put up a sheet or curtain in the classroom. Take turns at hiding **behind** it. B Play hide-and-seek. Hide **behind** and look **behind** objects.
5 **Review**	**Activity:** at group time, leave objects **behind** your chair. Talk about where they are and ask the children to find them. **Word Bag:** put three toy people in the bag. Place them in a line. Talk about who is **behind** another person. (Sometimes, ask about each person, eg sometimes nobody will be **behind**.) **Concept book:** see page 76 for details. **Family:** explore the home and let the child find places to go **behind**.

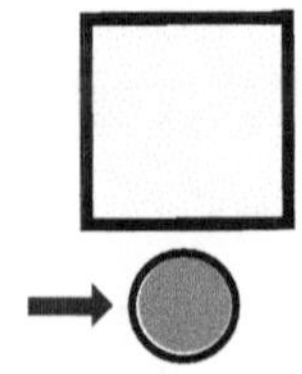

Below

1 **Teach**	 Use a <u>sign</u> or <u>gesture</u> for **below**. 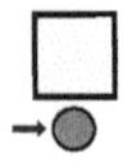 Look at the <u>symbol</u> together.  <u>Say</u> the word **below** to your partner.  <u>Sing</u> a Word Aware song including the word **below**.
2 **Teach** 	**Equipment: Concept Cat toy and a toy climbing frame. If the latter is not available, it can be imaginary.** Concept Cat is a clever, clever cat. He looks here, he looks there, learning as he goes and, when he comes home, he tells us a story. Concept Cat is a clever, clever cat. This story is all about **below**. Listen out for the word **below**. One day Concept Cat was playing outside. He was about to jump off the climbing frame when his teacher said, 'Watch out **below**. Before you jump, you need to look to see if anyone is **below** you.' (Concept Cat looks up.) 'That is <u>not</u> **below**. You need to look **below**.' (Concept Cat looks across.) 'That is still <u>not</u> **below**. Look **below** you.' (The teacher points. Concept Cat looks **below**.) 'That's it Concept Cat, now you are looking **below** you.' Looking like this (up) is <u>not</u> **below**. Looking like this (across) is <u>not</u> **below**. But looking like this (looking **below**) is **below**. Concept Cat, what a clever, clever cat. He knows all about **below**.
3 **Teach**	Allow the children to stand carefully on chairs or ladders so they can look **below** them. Talk about who is **below** and who is <u>not</u> **below**.
4 **Activate**	A In the water play area, look for fish and other sea creatures **below** the sea surface. B In the outdoor play area, climb on the apparatus and look at who and what is **below**.
5 **Review**	 **Activity:** choose an item on the wall and talk about what is **below** it.  **Word Bag:** put a toy ladder and a figure in the bag. Place the figure on the ladder and talk about and point to the step **below**.  **Concept book:** see page 76 for details.  **Family:** look at your child's bedroom window and talk about it, using the word **below**.

Bendy

1 **Teach**	 Use a sign or gesture for **bendy**.  Look at the symbol together.  Say the word **bendy** to your partner.  Sing a Word Aware song including the word **bendy**.
2 **Teach** 	**Equipment: Concept Cat toy, ice lolly sticks, hard plastic sticks, bendy twigs and pipe cleaners.** Concept Cat is a clever, clever cat. He looks here, he looks there, learning as he goes and, when he comes home, he tells us a story. Concept Cat is a clever, clever cat. This story is all about **bendy**. Listen out for the word **bendy**. Concept Cat is making a model. He wants to make special legs that are **bendy**. First, he finds some ice lolly sticks. That is no good. They are not **bendy**. Then he finds some plastic sticks. They are no good either as they are not **bendy**. Then he finds some twigs. The twigs are **bendy**. But wait, the pipe cleaners are really **bendy**. Look, they are **bendy**. The ice lolly sticks were not **bendy**. The plastic sticks were not **bendy**. The twigs were **bendy** and the pipe cleaners were **bendy** too. Concept Cat, what a clever, clever cat. He knows all about **bendy**.
3 **Teach**	A Ask the children to bend their elbows and bend their knees. They are **bendy**. B Select a few items and let the children explore them to discover whether they are **bendy** or not **bendy**.
4 **Activate**	A Go on a treasure hunt and find lots of things that are **bendy**. Place them on a table so the children can explore them at their leisure. B Do craft activities which include items that are **bendy**.
5 **Review**	 **Activity:** show the children several different items and ask them to identify which things are **bendy**.  **Word Bag:** put a **bendy** toy figure in the bag. Show how **bendy** he or she is.  **Concept book:** see page 76 for details.  **Family:** look through your child's toys and find a **bendy** toy. Label him Mr or Mrs **Bendy**.

Between

1 **Teach**	Use a <u>sign</u> or <u>gesture</u> for **between**. Look at the <u>symbol</u> together. <u>Say</u> the word **between** to your partner. <u>Sing</u> a Word Aware song including the word **between**.
2 **Teach**	**Equipment: Concept Cat toy, toy people ('Teddy' and 'Dolly') and small world furniture.** Concept Cat is a clever, clever cat. He looks here, he looks there, learning as he goes and, when he comes home, he tells us a story. Concept Cat is a clever, clever cat. This story is all about **between**. Listen out for the word **between**. One day, Concept Cat was watching television with his friends Teddy and Dolly. Teddy says, 'Come and sit **between** us.' Concept Cat does not know what **between** means. He will need to find out about **between**. He sits down (next to the toys). 'No, that is <u>not</u> **between**. Come and sit **between** us.' Concept Cat moves. (He sits on the other side.) 'No, that is <u>not</u> **between**. Come and sit **between** us.' Concept Cat moves again. (He now sits in front.) 'No, that is <u>not</u> **between**. Come and sit **between** us.' Concept Cat moves. (He is now **between**.) 'Great, now you are sitting **between** me and Dolly. You are **between** us,' says Teddy. Concept Cat, what a clever, clever cat. He knows all about **between**.
3 **Teach**	A Three children stand in front of the class. Ask 'Who is **between**?' Give the symbol to the child who is **between**. Change the children round. Ask 'Who is **between** now?' B Put out two pieces of furniture. Put a play figure **between** the chair and the bed. Let Concept Cat have a turn. If he makes mistakes, help him to find **between**.
4 **Activate**	A Look at your coat peg. Your coat peg is **between** two coat pegs. Whose pegs is yours **between**? B In the book area, place some interesting objects **between** books on the shelf. Find the things that are **between** the books.
5 **Review**	**Activity:** when the children are sitting on the carpet, talk about who is **between** two children. **Word Bag:** put four pieces of fruit in the bag. Put them in a line (eg apple, banana, orange, grape). Ask which one is **between** the apple and the orange, etc. **Concept book:** see page 76 for details. **Family:** squeeze up **between** family members on the sofa.

Big

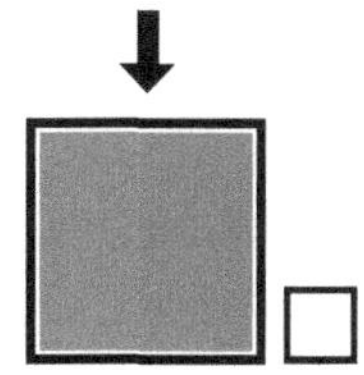

1 Teach	 Use a <u>sign</u> or <u>gesture</u> for **big**. 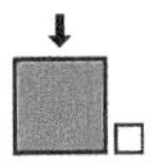 Look at the <u>symbol</u> together.  <u>Say</u> the word **big** to your partner.  <u>Sing</u> a Word Aware song including the word **big**.
2 Teach 	**Equipment: Concept Cat toy, a very big box and items which need to be either clearly big or clearly small (eg big and little spoon, big and little chair, big and little towel).** Concept Cat is a clever, clever cat. He looks here, he looks there, learning as he goes and, when he comes home, he tells us a story. Concept Cat is a clever, clever cat. This story is all about **big**. Listen out for the word **big**. Concept Cat has a **big** (use hand gesture to indicate **big**) box and he wants to find lots of **big** things to go in his **big** box. Help him find lots of **big** things to go in his **big** box. Concept Cat goes into the kitchen to find something **big**. Here is a spoon. It is not **big**. Concept Cat needs a **big** spoon. Oh! This one looks **big**, so **big** it goes in the **big** box. Here is a chair. It is not **big** and so it **cannot** go in the **big** box. Here is a **big** chair. The **big** chair can go in the **big** box. Concept Cat sees two towels. He needs the **big** one. This towel is not **big**. This towel is **big** and so it can go in the **big** box. Right, let's have a look at all of the **big** things Concept Cat has collected. A **big** spoon, a **big** chair and a **big** towel, all in a **big** box. Concept Cat, what a clever, clever cat. He knows all about **big**.
3 Teach	Gather some **big** items of clothing. Let the children try on the **big** items.
4 Activate	Have a selection of **big** and <u>not</u> **big** items. Sort them into two groups.
5 Review	 **Activity:** read the story of 'Goldilocks and the Three Bears'. Who has the **big** bowl, chair and bed?  **Word Bag:** put one **big** and one <u>not</u> **big** item in the bag. Take them out and compare them.  **Concept book:** see page 76 for details.  **Family:** ask family members to look out for **big** things on the way home.

Note: children need to confidently understand and use **all** and **lots**, before being introduced to **a bit**.

A bit

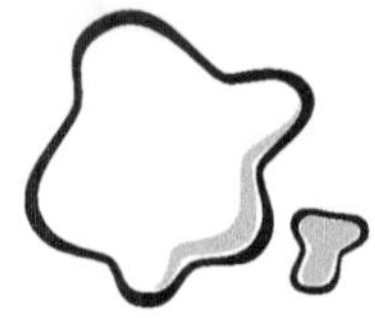

1 **Teach**	 Use a sign or gesture for **a bit**.  Look at the symbol together.  Say the word **a bit** to your partner.  Sing a Word Aware song including the word **a bit**.
2 **Teach** 	**Equipment: Concept Cat toy, two dolls ('Tom' and 'Katie'), a pretend sandwich, two glasses of water and something to tip the water into.** Concept Cat is a clever, clever cat. He looks here, he looks there, learning as he goes and, when he comes home, he tells us a story. Concept Cat is a clever, clever cat. This story is all about **a bit**. Listen out for the words **a bit**. Concept Cat: 'Tom, can I have **a bit** of your sandwich?' Tom: 'Yes, you can have **a bit**.' (Concept Cat eats the entire sandwich.) 'Oh no! I said that you could have **a bit** of my sandwich!' Concept Cat: 'I am thirsty! Oh look, Katie has a drink of water. Katie can I have **a bit** of your water?' Katie: 'Yes, you can have **a bit**.' (Concept Cat drinks all of the water, mimed by tipping it away.) 'Oh no! I said that you could have **a bit** of my water! I know, I will get some more water and we can share but this time you can only have **a bit** of water.' (Katie gets another glass of water.) Concept Cat: 'I will only take **a bit** this time.' (Adult sips a little water.) Concept Cat: 'Here, there is some for you because I only took **a bit**.' Concept Cat, what a clever, clever cat. He knows all about **a bit**.
3 **Teach**	Share a biscuit or cake with everyone taking **a bit**. Give a whole one to an adult. Have they got **a bit**? 'No, you can only have **a bit**!' Take it back and make sure the adult has **a bit**.
4 **Activate**	A At snack time, have the symbol for **a bit** on the table and talk about **a bit** of juice or **a bit** of apple. B At tidying up time, ask the children to pick up **a bit** of paper.
5 **Review**	 **Activity:** using play dough, ask the children to take **a bit**.  **Word Bag:** put a broken cracker in a plastic bag. Talk about **a bit**.  **Concept book:** see page 76 for details.  **Family:** share food at home, where each person gets **a bit**.

Both

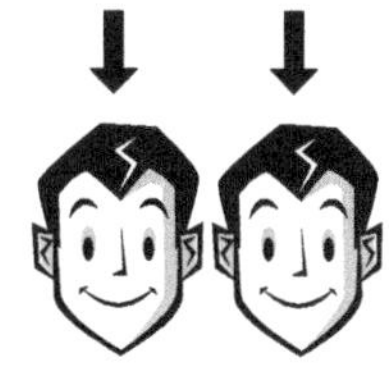

1 **Teach**	 Use a <u>sign</u> or <u>gesture</u> for **both**.  Look at the <u>symbol</u> together.  <u>Say</u> the word **both** to your partner.  <u>Sing</u> a Word Aware song including the word **both**.
2 **Teach** 	**Equipment: Concept Cat toy, a T-shirt, a pair of trousers, socks and gloves.** Concept Cat is a clever, clever cat. He looks here, he looks there, learning as he goes and, when he comes home, he tells us a story. Concept Cat is a clever, clever cat. This story is all about **both**. Listen out for the word **both**. Concept Cat is getting dressed. He puts on his T-shirt and trousers. Then he looks for his socks. He can only find one sock. That is <u>not</u> **both**. He needs **both** socks. He has two feet and so needs two socks! He needs **both** of his socks. He looks around. At last he finds two socks. He says, 'Oh good, now I have **both** of my socks!' It is very cold today. He needs his gloves. Concept Cat can only find one glove. That is <u>not</u> **both**. He needs **both** of his gloves. He has two hands, he needs two gloves. He needs **both** gloves. Then he finds **both** gloves and he says, 'Now I have **both** gloves'. Now Concept Cat has **both** socks and **both** gloves. Concept Cat, what a clever, clever cat. He knows all about **both**.
3 **Teach**	A Instruct the children to show **both** of their hands and **both** of their feet. B Put out a selection of shapes – two of each kind. Find **both** circles. If a child only gets one say, 'Oh yes, that is a circle. Now find **both** circles'.
4 **Activate**	Play outside with large items of equipment. Children need to use **both** hands to pick them up or catch a ball with **both** hands.
5 **Review**	 **Activity:** clap hands first with one hand and then with **both**. Ask 'Which one is better?'  **Word Bag:** put any two identical items in the bag. Ask a child to find **both** items from the bag.  **Concept book:** see page 76 for details.  **Family:** talk about **both** hands, feet, shoes, socks and gloves when getting dressed or going out.

Bottom

1 **Teach**	Use a <u>sign</u> or <u>gesture</u> for **bottom**. Look at the <u>symbol</u> together. <u>Say</u> the word **bottom** to your partner. <u>Sing</u> a Word Aware song including the word **bottom**.
2 **Teach**	**Equipment: Concept Cat toy and plastic plates, one of which is red. A pile of books including *The Gruffalo* (Donaldson & Scheffler, 1999). Five sheets of paper, one of which is yellow and not placed at the bottom.** Concept Cat is a clever, clever cat. He looks here, he looks there, learning as he goes and, when he comes home, he tells us a story. Concept Cat is a clever, clever cat. This story is all about **bottom**. Listen out for the word **bottom**. Concept Cat sees some plates. He wants a red one. It's at the **bottom**. Concept Cat will have to take off all the other ones so that he can get the plate which is at the **bottom**! Now Concept Cat wants to read a book. He's looking for *The Gruffalo*. It's at the **bottom**! He'll have to take the book from the **bottom**. Concept Cat needs some paper to do some drawing. He looks at the piece of paper that is at the **bottom**. (Point to the **bottom** sheet.) He does not want that one. He takes a yellow one. It is <u>not</u> at the **bottom**. Concept Cat, what a clever, clever cat. He knows all about **bottom**.
3 **Teach**	A Look at the **bottom** of your shoes. Can you see anything? B Use stacking cups or blocks. Talk about the one at the **bottom**. C Hide something at the **bottom** of a drawer. Go searching for what is at the **bottom**.
4 **Activate**	A Build towers with wooden bricks. What happens when the **bottom** brick is removed? B Take out items from **bottom** drawers. Ask children to put them away in the right **bottom** drawer.
5 **Review**	**Activity:** talk about what happened when the **bottom** brick was removed from the tower. **Word Bag:** tape three matchboxes together. Put something in the **bottom** box. Can they find what is in the **bottom** box? **Concept book:** see page 76 for details. **Family:** play Jenga or build towers and talk about the **bottom** pieces.

Corner

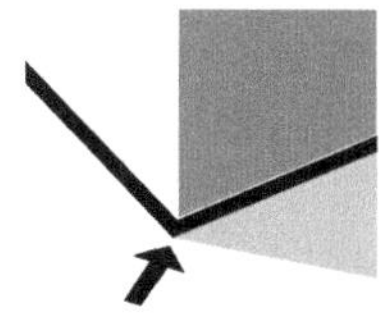

1 Teach

Use a sign or gesture for **corner**.

Look at the symbol together.

Say the word **corner** to your partner.

Sing a Word Aware song including the word **corner**.

2 Teach

Equipment: Concept Cat toy, a table and some toys.

Concept Cat is a clever, clever cat. He looks here, he looks there, learning as he goes and, when he comes home, he tells us a story. Concept Cat is a clever, clever cat. This story is all about **corner**. Listen out for the word **corner**.

Concept Cat is playing under the table. When he stands up Dad says, 'Watch your head on the **corner**.' But Concept Cat does not listen and bumps his head on the **corner**.

Concept Cat is tidying up and Mum says, 'Put your toys in the **corner**.' He tidies his toys away (put toys in the middle of the table), but Mum says, 'Not there. In the **corner**.' Concept Cat tidies the toys again (puts them on the side of the table), but Mum says, 'Put them in the **corner**!' Then Concept Cat moves all of his toys to the **corner**. His toys are now in the **corner**.

Concept Cat, what a clever, clever cat. He knows all about **corner**.

3 Teach

A Instruct the children to make **corners** with their bodies, eg with elbows and knees.

B Look at objects which have **corners**. Touch a **corner**. Touch a part of the table that is not a **corner**.

C Look at shapes. Ask the children to touch a **corner**. Find a shape with no **corners**.

4 Activate

A Make houses out of bricks. Collect them all together and explore **corners**.

B Send the children off to collect items with **corners** and put them all together and talk about them.

5 Review

Activity: look around the room and see what has **corners**.

Word Bag: put a toy table or brick in the bag. Can you find the **corners**?

Concept book: see page 76 for details.

Family: bring in an object which has **corners**.

Dark

1 **Teach**	Use a sign or gesture for **dark**. Look at the symbol together. Say the word **dark** to your partner. Sing a Word Aware song including the word **dark**.
2 **Teach** 	**Equipment: Concept Cat toy, a working lamp and a window with curtains (from a dolls' house).** Concept Cat is a clever, clever cat. He looks here, he looks there, learning as he goes and, when he comes home, he tells us a story. Concept Cat is a clever, clever cat. This story is all about **dark**. Listen out for the word **dark**. Concept Cat is going to bed but his room is not **dark**. To make his room **dark**, he closes the curtains. Now his room is **dark**. In the middle of the night, Concept Cat wakes up. Oh no! He can't see. It is so **dark**. Dad comes in and switches the light on. It is not **dark** now. Concept Cat can see. In the morning, the light is off and the curtains are closed. It is **dark**. Mum comes in and opens the curtains. It is not **dark** now! When the light was off, it was **dark**. When the curtains were closed, it was **dark**. Concept Cat, what a clever, clever cat. He knows all about **dark**.
3 **Teach**	A Turn the lights on and off and talk about **dark** and not **dark**. B Try on sunglasses or blindfolds to make things look **dark**.
4 **Activate**	A Put out the symbol for **dark** with blankets and a torch. Encourage children to make it **dark** and not **dark**. B In the role play area, play at opening and closing doors or curtains to make it **dark**.
5 **Review**	**Activity:** read *A **Dark**, **Dark** Tale* (Brown, 2012). **Word Bag:** put a blindfold in the bag and talk about **dark**. **Concept book:** see page 76 for details. **Family:** let children try on sunglasses indoors with the lights off so that it is **dark**.

Day

1 **Teach**	 Use a <u>sign</u> or <u>gesture</u> for **day**.  Look at the <u>symbol</u> together.  <u>Say</u> the word **day** to your partner.  <u>Sing</u> a Word Aware song including the word **day**.
2 **Teach** 	**Equipment: Concept Cat toy and another soft toy ('Mira'). Optional breakfast and lunch items and a toy bed.** Concept Cat is a clever, clever cat. He looks here, he looks there, learning as he goes and, when he comes home, he tells us a story. Concept Cat is a clever, clever cat. This story is all about **day**. Listen out for the word **day**. One **day**, Concept Cat is all confused about when it is **day** and when it is <u>not</u> **day**, so he asks his friend, Mira. She says it is **day** when it is light outside. When you can see the Sun it is **day** too. So Concept Cat learns that when he has breakfast, it is **day**. When he has lunch, it is **day**, if he has a nap that is **day** too, but when he goes to bed for a big sleep, that is <u>not</u> **day**. It is **day** when it is light outside. Breakfast is in the **day**. Lunch is in the **day**. A nap is in the **day**. Going to bed for a big sleep is <u>not</u> in the **day**. Concept Cat, what a clever, clever cat. He knows all about **day**.
3 **Teach**	A Look out of the window and decide whether it is **day** or <u>not</u> **day** now. B Talk about things the children do at home. Talk about whether they take place in the **day** or <u>not</u> **day**.
4 **Activate**	A Paint pictures of **day**, ensuring they include the Sun. B Bring in photos from home of events in the **day** and <u>not</u> **day**. C Read a book about **day**. It is a common theme in many books.
5 **Review**	 **Activity:** talk about all of the activities you do during the **day**. Make sure that you use the word **day**.  **Word Bag:** put a picture of the Sun in the bag. Talk about it being **day** when the Sun is in the sky.  **Concept book:** see page 76 for details.  **Family:** use the term **day** first thing in the morning and talk about what will happen in the **day**.

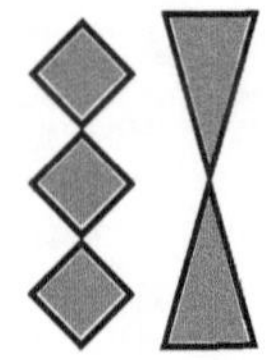

Different

1 **Teach**	 Use a sign or gesture for **different**. 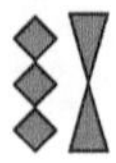 Look at the symbol together.  Say the word **different** to your partner.  Sing a Word Aware song including the word **different**.
2 **Teach** 	**Equipment: Concept Cat toy and four coloured pens, three of which should be red.** Concept Cat is a clever, clever cat. He looks here, he looks there, learning as he goes and, when he comes home, he tells us a story. Concept Cat is a clever, clever cat. This story is all about **different**. Listen out for the word **different**. Concept Cat wants to draw a picture. He has a red pen. 'I want a **different** pen.' He finds another pen. Is that **different**? No. He finds another pen. Is that **different**? No. Then he finds another pen. That is **different**. These two pens are **different**. This pen was not **different**. This pen was not **different**. This pen was **different**. Concept Cat, what a clever, clever cat. He knows all about **different**.
3 **Teach**	A Give one child a sparkly wig. Say, 'Oh look, you have **different** hair. You have pink hair. Your hair is **different** from Trisha's.' B Let's look at our eyes. I have blue eyes. Does anyone have **different** colour eyes?
4 **Activate**	A Put lots of objects and elastic bands on a table. The task is to tie together two items that are **different** from one another. B Play 'Snap!' slowly and talk about when the cards are **different**. 'Snap!' when they are not **different**.
5 **Review**	 **Activity:** present a series of items and judge whether they are **different**.  **Word Bag:** put any two items in the bag that are similar but a little **different** from one another.  **Concept book:** see page 76 for details.  **Family:** sort through a pile of clothing and talk about how the items are **different**.

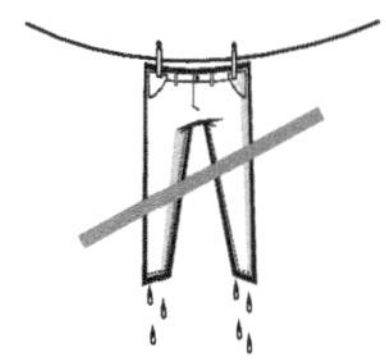

Dry

1 **Teach**	 Use a sign or gesture for **dry**.  Look at the symbol together.  Say the word **dry** to your partner.  Sing a Word Aware song including the word **dry**.
2 **Teach** 	**Equipment: Concept Cat toy and three pairs of socks, two of which should be damp.** Concept Cat is a clever, clever cat. He looks here, he looks there, learning as he goes and, when he comes home, he tells us a story. Concept Cat is a clever, clever cat. This story is all about **dry**. Listen out for the word **dry**. One day, Concept Cat needed to put on his socks. He needed some **dry** socks. He found a pair of socks. They were not **dry**. He found another pair of socks. When he touched them, they were not **dry**. Then he found another pair of socks. Yes, they were **dry**. These socks were not **dry**. These socks were not **dry**, but these socks were **dry**. Concept Cat, what a clever, clever cat. He knows all about **dry**.
3 **Teach**	Rub your hands together and note that they are **dry**. Touch the towels and note that they are also **dry**. Then dip your hands in water to make them not **dry** and then **dry** them with towels.
4 **Activate**	A Sort out objects that are **dry** and not **dry**. B Put the **dry** symbol up in the bathroom. Talk about hands that are **dry** and not **dry**. C Involve the children in washing clothes or dishes. Talk about **dry** and not **dry**.
5 **Review**	 **Activity:** talk about a rainy day and needing to put on **dry** clothes or having a bath and needing to **dry** yourself.  **Word Bag:** put pictures of two items that are **dry** and not **dry** in the bag.  **Concept book:** see page 76 for details.  **Family:** let the children help you to hang out the laundry or load the tumble dryer. Talk about the clothes being not **dry**. Then ask the children to feel the clothes when they are **dry**.

Early

1 Teach

Use a sign or gesture for **early**.

Look at the symbol together.

Say the word **early** to your partner.

Sing a Word Aware song including the word **early**.

2 Teach

Equipment: Concept Cat toy and several other soft toys, including one to be 'teacher'.

Concept Cat is a clever, clever cat. He looks here, he looks there, learning as he goes and, when he comes home, he tells us a story. Concept Cat is a clever, clever cat. This story is all about **early**. Listen out for the word **early**.

At school, the teacher told Concept Cat that he needed to come to school **early** but he did not know what **early** meant. The next day, Concept Cat went to school but it was not **early**; all of his friends were already working.

The teacher told him to come to school **early**. The next day, Concept Cat went to school but it was not **early**; all of his friends were already inside. That was not **early**.

The teacher told him to come to school **early**. The next day, Concept Cat got up **early** and made it to school **early**. He waited for his friends to come because he was **early**. Concept Cat was **early** for school.

Concept Cat, what a clever, clever cat. He knows all about **early**.

3 Teach

A Talk about who was **early** at school today.

B Talk about what children do **early** in the morning (before parents are awake).

4 Activate

A Start school a little **early** one day, so that you can share breakfast at school.

B On regular days, talk about all of the children who were **early**.

C Talk about what would happen if school finished **early** today.

5 Review

Activity: talk about your morning routine, waking up **early** and getting to school **early**. What would happen if you were not **early**?

Word Bag: include a piece of toy toast in the bag as the object representing **early** (it is eaten **early** in the morning).

Concept book: see page 76 for details.

Family: use the word **early** when waking children and as they get ready for school. They want to be **early** at school.

Empty

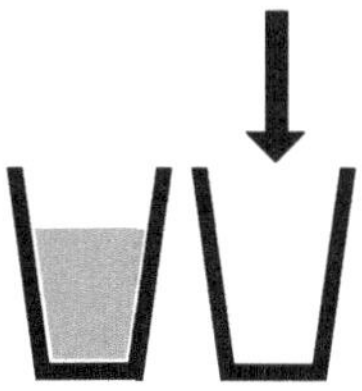

1 **Teach**	 Use a sign or gesture for **empty**.  Look at the symbol together.  Say the word **empty** to your partner.  Sing a Word Aware song including the word **empty**.
2 **Teach** 	**Equipment: Concept Cat toy, an empty cereal box, an empty biscuit tin and a full fruit bowl.** Concept Cat is a clever, clever cat. He looks here, he looks there, learning as he goes and, when he comes home, he tells us a story. Concept Cat is a clever, clever cat. This story is all about **empty**. Listen out for the word **empty**. Concept Cat is hungry. He really wants something to eat. He goes into the kitchen and finds a box of cereal. He looks inside. Oh no! It is **empty**. No cereal! He looks for a biscuit. He opens the biscuit tin. Oh no, it is **empty**! No biscuits! He looks in the fruit bowl. Oh wonderful, it's not **empty**. There is fruit to eat! The cereal packet was **empty**. The biscuit tin was **empty**. The fruit bowl was not **empty**. Concept Cat, what a clever, clever cat. He knows all about **empty**.
3 **Teach**	A Give out boxes to a few children, some with an object in them and some **empty**. Talk about which ones are **empty** and not **empty**. B Give a few children an **empty** cup. Add water to them all. Now they are not **empty**. The children drink the water and now the cups are **empty** again.
4 **Activate**	A Place the symbol for **empty** next to the sand or water tray. Encourage all staff members to use **empty** and not **empty** while children play. B At snack time also talk about cups being **empty** and not **empty**.
5 **Review**	 **Activity:** present a range of containers and discuss which ones are **empty**.  **Word Bag:** have two small transparent bags; one that has something in and one that does not. Talk about which one is **empty**.  **Concept book:** see page 76 for details.  **Family:** find things that are **empty** and not **empty** at home.

Enough

1 Teach

Use a sign or gesture for **enough**.

Look at the symbol together.

Say the word **enough** to your partner.

Sing a Word Aware song including the word **enough**.

2 Teach

Equipment: Concept Cat toy, a teddy bear, play food, a cup and a jug.

Concept Cat is a clever, clever cat. He looks here, he looks there, learning as he goes and, when he comes home, he tells us a story. Concept Cat is a clever, clever cat. This story is all about **enough**. Listen out for the word **enough**.

Concept Cat and Teddy are having something to eat. Concept Cat asks, 'Would you like some more food?'

Teddy says, 'I have **enough**.' Concept Cat isn't sure what **enough** means, so he gives Teddy some more.

Teddy responds, 'No, I said I had **enough**.' So Concept Cat asks Teddy, 'Would you like some more to drink?'

Teddy replies, 'No thank you. I have had **enough**.'

Then Concept Cat thinks, 'I know what **enough** means. I won't give Teddy any more. He has **enough**. Teddy has **enough** food. Teddy has **enough** drink.'

Concept Cat, what a clever, clever cat. He knows all about **enough**.

3 Teach

Show the children some cotton wool and a small bag. Ask, 'Do I have **enough** cotton wool to fill the bag?'

4 Activate

A At snack time, talk about having **enough** to eat and drink. Ask, 'Is that **enough**?'

B When cooking, use the word **enough** when adding liquid, when stirring or when dishing out servings.

5 Review

Activity: make a picture of a sheep. Give the children a tiny piece of cotton wool. Ask 'Is that **enough**?'

Word Bag: take a bowl and several items of play food out of the bag. Put **enough** of the items in the bowl to fill it.

Concept book: see page 76 for details.

Family: talk about having **enough** money to buy an item or **enough** food for dinner.

Fast

1 **Teach**	 Use a sign or gesture for **fast**.  Look at the symbol together.  Say the word **fast** to your partner.  Sing a Word Aware song including the word **fast**.
2 **Teach** 	**Equipment: Concept Cat toy, Frog, Pig and Fish (or other characters).** Concept Cat is a clever, clever cat. He looks here, he looks there, learning as he goes and, when he comes home, he tells us a story. Concept Cat is a clever, clever cat. This story is all about **fast**. Listen out for the word **fast**. One day Concept Cat was watching a race. He saw Frog. Zoom! (Frog zooms past.) Frog was so **fast**! Then he saw Pig. (Pig goes past very slowly.) Pig was not **fast**. Then he saw Fish. (Fish goes past **fast**.) Fish went **fast**. Concept Cat joins in the race because he wants to go **fast**. (Cat rushes past.) Concept Cat was **fast**. Here they go again. Frog is **fast**. Fish is **fast**. Concept Cat is **fast**. But Pig is not **fast**. Concept Cat, what a clever, clever cat. He knows all about **fast**.
3 **Teach**	A Run around in the hall **fast** and not **fast**. B Make a sign for the bike area that has **fast** and not **fast** on it. One child is the caller and tells the others to move **fast** and not **fast**.
4 **Activate**	Play with a selection of toy transport vehicles. Push them along and see which ones are **fast** and not **fast**.
5 **Review**	 **Activity:** move either **fast** or not **fast** and ask the children to label your actions.  **Word Bag:** put a toy sports car in the bag.  **Concept book:** see page 76 for details.  **Family:** on the way home from school, walk **fast** and not **fast**. Find a toy that is **fast**.

Fat

1 Teach

Use a <u>sign</u> or <u>gesture</u> for **fat**.

Look at the <u>symbol</u> together.

<u>Say</u> the word **fat** to your partner.

<u>Sing</u> a Word Aware song including the word **fat**.

2 Teach

Equipment: Concept Cat toy, a boy doll ('Harry'), several fat toy animals (eg a pig, hippopotamus or seal) and several which are not fat (eg a zebra and a monkey).

Concept Cat is a clever, clever cat. He looks here, he looks there, learning as he goes and, when he comes home, he tells us a story. Concept Cat is a clever, clever cat. This story is all about **fat**. Listen out for the word **fat**.

One day, Concept Cat was playing with his friend Harry. His friend asked for a **fat** animal but Concept Cat did not know what **fat** meant. He gave Harry a zebra, but Harry said that was <u>not</u> **fat**. He gave Harry a monkey, but he said that was <u>not</u> **fat**. Concept Cat found a hippo. He gave that to Harry. His friend said the hippo was **fat**. Then Concept Cat found a pig. The pig was **fat**. Seals are also **fat**.

The zebra was <u>not</u> **fat**. The monkey was <u>not</u> **fat**. The hippo was **fat** and the pig was **fat** too. Seals are also **fat**.

Concept Cat, what a clever, clever cat. He knows all about **fat**.

3 Teach

A Instruct the children to place their hands on their stomach. Then expand their belly so that they are '**fat**' and then <u>not</u> **fat** again.

B Fill a sock or stocking with pieces of fabric until it is **fat**. Take the fabric out and repeat the activity.

4 Activate

A Sort pictures of animals into **fat** and <u>not</u> **fat**.

B Look at pictures in books and find characters who are **fat**.

5 Review

Activity: make a 'lucky dip' bag filled with toy animals that are **fat** or <u>not</u> **fat**. Encourage the children to take turns and select a toy and label it as **fat** or <u>not</u> **fat**.

Word Bag: put a picture of a pig, or a soft toy, in the bag. Talk about the pig being **fat**.

Concept book: see page 76 for details.

Family: talk about animals that are **fat** and <u>not</u> **fat**.

Few

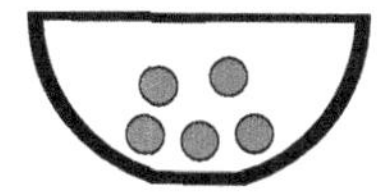

1 **Teach**	 Use a <u>sign</u> or <u>gesture</u> for **few**.  Look at the <u>symbol</u> together.  <u>Say</u> the word **few** to your partner.  <u>Sing</u> a Word Aware song including the word **few**.
2 **Teach** 	**Equipment: Concept Cat toy, something to represent strawberries (eg toy bricks) and blueberries (eg beads) and a plate.** Concept Cat is a clever, clever cat. He looks here, he looks there, learning as he goes and, when he comes home, he tells us a story. Concept Cat is a clever, clever cat. This story is all about a **few**. Listen out for the word **few**. Mum says, 'Would you like a **few** strawberries?' Concept Cat replies, 'Yes please. I love strawberries!' (Takes lots of them.) Mum is a bit cross and says, 'Oh no. Please only take a **few**. Here, this is a **few**.' (Puts three strawberries on Concept Cat's plate.) 'Would you like a **few** blueberries too?' Concept Cat wants a **few** blueberries and takes a **few** (four). Mum is happy now because Concept Cat has taken a **few**. Mum takes a **few** strawberries (four) and a **few** blueberries (three). Concept Cat, what a clever, clever cat. He knows all about **few**.
3 **Teach**	A Instruct the children to hold a **few** strands of their own hair. B Give out strawberries and blueberries to the children. Vary the amount but make sure it is a **few**. Then give lots to one child and none to some others. Talk about who has a **few**.
4 **Activate**	A Share out the pens in a craft activity. Get each child to choose a **few** each. Change colours after a while but remember that everyone only has a **few** each. B Anytime when sharing is required, talk about a **few**.
5 **Review**	 **Activity:** place different numbers of counters in bowls. Talk about which one has a **few**.  **Word Bag:** put a **few** items such as toy bricks or counters in the bag.  **Concept book:** see page 76 for details.  **Family:** when sharing food, talk about having a **few** each, eg when serving berries, sweets or mini-biscuits.

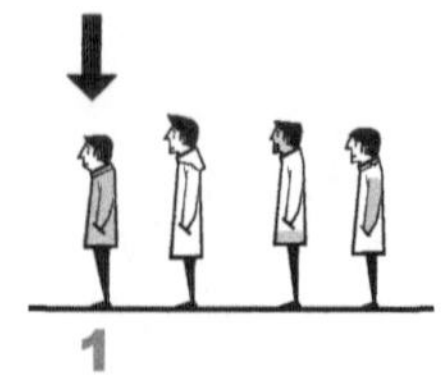

First

1 **Teach**	 Use a <u>sign</u> or <u>gesture</u> for **first**. 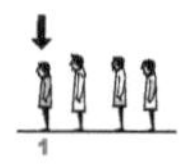 Look at the <u>symbol</u> together.  <u>Say</u> the word **first** to your partner.  <u>Sing</u> a Word Aware song including the word **first**.
2 **Teach** 	**Equipment: Concept Cat toy, a teddy bear and a doll.** Concept Cat is a clever, clever cat. He looks here, he looks there, learning as he goes and, when he comes home, he tells us a story. Concept Cat is a clever, clever cat. This story is all about **first**. Listen out for the word **first**. Concept Cat loves to be **first**. One day it was time to line up for play. Concept Cat ran as fast as he could but Teddy got there **first**. Concept Cat was sad. Teddy was **first**. Concept Cat was <u>not</u> **first**. Dolly lined up too. Dolly was <u>not</u> **first**. Dolly said, 'Don't worry Concept Cat, Teddy is **first** today. You will be **first** another day.' Dolly, Teddy and Concept Cat went out to play. They wanted to play buses. Dolly said, 'Let's all line up and wait for the bus. Concept Cat, you come and be **first**.' They all lined up. Concept Cat was **first**. Dolly was <u>not</u> **first**. Teddy was <u>not</u> **first** but they all had a good time playing buses. Concept Cat, what a clever, clever cat. He knows all about **first**.
3 **Teach**	A Line up the children. Talk about who is **first**. Mix up the order and identify again who is **first** and <u>not</u> **first**. B Line up the children again. Instruct the **first** child to do an action. The others then copy it. Change the order around and again everyone copies the new child who is **first**.
4 **Activate**	A Put up a symbol for **first** next to the door where you line up. Comment on who is **first** referring to the symbol. B When doing any small group activity, comment on who is **first** to have a turn.
5 **Review**	 **Activity:** place some soft toys in a row and talk about which one is **first**.  **Word Bag:** no specific items are needed. Just talk about which item comes out of the bag **first**.  **Concept book:** see page 76 for details.  **Family:** play a board game and talk about who goes **first**. On the way home, see who can run to a tree **first**.

Forwards

1 **Teach**	 Use a <u>sign</u> or <u>gesture</u> for **forwards**.  Look at the <u>symbol</u> together.  <u>Say</u> the word **forwards** to your partner.  <u>Sing</u> a Word Aware song including the word **forwards**.
2 **Teach** 	**Equipment: Concept Cat toy and several other soft toys.** Concept Cat is a clever, clever cat. He looks here, he looks there, learning as he goes and, when he comes home, he tells us a story. Concept Cat is a clever, clever cat. This story is all about **forwards**. Listen out for the word **forwards**. One day, Concept Cat was going on a school trip. He was excited. While he waited on the carpet, Concept Cat did <u>not</u> look **forwards**. In the line to get on the bus, Concept Cat did <u>not</u> look **forwards**. On the bus, Concept Cat did <u>not</u> look **forwards**. Then the teacher told Concept Cat to go down the bus steps **forwards**. Concept Cat walked **forwards** down the steps. When he waited on the carpet, Concept Cat did <u>not</u> look **forwards**. In the line to get on the bus, Concept Cat did <u>not</u> look **forwards**. On the bus, Concept Cat did <u>not</u> look **forwards**. When he walked down the steps, he went **forwards**. Concept Cat, what a clever, clever cat. He knows all about **forwards**.
3 **Teach**	A Form a conga line, adding one child at a time. Each time a child is added, talk about how they will move **forwards**. B Arrange chairs like on a bus. Everyone pretends to be on the bus. The bus moves **forwards** and the people all face **forwards**.
4 **Activate**	A In the playground, draw a chalk line for the children to follow, moving **forwards** as they do so. B March around the playground with one child being the 'sergeant major', telling the others to move **forwards**. C Play with toy trains, moving them **forwards** and <u>not</u> **forwards**.
5 **Review**	 **Activity:** walk in different directions and ask the children to say when you are moving **forwards**.  **Word Bag:** put a toy slide and person in the bag. Talk about the safest way to go down a slide, which is facing **forwards**.  **Concept book:** see page 76 for details.  **Family:** in a safe space, walk in different directions – **forwards** and <u>not</u> **forwards**.

Front

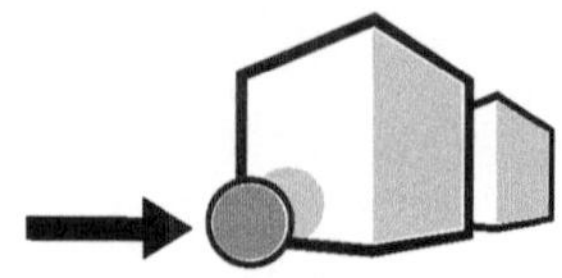

1 **Teach**	 Use a sign or gesture for **front**. 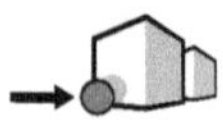 Look at the symbol together.  Say the word **front** to your partner.  Sing a Word Aware song including the word **front**.
2 **Teach** 	**Equipment: Concept Cat toy, several chairs for acting out a cinema, a car and a bus, and several soft toys.** Concept Cat is a clever, clever cat. He looks here, he looks there, learning as he goes and, when he comes home, he tells us a story. Concept Cat is a clever, clever cat. This story is all about **front**. Listen out for the word **front**. One day, Concept Cat went to see a movie (film). In the car on the way to the cinema, Concept Cat was not allowed to sit in the **front** seat. In the queue to buy tickets, he was not allowed to push in at the **front**. In the cinema, there were no seats left at the **front**. In the car on the way home, Concept Cat was still not allowed to sit in the **front**. On the bus the next day, he was allowed to sit at the **front**. Concept Cat liked sitting at the **front**. In the car, Concept Cat could not sit in the **front**. In the queue, he could not go to the **front**. In the cinema, he could not sit at the **front**. On the bus, Concept Cat could sit at the **front**. Concept Cat, what a clever, clever cat. He knows all about **front**.
3 **Teach**	A Show the children where their **front** is and then ask them to pat their **front**. Next, ask them to spin round for a moment. When they stop, they may be facing in a different direction but ask them again to show their **front**. Repeat this activity several times. B Make a small playhouse which has several doors, one of which is the **front**. Ask the children to walk play people through the **front** door.
4 **Activate**	A Make play dens and emphasise the **front** door, eg with a bell. B At carpet time, place a row of cushions or markers at the **front**. The children who sit on those are at the **front**.
5 **Review**	 **Activity:** look at objects with an obvious **front**, eg a microwave oven, a radio or a food packet. Talk about the **front**.  **Word Bag:** place any small product that has an obvious **front** in the bag, eg a shampoo bottle. Talk about **front**.  **Concept book:** see page 76 for details.  **Family:** when in the car, or on the bus, talk about who is in the **front**.

Full

1 Teach	Use a <u>sign</u> or <u>gesture</u> for **full**. Look at the <u>symbol</u> together. <u>Say</u> the word **full** to your partner. <u>Sing</u> a Word Aware song including the word **full**.
2 Teach 	**Equipment: Concept Cat toy, a bottle of water and a cup (and maybe a tray to keep things tidy).** Concept Cat is a clever, clever cat. He looks here, he looks there, learning as he goes and, when he comes home, he tells us a story. Concept Cat is a clever, clever cat. This story is all about **full**. Listen out for the word **full**. Concept Cat is thirsty. He finds a bottle of water that is **full**. He pours himself a drink. He wants it really **full**. He pours some water into a cup. (Pour in a little water.) The cup is <u>not</u> **full**. He pours some more in. (Pour in more water.) No, it is still <u>not</u> **full**. He fills it right up to the top. Now the cup is **full**. Concept Cat likes his cup to be **full**. But look, now the bottle is <u>not</u> **full**. Concept Cat drinks the water. Now the cup is <u>not</u> **full**. (Repeat the actions to accompany the retelling.) First, the bottle was **full** and the cup was <u>not</u> **full**. Then the cup was <u>not</u> **full**. Then it was **full** and the bottle was <u>not</u> **full**. Concept Cat drank the water and the cup was <u>not</u> **full**. Concept Cat, what a clever, clever cat. He knows all about **full**.
3 Teach	A Give several children a cup each. Put various amounts of water in each cup. Talk about whose cup is **full**. Fill up all of the cups. Then drink some water. Discuss again **full** and <u>not</u> **full**. B Put a selection of containers and rice or dried beans on the table. Make the containers **full** and <u>not</u> **full**.
4 Activate	A Put the symbol for **full** in the wet play or sand area. Comment on objects when they get **full**. B When playing with play dough, fill containers until they are **full**. Make them <u>not</u> **full** and start all over again.
5 Review	**Activity:** place several objects on the table that are **full** and <u>not</u> **full** of various materials (rice, lentils, water, play dough, etc). Encourage the children to identify and talk about which ones are **full** and <u>not</u> **full**. **Word Bag:** take a beaker and some cotton wool out of the bag. Talk about when it is **full** and <u>not</u> **full**. **Concept book:** see page 76 for details. **Family:** talk about **full** and <u>not</u> **full** when having a drink at home.

Half

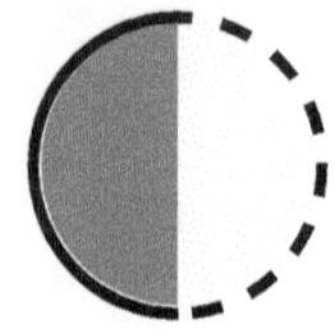

1 Teach	Use a <u>sign</u> or <u>gesture</u> for **half**. Look at the <u>symbol</u> together. <u>Say</u> the word **half** to your partner. <u>Sing</u> a Word Aware song including the word **half**.
2 Teach 	**Equipment: Concept Cat toy, another toy ('Sammy'), a biscuit, a piece of bread and two apples.** Concept Cat is a clever, clever cat. He looks here, he looks there, learning as he goes and, when he comes home, he tells us a story. Concept Cat is a clever, clever cat. This story is all about **half**. Listen out for the word **half**. Concept Cat says, 'I'm hungry.' Sammy says, 'I'm hungry too. Let's look for something to eat.' They look in the biscuit tin. There is one biscuit. 'I want it,' says Concept Cat. 'I want it,' says Sammy. 'I know,' says Concept Cat. 'Let's have **half** each.' 'OK,' says Sammy. (They break the biscuit in **half** and eat it.) 'I'm still hungry! Let's look for some bread,' says Concept Cat. 'There is one piece of bread. Let's have **half** each.' Sammy says, 'I'm still hungry. Let's have an apple. This time we <u>don't</u> need to have **half** each.' (They eat an apple each.) We had **half** a biscuit, **half** a piece of bread, but <u>not</u> **half** an apple. Concept Cat, what a clever, clever cat. He knows all about **half**.
3 Teach	A Divide the class in **half**. Mix up the children again and repeat. B Bring out a pile of objects. Ask the children to collect **half** of them.
4 Activate	A Ask two children to share out the toys or pens between them so that each child has **half**. B Cut play dough 'pizzas' in **half**.
5 Review	**Activity:** talk about sharing using the word **half**. Ask, 'If there are two people and only one biscuit, what should you do?' **Word Bag:** put **half** a biscuit in the bag. Talk about **half** being eaten, but **half** being left, when you take it out of the bag. **Concept book:** see page 76 for details. **Family:** share some food that can be cut or broken in **half**, eg apples or biscuits. Make sure that everyone has **half**.

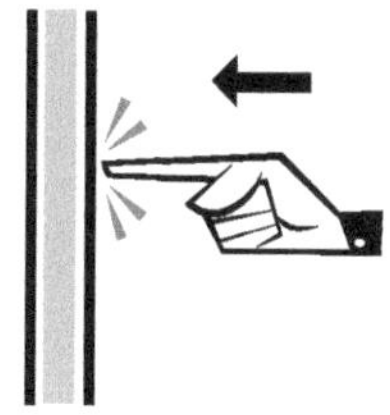

Hard

1 **Teach**	 Use a sign or gesture for **hard**.  Look at the symbol together.  Say the word **hard** to your partner.  Sing a Word Aware song including the word **hard**.
2 **Teach** 	**Equipment: Concept Cat toy, a bouncy ball, hard floor, a cushion, a chair and a jumper (sweater).** Concept Cat is a clever, clever cat. He looks here, he looks there, learning as he goes and, when he comes home, he tells us a story. Concept Cat is a clever, clever cat. This story is all about **hard**. Listen out for the word **hard**. Concept Cat likes playing with a ball. He wants to bounce the ball on something **hard**. He bounces it on the floor. It bounces! The floor is **hard**. He tries to bounce the ball on a cushion. No, the cushion is not **hard**! Concept Cat wants something **hard** for his ball to bounce on. He tries a chair. The chair is **hard**. He tries his jumper. No, the jumper is not **hard**. Concept Cat touches the floor and the chair to feel that they are **hard**. He touches the jumper and the cushion to feel that they are not **hard**. Concept Cat, what a clever, clever cat. He knows all about **hard**.
3 **Teach**	A Use a variety of objects that are **hard** and not **hard**. B Feel objects that are both **hard** and not **hard**. C Sort objects into **hard** and not **hard**.
4 **Activate**	Explore chairs and beds that are **hard** and not **hard**.
5 **Review**	 **Activity:** read 'Goldilocks and the Three Bears' at story time. Ask the children to listen out for the word **hard**.  **Word Bag:** put any **hard** object in the bag, eg a book, a toy brick or a play person. Talk about the object being **hard**.  **Concept book:** see page 76 for details.  **Family:** take it in turns to be blindfolded. Get the person who cannot see to sit on objects that are **hard** and not **hard**. Can they say which ones are **hard**?

Heavy

1 Teach

Use a sign or gesture for **heavy**.

Look at the symbol together.

Say the word **heavy** to your partner.

Sing a Word Aware song including the word **heavy**.

2 Teach

Equipment: Concept Cat toy, a balloon (inflated, ideally with helium) with string attached, a feather, paper and a chair.

Concept Cat is a clever, clever cat. He looks here, he looks there, learning as he goes and, when he comes home, he tells us a story. Concept Cat is a clever, clever cat. This story is all about **heavy**. Listen out for the word **heavy**.

Concept Cat has a balloon. He does not want the balloon to fly away. He needs something **heavy** to hold it down. He ties a feather to it. That is not **heavy**. He ties a piece of paper to it. That is not **heavy**. He finds a chair. He ties the balloon to the chair. The chair is **heavy**. He wants something else **heavy**.

I know, let's use one of you. (Choose a child of medium weight.) Are you **heavy**? Will you keep the balloon down? Let's try. I will tie the balloon on to you. Are you **heavy**? Yes. You are **heavy**.

The feather was not **heavy**. The paper was not **heavy**. The chair was **heavy** and you are **heavy**.

Concept Cat, what a clever, clever cat. He knows all about **heavy**.

3 Teach

Put Concept Cat, a balloon, a range of objects of different weights and a symbol for **heavy** on a table. Encourage the children to pick up objects and sort them into **heavy** and not **heavy**.

4 Activate

In the outdoor play area, have some bricks, stones and foam cubes or other not **heavy** objects. Mime picking up **heavy** and not **heavy** objects.

5 Review

Activity: go looking for things that are **heavy**.

Word Bag: put a rock in the bag. Talk about it being **heavy**.

Concept book: see page 76 for details.

Family: get children to help with carrying the shopping. Which bags are **heavy**? Do they want to carry one that is **heavy** or not **heavy**?

In

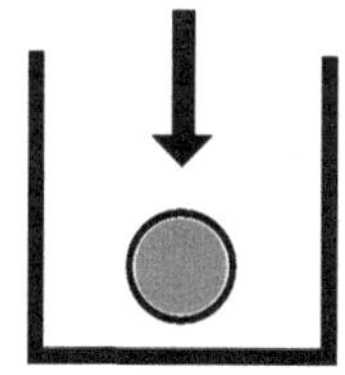

1 **Teach**	Use a <u>sign</u> or <u>gesture</u> for **in**. Look at the <u>symbol</u> together. <u>Say</u> the word **in** to your partner. <u>Sing</u> a Word Aware song including the word **in**.
2 **Teach** 	**Equipment: Concept Cat toy, a pair of shoes and gloves, and a box with a lid.** Concept Cat is a clever, clever cat. He looks here, he looks there, learning as he goes and, when he comes home, he tells us a story. Concept Cat is a clever, clever cat. This story is all about **in**. Listen out for the word **in**. Mum asks Concept Cat to put his shoes **in** the box. Concept Cat does not know what **in** means. 'Is this **in**?' (He puts the shoes on top of the box.) '<u>No</u>, that's <u>not</u> **in**. Put them **in**.' (Adult gestures **in**.) Concept Cat puts the shoes **in** the box. Mum says, 'Put your gloves **in** the box.' (Place the gloves behind the box.) 'Oh no, Concept Cat! Put them **in** the box. That is <u>not</u> **in**. Put them **in**!' (Adult gestures again.) Concept Cat puts the gloves **in** the box. Concept Cat put the shoes here (point to on top). That was <u>not</u> **in**. Then he put the shoes **in** (point **in**). Then Concept Cat put the gloves here (point to behind). That was <u>not</u> **in**. Then he put it here (point **in**). That was **in** the box. Concept Cat, what a clever, clever cat. He knows all about **in**.
3 **Teach**	A Children need to wash their hands first. Then ask them to put a finger **in** their mouth. Then to put a finger <u>not</u> **in** their mouth. B Have a box and various items **in** and around it. Talk about what is **in** and <u>not</u> **in** the box.
4 **Activate**	A Put the symbol for **in** near the sand or water tray and talk about things going **in** and <u>not</u> **in**. B Have a selection of boxes and items to go **in**. Encourage the children to use the word **in**.
5 **Review**	**Activity:** put an object **in** a box. Talk about what might be **in** it and then look **in** the box. **Word Bag:** put a small interesting object **in** a small box. Open the box and show what is **in** it. Keep changing the object so that it is exciting to see what is **in** the box. **Concept book:** see page 76 for details. **Family:** see how many places you can climb **in** at home. Can adults get **in** as many places as a child?

Note: **large** should only be introduced when children have firmly established the concept of **big**.

Large

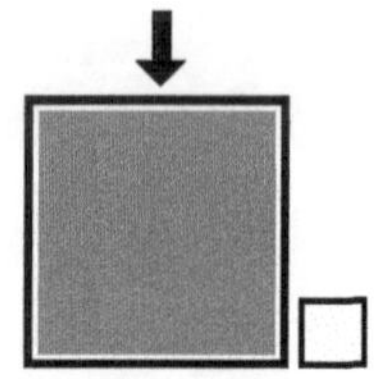

1 **Teach**	 Use a sign or gesture for **large**. 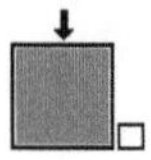 Look at the symbol together.  Say the word **large** to your partner.  Sing a Word Aware song including the word **large**.
2 **Teach** 	**Equipment: Concept Cat toy, a large toy dog (or similar), three cups (one large and two not large).** Concept Cat is a clever, clever cat. He looks here, he looks there, learning as he goes and, when he comes home, he tells us a story. Concept Cat is a clever, clever cat. This story is all about **large**. Listen out for the word **large**. Concept Cat and his friend have been playing and are now thirsty. They want a drink. The **large** dog says, 'I am a **large** dog, and so I need a **large** drink. Concept Cat, please bring me a **large** drink.' Concept Cat goes off to get a drink, but does not know what **large** means. He returns with a drink. The **large** dog says, 'That drink is not **large**. Please bring me a **large** drink.' Concept Cat comes back with another drink. This time, the **large** dog shakes his head and says, 'That drink is not **large**. Please bring a **large** drink.' Concept Cat brings back another drink. The **large** dog smiles and says, 'Thank you, this drink is **large**.' This drink was not **large**. This drink also was not **large**. This drink was **large**. Concept Cat, what a clever, clever cat. He knows all about **large**.
3 **Teach**	A Have some **large** and not **large** boxes. Explore them by going inside the **large** boxes. B Sort different objects into **large** and not **large**.
4 **Activate**	A In the home corner, put out oversized clothes so that the children can dress dolls in **large** clothes. B Adults should occasionally substitute **large** for 'big' in their speech as well.
5 **Review**	 **Activity:** talk about animals that are **large**.  **Word Bag:** put a **large** and a not **large** toy brick in the bag. Talk about them, using **large** and not **large**, when you take them out of the bag.  **Concept book:** see page 76 for details.  **Family:** when you are walking home, look for and talk about things that are **large**, such as **large** houses, **large** trees, **large** gardens or **large** cars.

Last

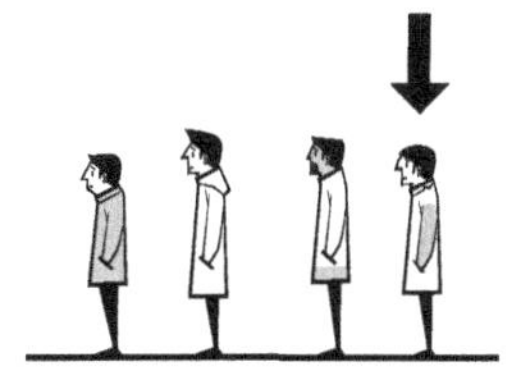

1 Teach

 Use a <u>sign</u> or <u>gesture</u> for **last**.

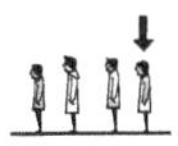 Look at the <u>symbol</u> together.

 <u>Say</u> the word **last** to your partner.

 <u>Sing</u> a Word Aware song including the word **last**.

2 Teach

Equipment: Concept Cat toy, a large toy bus and five toy animals or dolls.

Concept Cat is a clever, clever cat. He looks here, he looks there, learning as he goes and, when he comes home, he tells us a story. Concept Cat is a clever, clever cat. This story is all about **last**. Listen out for the word **last**.

Concept Cat and his class are going on a trip. The teacher says, 'Everyone needs to get in a line. Concept Cat you will be **last**.' Everyone gets in the line, but Concept Cat does not know where to go. He does not know what **last** means. Concept Cat gets in the line (at the front). The teacher says, 'That is <u>not</u> **last**.'

Concept Cat finds another place in the line (in the middle). His friend says, 'That is <u>not</u> **last**. I'll show you **last**.' She takes him by the paw and shows him **last**. The teacher says, 'Well done Concept Cat. Now you are **last**.'

(Place Concept Cat at corresponding places in the line.) Say: This is <u>not</u> **last**. This is <u>not</u> **last**. This is **last**.

Concept Cat, what a clever, clever cat. He knows all about **last**.

3 Teach

A Line up by the door or by the slide. Take turns at being **last**. Label different children as being **last** or <u>not</u> **last**.

B Take a photograph of the children in a line with the child who is **last** holding Concept Cat and the symbol for **last**.

4 Activate

At snack time, use the word **last**, eg 'I have one **last** piece of fruit. Who wants this **last** piece of fruit?' Also encourage children to use the word.

5 Review

 **Activity:** talk about a time when a child was **last**.

Word Bag: put three toy people in the bag. Take them out, put them in a line and talk about who is **last**.

 **Concept book:** see page 76 for details.

 **Family:** talk about the **last** thing that you do, eg the **last** thing before bed, the **last** thing to go in the lunch-box, the **last** time you throw the ball.

Note: **now** must be established before introducing **later**.

Later

1 Teach

Use a sign or gesture for **later**.

Look at the symbol together.

Say the word **later** to your partner.

Sing a Word Aware song including the word **later**.

2 Teach

Equipment: Concept Cat toy, a toy to act as Dad, something to play with, a book and a toy bed.

Concept Cat is a clever, clever cat. He looks here, he looks there, learning as he goes and, when he comes home, he tells us a story. Concept Cat is a clever, clever cat. This story is all about **later**. Listen out for the word **later**.

It is Concept Cat's bedtime, but he does not want to go to bed right now. He wants to go **later**. Concept Cat is playing. Dad says, 'Time for bed.' Concept Cat says, 'I'll go to bed **later**.' Concept Cat is watching television. Dad says, 'Time for bed.' Concept Cat says, 'I'll go to bed **later**.' Concept Cat is reading a book. Dad says, 'Time for bed.' Concept Cat says, 'I'll go to bed **later**.' Dad is cross and says, 'Not **later** Concept Cat. It's time for bed. Go to your bed.'

When Concept Cat was playing, he said, **later**. When Concept Cat was watching television, he said **later**. When Concept Cat was reading a book, he said, **later**. Then Dad said 'Not **later**. It's time for bed.'

Concept Cat, what a clever, clever cat. He knows all about **later**.

3 Teach

Present the visual timetable to the class and indicate the activities that they will be doing **later**.

4 Activate

Cook biscuits or cakes. Stop occasionally and talk about whether they are ready, ensuring that you say, 'We will eat them **later**.'

5 Review

Activity: talk about things the children would like to do **later**.

Word Bag: put an object in the bag that represents something that will happen **later**, eg a story you are going to read **later**, or a biscuit you will eat **later**. Obviously, the objects need to change as things happen.

Concept book: see page 76 for details.

Family: talk about what will happen **later**. It is always fun to think about nice things that are going to happen **later**.

Less

1 **Teach**	 Use a <u>sign</u> or <u>gesture</u> for **less**.  Look at the <u>symbol</u> together.  <u>Say</u> the word **less** to your partner.  <u>Sing</u> a Word Aware song including the word **less**.
2 **Teach** 	**Equipment: Concept Cat toy, a clear container with a lid, and material such as rice, pasta or marbles.** Concept Cat is a clever, clever cat. He looks here, he looks there, learning as he goes and, when he comes home, he tells us a story. Concept Cat is a clever, clever cat. This story is all about **less**. Listen out for the word **less**. One day, Concept Cat wants to make a musical instrument. He wants to make a shaker. So he gets a pot and some rice. He fills the pot with rice and puts the lid on. When he shakes the pot, it does not make much noise. Concept Cat thinks he needs **less** rice. (Take out a small amount of rice, put the lid back on and shake the pot.) Concept Cat tries again. It still does not work. He needs **less** rice. (Take out a small amount of rice, put the lid back on and shake the pot.) Concept Cat tries again. It does not sound right. He needs **less**. (Take all but a small amount of rice out, put the lid back on and shake the pot.) Concept Cat tries again. That sounds good. He needed **less**. Fill up the container again and, as you remove some rice, say, 'To make a shaker, Concept Cat needed **less**. To make the sound, he needed **less**. He needed **less** rice. Then he needed **less** rice.' Concept Cat, what a clever, clever cat. He knows all about **less**.
3 **Teach**	Give two children some play dough, one with **less** than the other. Talk about who has **less**. Give a third child a smaller amount and now talk about this child having **less**. Repeat with a fourth child, having **less**. Compare any two children and talk about who has **less**.
4 **Activate**	At snack time, repeat the above activity with raisins. Or have a teddy bears' picnic. Use small toy bricks for food. Give out the 'food' and talk about who has **less**.
5 **Review**	 **Activity:** talk about a time when the children had **less** of something.  **Word Bag:** put two see-through bags containing coins in the bag. Talk about which one has **less**.  **Concept book:** see page 76 for details.  **Family:** get your child to help serve the meal. Talk about who has got **less**. Would they like **less** pudding?

Routledge Taylor & Francis Group

Note: it is important to teach only one meaning of **light** at a time.

Light (not heavy)

1 **Teach**	Use a sign or gesture for **light**. Look at the symbol together. Say the word **light** to your partner. Sing a Word Aware song including the word **light**.
2 **Teach** 	**Equipment: Concept Cat toy, a leaf, some cotton wool, a stone and a piece of heavy wood.** Concept Cat is a clever, clever cat. He looks here, he looks there, learning as he goes and, when he comes home, he tells us a story. Concept Cat is a clever, clever cat. This story is all about **light**. Listen out for the word **light**. One day, Concept Cat and his friends are playing with bricks. They are making towers. One friend says, 'Concept Cat, please find me something **light** to go on the top.' Concept Cat agrees but he does not know what **light** means. He finds a stone but his friend says, 'No, that is not **light**. I need something **light**.' Concept Cat finds some wood but his friend says, 'No, that is not **light**. I need something **light**.' Concept Cat finds a leaf. He hopes that is **light**. 'Thank you,' says his friend. 'That is **light**.' Concept Cat's other friend has made a tower and also wants something **light** to go on the top. This time, Concept Cat finds some cotton wool. He knows that is **light**. 'Thank you,' says his friend. 'That is **light**.' Concept Cat found a stone. That was not **light**. The wood was not **light**. The leaf was **light**. The cotton wool was **light**. Concept Cat, what a clever, clever cat. He knows all about **light**.
3 **Teach**	Present a range of **light** and not **light** objects to the children. Take turns to feel them. When holding **light** objects, mime holding them high above your head. Sort the items into **light** and not **light**.
4 **Activate**	When playing outside, place **light** and not **light** objects in the children's hands and blow gently to see what happens. Very **light** objects will blow away. Look for more **light** objects that will blow away.
5 **Review**	**Word Bag and activity:** put a feather in the bag. Can the children think of something else that is **light**? **Concept book:** see page 76 for details. **Family:** put a few objects in a bag, some of which are **light** and some not **light**, eg a stone, a feather, a plastic piece of fruit, an empty matchbox, a big book. Take turns putting your hands into the bag. Hold the object without taking it out. Can you guess what it is? Is it **light** or not **light**?

Note: it is important to teach only one meaning of **light** at a time.

Light (not dark)

1 **Teach**	 Use a <u>sign</u> or <u>gesture</u> for **light**.  Look at the <u>symbol</u> together.  <u>Say</u> the word **light** to your partner.  <u>Sing</u> a Word Aware song including the word **light**.
2 **Teach** 	**Equipment: an old coin (or something hard to see), a toy 'Grandad', light through a window, a lamp and a torch (turn off the room lights).** Concept Cat is a clever, clever cat. He looks here, he looks there, learning as he goes and, when he comes home, he tells us a story. Concept Cat is a clever, clever cat. This story is all about **light**. Listen out for the word **light**. One day, Concept Cat is helping his Grandad and finds an old coin. He shows it to his Grandad who says, 'It's <u>not</u> **light** in here. You'll need to go somewhere **light**. Then we can see it.' Concept Cat goes to the corner but it's <u>not</u> **light**. He goes under the chair, but it's <u>not</u> **light**. He goes to the window. It is **light**. Then Grandad switches on the lamp. That's **light** too. And how about the torch? That's **light** too. In the corner, it was <u>not</u> **light**. Under the chair, it was <u>not</u> **light**. Next to the window, it was **light**. By the lamp it was **light**. The torch made it **light** too. Concept Cat, what a clever, clever cat. He knows all about **light**.
3 **Teach**	Go into a room which has blinds at the windows. Turn off the lights and close the blinds. Say, 'It is <u>not</u> **light**.' Then open the blinds, switch on the lights and talk about it being **light**. Repeat this activity several times.
4 **Activate**	Place some blankets and fabric in a well-lit area. Encourage the children to explore **light** and <u>not</u> **light** as they hide under the blankets.
5 **Review**	 **Activity:** what time of day would it be **light** or <u>not</u> **light**? Which place might be **light**? A cave or a beach?  **Word Bag:** put a torch in the bag. Turn it on to show that it gives **light**.  **Concept book:** see page 76 for details.  **Family:** open and close the curtains. Talk about it being **light** and <u>not</u> **light**.

Little

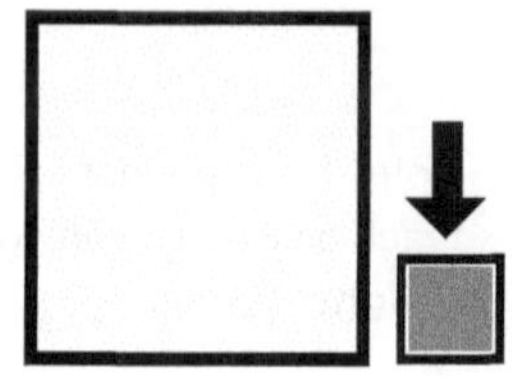

1 Teach

Use a sign or gesture for **little**.

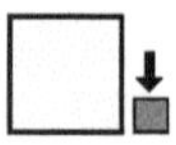
Look at the symbol together.

Say the word **little** to your partner.

Sing a Word Aware song including the word **little**.

2 Teach

Equipment: Concept Cat toy, a small doll, and doll's clothes and larger clothes, all in a bag.

Concept Cat is a clever, clever cat. He looks here, he looks there, learning as he goes and, when he comes home, he tells us a story. Concept Cat is a clever, clever cat. This story is all about **little**. Listen out for the word **little**.

Concept Cat has a **little** doll. He wants to find some **little** clothes that his **little** doll can wear. He pulls something out of the bag. Is this **little**? No, that's not **little**. Is this **little**? Yes, that's **little**. The **little** doll can wear these **little** clothes. No, that's not **little**. Is this **little**? No, that's not **little**. Is this **little**? Yes, that's **little**. The **little** doll can wear these **little** clothes. Yes, that's **little**. The **little** doll can wear these **little** clothes. Now the **little** doll is dressed in the **little** clothes.

Concept Cat, what a clever, clever cat. He knows all about **little**.

3 Teach

A Line up children's and teachers' shoes in a mixed order. Go along the line saying, '**little, little, little,** not **little, little, little.**' Encourage the children to repeat using the word **little**.

B Collect a range of matching pairs of objects, one big, one **little**. Where possible, the only difference should be the size. For instance, find one red ball that is not **little** and one **little** red ball.

C Sort objects by size. Place the **little** objects together and the not **little** objects together. Sign **little** and not **little** whenever you use these terms.

4 Activate

A Go on a treasure hunt looking for **little** things.

B Leave out the Concept Cat toy and equipment for the children to explore.

5 Review

Activity: talk about your favourite **little** things.

Word Bag: put some **little** biscuits in the bag. Talk about them being **little**.

Concept book: see page 76 for details.

Family: find a small bag. How many **little** things can you find to put in it?

Long

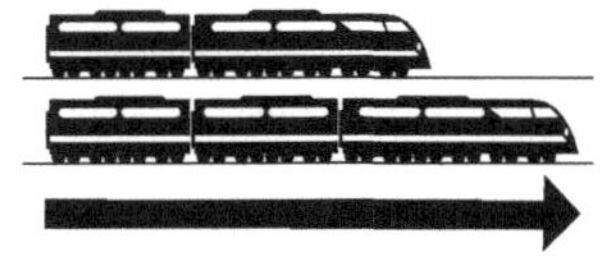

1 Teach

Use a sign or gesture for **long**.

Look at the symbol together.

Say the word **long** to your partner.

Sing a Word Aware song including the word **long**.

2 Teach

Equipment: Concept Cat toy, a ball, a small spade (must not have a long handle), a long stick, and a long piece of string.

Concept Cat is a clever, clever cat. He looks here, he looks there, learning as he goes and, when he comes home, he tells us a story. Concept Cat is a clever, clever cat. This story is all about **long**. Listen out for the word **long**.

At home one day, Concept Cat was helping Mum in the garden. She said, 'Please go and find something **long**. I need a **long** thing.' Concept Cat nodded but he did not know what **long** meant. So he set off to find out all about **long**.

First, Concept Cat found a ball. Maybe that was **long**. He showed it to Mum. 'No,' she said, 'I need something **long**. The ball is not **long**.' Concept Cat went off again and found a spade. He showed it to Mum. 'No,' she said, 'I need something **long**. That spade is not **long**.' Next, Concept Cat found a stick. He showed it to Mum. 'Yes,' she said, 'that stick is **long**. This string is **long** too.'

The ball was not **long**. The spade was not **long**. The stick was **long**.

Concept Cat, what a clever, clever cat. He knows all about **long**.

3 Teach

A Talk about who has **long** hair and who does not have **long** hair.

B Peg one **long** paper or ribbon and one not **long** item to the clothes line. The children take turns selecting strips of paper and ribbon and match them to either **long** or not **long**.

4 Activate

Build toy train tracks of varying length. Take turns to talk about the tracks being either **long** or not **long**.

5 Review

Activity: talk about what **long** things you can play with or make, eg train tracks, threading beads, paper, snakes.

Word Bag: put a **long** and a not **long** piece of string in the bag. Talk about them when you take them out of the bag.

Concept book: see page 76 for details.

Family: have jumping competitions. Who can do a very **long** jump? Or ask children to bring in anything **long** from home.

Lots

1 Teach

Use a sign or gesture for **lots**.

Look at the symbol together.

Say the word **lots** to your partner.

Sing a Word Aware song including the word **lots**.

2 Teach

Equipment: Concept Cat toy and lots of building bricks.

Concept Cat is a clever, clever cat. He looks here, he looks there, learning as he goes and, when he comes home, he tells us a story. Concept Cat is a clever, clever cat. This story is all about **lots**. Listen out for the word **lots**.

One day, Concept cat is helping his friend build a house. The friend says, 'Concept Cat, I need **lots** of bricks. Please bring me **lots** of bricks.' Concept Cat wants to help, but he does not know what **lots** means. Concept Cat brings back a brick. His friend says, 'That is not **lots**. I need **lots** of bricks.'

Concept Cat brings back some bricks. His friend says again, 'That is not **lots**. I need **lots** of bricks.' This time, Concept Cat brings some more bricks. His friend is very happy. 'Concept Cat, that is **lots** of bricks! Now we have **lots** and **lots** of bricks.'

First, Concept Cat did not bring back **lots**. Then Concept cat did not bring back **lots** of bricks. Then he did bring back **lots** of bricks.

Concept Cat, what a clever, clever cat. He knows all about **lots**.

3 Teach

A Look at your body. What do you have **lots** of? (For example, hair, fingers and toes.) Do you have **lots** of noses or legs?

B Start with a large bowl and **lots** of rice or dried pasta. Explore **lots** and not **lots** by placing various amounts in the bowl. Later, encourage the children to label things **lots** and not **lots**.

4 Activate

A Blow bubbles and talk about **lots** and not **lots**.

B Leave out the Concept Cat toy and equipment for the children to explore. Join in their play, using the word **lots**.

5 Review

Activity: look at any book with **lots** of animals in it.

Word Bag: put a selection of coins in the bag, so that you can talk about **lots** of money.

Concept book: see page 76 for details.

Family: what can you spot **lots** of on the way home? For example, **lots** of cars, cats, trees, houses and lamp posts.

Loud

1 **Teach**	 Use a <u>sign</u> or <u>gesture</u> for **loud**.  Look at the <u>symbol</u> together.  <u>Say</u> the word **loud** to your partner.  <u>Sing</u> a Word Aware song including the word **loud**.
2 **Teach** 	**Equipment: Concept Cat toy and a drum.** Concept Cat is a clever, clever cat. He looks here, he looks there, learning as he goes and, when he comes home, he tells us a story. Concept Cat is a clever, clever cat. This story is all about **loud**. Listen out for the word **loud**. One day, Concept Cat was trying to sleep. He was very tired. Then he heard a **loud** noise (bang on the drum). 'Oh, that is so **loud**! I will try to sleep again.' Then Concept Cat heard a **loud** noise (stamp feet loudly). 'Oh, what a **loud** noise! I just want to sleep.' Then he heard some **loud** talking (say 'Hello' loudly). 'Oh, that is very **loud**! It is very hard to sleep with all these **loud** noises. I need you to help me to sleep.' Do <u>not</u> make **loud** noises. Do <u>not</u> be **loud**. (Ensure that the children are <u>not</u> **loud**.) Now let's play a trick on Concept Cat. Let's all make lots of **loud** noises. We can all stamp, bang and say 'Hello' all at the same time Concept Cat: Oh no, that is so **loud**! Concept Cat, what a clever, clever cat. He knows all about **loud**.
3 **Teach**	A Let's clap **loudly**. Now let's clap <u>not</u> **loudly**. Now clap **loudly** again. B Let's talk **loudly**. Now let's talk <u>not</u> **loudly**. Now talk **loudly** again. C Let's walk **loudly**. (Stamp feet.) Now let's walk <u>not</u> **loudly**. (Walk on tiptoes.) Now walk **loudly** again.
4 **Activate**	Play musical instruments. Play them **loud** and <u>not</u> **loud**.
5 **Review**	 **Activity:** talk about a time when you heard something **loud**.  **Word Bag:** put a bell in the bag. Make a **loud** sound.  **Concept book:** see page 76 for details.  **Family:** see how **loudly** you can talk when you are going home.

More

1 **Teach**	 Use a sign or gesture for **more**.  Look at the symbol together.  Say the word **more** to your partner.  Sing a Word Aware song including the word **more**.
2 **Teach** 	**Equipment: Concept Cat toy, a toy baby and play dough.** Concept Cat is a clever, clever cat. He looks here, he looks there, learning as he goes and, when he comes home, he tells us a story. Concept Cat is a clever, clever cat. This story is all about **more**. Listen out for the word **more**. Concept Cat and Baby are playing with play dough. (Give each some play dough.) Baby wants **more**. Concept Cat gives him **more**. (Give Baby a bit **more** play dough). Baby wants **more**, so Concept Cat gives him **more**. (Give Baby a bit **more** play dough.) Baby wants **more** but Concept Cat says, 'No **more**.' Baby holds up his play dough and says, 'I have **more** play dough than you.' (Give Concept Cat **more** play dough.) Concept Cat finds some **more** play dough and says, 'I have **more** play dough than you.' Concept Cat, what a clever, clever cat. He knows all about **more**.
3 **Teach**	A Children hold up varying numbers of fingers. Talk about who is holding up **more** fingers. B Give the children bowls and put items in them. Talk about who has **more**.
4 **Activate**	A At snack time, give the children varying amounts of food and drink. Talk about who has **more** and not **more** and who wants **more**. B Put out a few building bricks and talk about needing **more**.
5 **Review**	 **Activity:** put objects into two sacks. Talk about which one has **more**.  **Word Bag:** put two transparent containers containing small items (eg counters) in the bag. Have **more** items in one container than in the other.  **Concept book:** see page 76 for details.  **Family:** using several cups, pour water from one to another and talk about which one has **more**.

Most

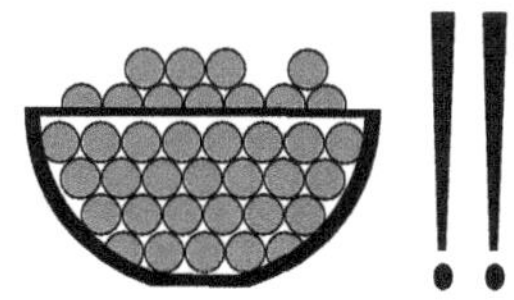

1 Teach	 Use a sign or gesture for **most**. 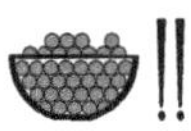 Look at the symbol together.  Say the word **most** to your partner.  Sing a Word Aware song including the word **most**.
2 Teach 	**Equipment: Concept Cat toy, lots of toy bricks in a box, a boy doll ('Jack') and a girl doll ('Kisha').** Concept Cat is a clever, clever cat. He looks here, he looks there, learning as he goes and, when he comes home, he tells us a story. Concept Cat is a clever, clever cat. This story is all about **most**. Listen out for the word **most**. One day, Concept Cat is playing with bricks with his friends. He gives five bricks to Jack and three bricks to Kisha and keeps the rest for himself. Concept Cat has the **most** bricks. Jack does not have the **most** bricks. Kisha does not have the **most** bricks. Concept Cat has the **most** bricks. When Concept Cat isn't looking, Kisha takes **most** of his bricks. Now Kisha has the **most** bricks. Then Jack takes bricks out of the box. Now Jack has the **most** bricks! Concept Cat looks at Jack's bricks and says, 'Jack, you have the **most** bricks!' First, Concept Cat had the **most** bricks. Then Kisha had the **most** bricks. Then Jack had the **most** bricks. Concept Cat, what a clever, clever cat. He knows all about **most**.
3 Teach	Use a large piece of play dough. Give a small amount to one child and a large amount to another. Discuss who has **most** and not **most**. Mix all of the play dough back together. Break off small amounts and keep one large amount. Redistribute it. Discuss who has the **most** and not **most**. Repeat the activity several times.
4 Activate	At snack time, pour water into several cups and compare who has the **most** and not **most**.
5 Review	 **Activity:** involve the children in carrying books. Talk about who has the **most** books.  **Word Bag:** put several small toys in the bag. Give them out to two children. Talk about who has the **most**.  **Concept book:** see page 76 for details.  **Family:** talk about who has the **most** at dinner-time. It might be the **most** broccoli or the **most** ice-cream.

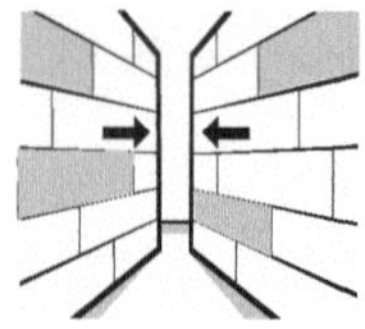

Narrow

1 **Teach**	 Use a sign or gesture for **narrow**. 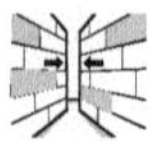 Look at the symbol together.  Say the word **narrow** to your partner.  Sing a Word Aware song including the word **narrow**.
2 **Teach** 	**Equipment: Concept Cat toy, a small ball and two large items such as boxes.** Concept Cat is a clever, clever cat. He looks here, he looks there, learning as he goes and, when he comes home, he tells us a story. Concept Cat is a clever, clever cat. This story is all about **narrow**. Listen out for the word **narrow**. One day, Concept Cat is playing with a ball. It bounces away and gets stuck in a **narrow** place. Concept Cat tries to get the ball but the space is too **narrow**. He moves one box but the space is still **narrow**. Then he moves the box gain. That's better, the space is not **narrow**. Concept Cat now has a new game. He can make the space **narrow** and not **narrow**. He makes it **narrow**, so he can just get through, and then not **narrow**, so he can easily get through. Concept Cat, what a clever, clever cat. He knows all about **narrow**.
3 **Teach**	A Make your hands **narrow** together and not **narrow**. B Go to a door. Close it so it is **narrow**. Continue making the door **narrow** and not **narrow**, and explore the space by encouraging the children to walk through.
4 **Activate**	A Two children face each other and hold hands to make a **narrow** arch. Another two children make a not **narrow** arch. The remaining children can choose whether they want to go through the **narrow** arch or the not **narrow** arch. B When it is playtime, leave the door open so it is **narrow**. Talk about the gap being **narrow**.
5 **Review**	 **Activity:** talk about who could get through a **narrow** space – an elephant or a small bird?  **Word Bag:** put two small chairs and a teddy bear in the bag. Make the gap between the chairs **narrow** and not **narrow**. Can Teddy get through?  **Concept book:** see page 76 for details.  **Family:** on the way home, look out for roads that are **narrow** and not **narrow**. Look out for any **narrow** paths.

Near

1 Teach	 Use a sign or gesture for **near**.  Look at the symbol together.  Say the word **near** to your partner.  Sing a Word Aware song including the word **near**.
2 Teach 	**Equipment: Concept Cat toy, a toy cooker and two non-identical spoons, forks and knives. Arrange them so that one of each fork, knife and spoon is near the cooker and the other is further away.** Concept Cat is a clever, clever cat. He looks here, he looks there, learning as he goes and, when he comes home, he tells us a story. Concept Cat is a clever, clever cat. This story is all about **near**. Listen out for the word **near**. One day, Concept Cat is helping in the kitchen. Dad asks him to get the spoon that is **near** the cooker. Dad says, 'Not that one. That spoon is not **near** the cooker. Get the spoon that is **near** the cooker. Here's the spoon that is **near** the cooker.' Next, Dad asks for the fork that is **near** the cooker. Dad says, 'Not that one. That fork is not **near** the cooker. Get the fork that is **near** the cooker. Here's the fork that is **near** the cooker.' Dad asks for the knife. He wants the knife that is **near** the cooker. Dad says, 'That's right, Concept Cat, you got the knife that is **near** the cooker.' Concept Cat, what a clever, clever cat. He knows all about **near**.
3 Teach	Place one soft toy **near** a child and another one not **near**. Ensure you show that **near** can be front, next to or behind, but is still **near**. Talk about the toy being **near** or not **near**. Avoid using 'front', 'next to' or 'behind'. If objects are touching, they are also not **near**.
4 Activate	When playing with toy cars, talk about the cars that are **near** and not **near** to each other.
5 Review	 **Activity:** when all of the children are seated for story-time, ask one child to stand **near** the group and then not **near**. Repeat with the other children.  **Word Bag:** place two toy bears in the bag. Take them out and put them in different positions from each other so they are **near** and not **near**.  **Concept book:** see page 76 for details.  **Family:** play 'Grandmother's Footsteps'. One person turns away at one end of the room. The others have to creep up behind them. The first person looks around suddenly and sees whether anyone is moving. If they are moving, they have to start again. How **near** can you get?

New

1 **Teach**	 Use a <u>sign</u> or <u>gesture</u> for **new**.  Look at the <u>symbol</u> together.  <u>Say</u> the word **new** to your partner.  <u>Sing</u> a Word Aware song including the word **new**.
2 **Teach** 	**Equipment: Concept Cat toy, two pairs of shoes (one new and one old).** Concept Cat is a clever, clever cat. He looks here, he looks there, learning as he goes and, when he comes home, he tells us a story. Concept Cat is a clever, clever cat. This story is all about **new**. Listen out for the word **new**. One day, Concept Cat went to the shop with his Dad and bought **new** shoes. The **new** shoes were in a box. The **new** shoes were clean. The **new** shoes did not have holes in them. The shop assistant said, 'Do you want to put on the **new** shoes?' Concept Cat did not want to. He liked his shoes that were <u>not</u> **new**. At home, Concept Cat looked at the **new** shoes. The **new** shoes looked great. He tried on the **new** shoes. The **new** shoes felt great too. He said goodbye to his <u>not</u> **new** shoes and kept his **new** shoes on. Concept Cat, what a clever, clever cat. He knows all about **new**.
3 **Teach**	A Present two similar items, one **new** and one <u>not</u> **new**. Talk about them. B Talk about a time when the children got something **new**.
4 **Activate**	A If you get a **new** piece of equipment, have an unveiling and talk about it being **new**. Compare it with any equipment it is replacing. This could be as simple as **new** pencils. B Change displays in the classroom, taking down the one that is <u>not</u> **new** and replacing it with one that is **new**.
5 **Review**	 **Activity:** collect several items, some of which are **new** and some <u>not</u> **new**. Talk about them, using the word **new**.  **Word Bag:** place two items in the bag, one that is **new** and one that is <u>not</u> **new**.  **Concept book:** see page 76 for details.  **Family:** look at your child's book or toys together. Which ones look **new** and which ones do <u>not</u> look **new**?

Note: children need to understand the concept of **first** before they learn about **next**.

Next

1 **Teach**	 Use a sign or gesture for **next**.  Look at the symbol together.  Say the word **next** to your partner.  Sing a Word Aware song including the word **next**.
2 **Teach** 	**Equipment: Concept Cat toy, three other soft toys ('Marco', 'Daisy' and 'Ben'), a cup and a ball.** Concept Cat is a clever, clever cat. He looks here, he looks there, learning as he goes and, when he comes home, he tells us a story. Concept Cat is a clever, clever cat. This story is all about **next**. Listen out for the word **next**. Everyone wants a turn with the ball. 'Stop fighting!' says Mum. 'Everyone needs to have a turn. Marco you can have a go. Everyone else needs to get in a line. Right, Concept Cat, you can be **next**. Then Daisy, you can be **next**. Ben, you can be **next**.' 'OK, who would like a drink?' says Mum. 'Me!' shouts everyone. 'OK. Daisy, you can get a drink. Then Ben can be **next**. Then Marco is **next** and Concept Cat is **next**. Now get in line!' They all get in line so that Ben is **next**. Then Marco is **next** and then Concept Cat is **next**. Concept Cat, what a clever, clever cat. He knows all about **next**.
3 **Teach**	A Ask a few children to stand in a line. The first child does an action. Then each one copies the action in turn. Each time, talk about who is **next**. B Have a choice of toys out. Select a child to choose one. Each time say, 'I wonder which toy is going to be chosen **next**?' Then recap. For example, 'Amy chose the teddy. **Next** Federico chose the horse. **Next** Emile chose the car.'
4 **Activate**	A Talk about what is happening **next** on the visual timetable. B At snack time, talk about who is going to be **next** to get their fruit or drink.
5 **Review**	 **Activity:** put a set of sequencing cards in order and talk about what happens **next**.  **Word Bag:** put a cup and a bottle in the bag. Mime the sequence of pouring and drinking and then retell the sequence using **next**.  **Concept book:** see page 76 for details.  **Family:** look out for vehicles on the way home. Guess what the **next** one will be, eg 'I think the **next** one will be a bike.'

Next to

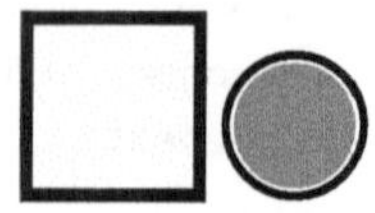

1 **Teach**	 Use a <u>sign</u> or <u>gesture</u> for **next to**. 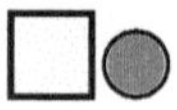 Look at the <u>symbol</u> together.  <u>Say</u> the words **next to** to your partner.  <u>Sing</u> a Word Aware song including the words **next to**.
2 **Teach** 	**Equipment: Concept Cat toy, a hat and a pair of sunglasses.** Concept Cat is a clever, clever cat. He looks here, he looks there, learning as he goes and, when he comes home, he tells us a story. Concept Cat is a clever, clever cat. This story is all about **next to**. Listen out for the words **next to**. (Ask one child to come to the front. Place the hat **next to** the child.) Concept Cat wants to find his hat and sunglasses. He can't find them anywhere! Concept Cat asks, 'Where is my hat, Mrs Brown?' Mrs Brown tells him, 'It's **next to** Lily.' Concept Cat does <u>not</u> look **next to** Lily. Mrs Brown says, 'Look **next to** Lily'. Concept Cat does not look **next to** Lily. Mrs Brown says again, 'Look **next to** Lily.' Then Concept Cat sees his hat. It is **next** to Lily! (Place the sunglasses **next to** a chair.) Concept Cat is looking for his sunglasses. He remembers that Mrs Brown said they were **next to** the chair. He looks here but that is <u>not</u> **next to** the chair. He looks there but that is <u>not</u> **next to** the chair. Then he looks **next to** the chair. He finds his sunglasses. The sunglasses were **next to** the chair. Concept Cat, what a clever, clever cat. He knows all about **next to**.
3 **Teach**	Ask the children to look at who they are sitting **next to**. Then move them around and see who they are **next to** now.
4 **Activate**	A At the start of any small group activity, talk about who the children are sitting **next to**. B When playing with building bricks, position them **next to** each other.
5 **Review**	 **Activity:** talk about what is **next to** the children's beds at home.  **Word Bag:** put a toy bed and a play person in the bag. Place the person **next to** the bed.  **Concept book:** see page 76 for details.  **Family:** play the '**next to**' game. When you are out and about, see if you can spot any two things together. For example, Say 'I can see a man **next to** a dog.'

Night

1 **Teach**	 Use a <u>sign</u> or <u>gesture</u> for **night**.  Look at the <u>symbol</u> together.  <u>Say</u> the word **night** to your partner.  <u>Sing</u> a Word Aware song including the word **night**.
2 **Teach** 	**Equipment: Concept Cat toy, a toy bed, pictures of a moon, stars and fireworks.** Concept Cat is a clever, clever cat. He looks here, he looks there, learning as he goes and, when he comes home, he tells us a story. Concept Cat is a clever, clever cat. This story is all about **night**. Listen out for the word **night**. Concept Cat was awake at **night** time. He looked at the **night** sky. It was **night**, so Concept Cat could see the stars. It was **night**, so Concept Cat could see the Moon. It was **night**, so Concept Cat could see some fireworks. Mum came in and said, 'Because it is **night**, Concept Cat, you should be in bed and because it is **night** you should be asleep. Good **night** Concept Cat,' said Mum. Concept Cat, what a clever, clever cat. He knows all about **night**.
3 **Teach**	A Ask the children to pretend to go to sleep because it is **night**-time. B Talk about bedtime routines using the word **night**.
4 **Activate**	A In the home corner, put teddy bears to bed because it is **night** time. B Read a book about bedtime. Talk about it, using the word **night**.
5 **Review**	 **Activity:** look at pictures of day and **night** and talk about them, using the words **night** and <u>not</u> **night**.  **Word Bag:** put a toy pillow in the bag and talk about going to bed at **night**.  **Concept book:** see page 76 for details.  **Family:** look out of the window at **night** time. Talk about having no sunshine at **night** time. Read a book that ends with 'good **night**'.

Noisy

1 **Teach**	 Use a <u>sign</u> or <u>gesture</u> for **noisy**.  Look at the <u>symbol</u> together.  <u>Say</u> the word **noisy** to your partner.  <u>Sing</u> a Word Aware song including the word **noisy**.
2 **Teach** 	**Equipment: Concept Cat toy, a drum, a tea towel and a table.** Concept Cat is a clever, clever cat. He looks here, he looks there, learning as he goes and, when he comes home, he tells us a story. Concept Cat is a clever, clever cat. This story is all about **noisy**. Listen out for the word **noisy**. Concept Cat wants to make some noise. He starts to look for **noisy** things. He finds a drum and bangs on it to see if it is **noisy**. It is very **noisy**! Concept Cat wants something else that is **noisy**. He finds a tea towel. He shakes the tea towel. It is <u>not</u> **noisy**. Concept Cat sees a table. He bangs on the table to see if that is **noisy**. It is **noisy**! Concept Cat wants everyone to be **noisy** when they stamp their feet. It is **noisy** when everyone stamps their feet. Banging on the drum was **noisy**. Shaking the tea towel was <u>not</u> **noisy**. Banging on the table was **noisy**. Stamping feet was **noisy**. Concept Cat, what a clever, clever cat. He knows all about **noisy**.
3 **Teach**	Encourage all of the children to be **noisy** by stamping their feet, clapping their hands and calling out. Between each episode, remember to be <u>not</u> **noisy**.
4 **Activate**	A Collect a range of silent, quiet and **noisy** items. Explore each one in turn and then categorise them into **noisy** and <u>not</u> **noisy**. B Give each child a musical instrument and alternate between being **noisy** and <u>not</u> **noisy**. The instruments can still be played and <u>not</u> be **noisy**.
5 **Review**	 **Activity:** several children play instruments or call out. Discuss whether they were **noisy**.  **Word Bag:** put a musical instrument in the bag. Make it **noisy** and <u>not</u> **noisy**.  **Concept book:** see page 76 for details.  **Family:** do a range of activities in a **noisy** manner followed by being <u>not</u> **noisy**. For example, walking, banging bricks together or playing music.

Old

1 Teach

 Use a sign or gesture for **old**.

 Look at the symbol together.

 Say the word **old** to your partner.

 Sing a Word Aware song including the word **old**.

2 Teach

Equipment: Concept Cat toy, an old jumper, an old doll, an old toy and a mobile phone (which is not old).

Concept Cat is a clever, clever cat. He looks here, he looks there, learning as he goes and, when he comes home, he tells us a story. Concept Cat is a clever, clever cat. This story is all about **old**. Listen out for the word **old**.

One day, Concept Cat was at his grandparents' house. He looked in a box and found lots of **old** things. Concept Cat found an **old** jumper. Granny made the **old** jumper for Mum. Concept Cat found an **old** doll. The **old** doll was a little bit broken. Then he found an **old** toy. The toy looked really **old**. 'But look, there's something else in here. It's Mum's phone. That's not **old**.'

The jumper was **old**. The doll was **old**. The toy was **old**. The phone was not **old**.

Concept Cat, what a clever, clever cat. He knows all about **old**.

3 Teach

A Collect a range of objects and discuss which ones are **old** and not **old**.

B Look at pictures of **old** people and not **old** people and compare them.

4 Activate

A Ask the children to bring in something of theirs that is **old**. Talk about how the objects look.

B Go on a walk to see buildings which are **old** and not **old**.

5 Review

 **Activity:** ask the children to choose which items in the classroom are **old**.

Word Bag: put in the bag any object which is obviously **old**.

 **Concept book:** see page 76 for details.

 **Family:** look in the child's toy box and find things that are **old** and not **old**. Talk to an **old** person about their childhood.

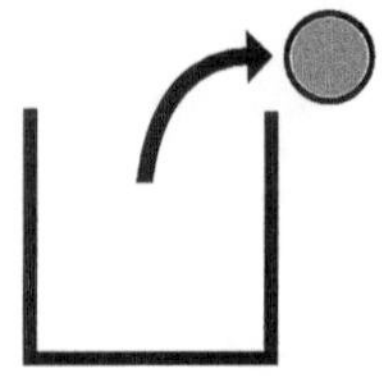

Out

1 Teach	 Use a <u>sign</u> or <u>gesture</u> for **out**. 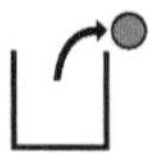 Look at the <u>symbol</u> together.  <u>Say</u> the word **out** to your partner.  <u>Sing</u> a Word Aware song including the word **out**.
2 Teach 	**Equipment: Concept Cat toy, a biscuit in a tin and a bin.** Concept Cat is a clever, clever cat. He looks here, he looks there, learning as he goes and, when he comes home, he tells us a story. Concept Cat is a clever, clever cat. This story is all about **out**. Listen for the word **out**. One day, Concept Cat wanted a biscuit. Mum said, 'Don't take any biscuits **out** of the biscuit tin.' Concept Cat took a biscuit **out** of the biscuit tin. Mum was cross. She shouted, 'Because you took a biscuit **out** of the tin, you can <u>not</u> go **out** to play!' Concept Cat stayed at home and looked **out** of the window. He saw someone putting their rubbish bin **out**. Concept Cat took a biscuit **out** of the tin. He was not allowed to go **out** to play. He looked **out** of the window and he saw the rubbish being put **out**. Concept Cat, what a clever, clever cat. He knows all about **out**.
3 Teach	A Instruct the children to poke their tongues **out** (and then <u>not</u> **out**). B Collect several containers with small objects in them. Ask the children to take objects **out**.
4 Activate	A Before free play, talk about who is going **out** and who is <u>not</u> going **out**. B Using a doll's house, talk about what is **out** and <u>not</u> **out**.
5 Review	 **Activity:** look **out** of the window and describe what you see.  **Word Bag:** put in the bag a small container and objects that can be taken **out**.  **Concept book:** see page 76 for details.  **Family:** at snack time, put mini-biscuits in containers and then take them **out**. On the bus or in the car, look **out** of the window.

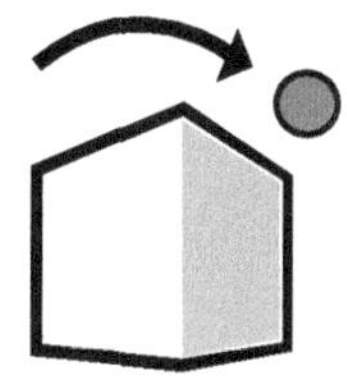

Over

1 **Teach**	 Use a <u>sign</u> or <u>gesture</u> for **over**.  Look at the <u>symbol</u> together.  <u>Say</u> the word **over** to your partner.  <u>Sing</u> a Word Aware song including the word **over**.
2 **Teach** 	**Equipment: Concept Cat toy and objects to represent dog poo (eg play dough), rubbish, pavement cracks and a puddle.** Concept Cat is a clever, clever cat. He looks here, he looks there, learning as he goes and, when he comes home, he tells us a story. Concept Cat is a clever, clever cat. This story is all about **over**. Listen out for the word **over**. One day, Concept Cat was walking down the street when he saw some dog poo. He stepped **over** the dog poo. Concept Cat saw some rubbish. He stepped **over** the rubbish. Concept Cat saw some cracks in the pavement. He stepped **over** the cracks. Concept Cat saw a puddle. He did <u>not</u> step **over** the puddle. Splash! Concept Cat stepped **over** the dog poo. Concept Cat stepped **over** the rubbish. Then Concept Cat stepped **over** the cracks. But Concept Cat did <u>not</u> step **over** the puddle. Concept Cat, what a clever, clever cat. He knows all about **over**.
3 **Teach**	A Ask one child to lie on the floor and another child to step **over** him. Swap places and repeat the stepping **over**. B Select an object such as a chair or table and give children the option of going **over** or <u>not</u> **over** it.
4 **Activate**	A Build an obstacle course, or a series of hurdles, for children to climb **over**. B In the playground, talk about going **over** the apparatus.
5 **Review**	 **Activity:** place a cushion on the floor and ask the children to say how they are going to get past it, emphasising **over**.  **Word Bag:** put a play person and a toy log or a stick in the bag. Make the person step **over** the log.  **Concept book:** see page 76 for details.  **Family:** when walking down the street, jump **over** the cracks in the pavement.

Quick

1 Teach

Use a sign or gesture for **quick**.

Look at the symbol together.

Say the word **quick** to your partner.

Sing a Word Aware song including the word **quick**.

2 Teach

Equipment: Concept Cat toy, a ball and a cup.

Concept Cat is a clever, clever cat. He looks here, he looks there, learning as he goes and, when he comes home, he tells us a story. Concept Cat is a clever, clever cat. This story is all about **quick**. Listen out for the word **quick**.

One day, Concept Cat was going to the park with Mum. He wanted to take a ball. Mum said, 'Go and get your ball, but you need to be **quick**.' Before they left, Concept Cat wanted a drink. Mum said, 'You can have a drink, but be **quick**.' Then Concept Cat needed the toilet and Mum said, 'Be **quick**.'

When they got to the park, Mum saw her friend and went for a **quick** chat. Concept Cat said, 'I do not want a **quick** play. I want to play on the slide, the swings and the climbing frame.'

Concept Cat was **quick** when he got his ball. He was **quick** when he had a drink and he was **quick** when he went to the toilet. Mum had a **quick** chat with her friend. Concept Cat was not **quick** when he went to the park.

Concept Cat, what a clever, clever cat. He knows all about **quick**.

3 Teach

A Ask the children to do a simple action such as brushing teeth or hair, but to be **quick** and not **quick**.

B In a long line, be **quick** when you walk to play and then not **quick**.

4 Activate

A Be **quick** when you tidy up.

B Go on a treasure hunt. Be **quick**.

5 Review

Activity: do actions for **quick** and not **quick** and ask the children to label them.

Word Bag: put a pen and a piece of paper in the bag and draw a picture but be **quick**!

Concept book: see page 76 for details.

Family: on the way home, walk **quickly** and not **quick**.

Quiet

1 **Teach**	 Use a sign or gesture for **quiet**.  Look at the symbol together.  Say the word **quiet** to your partner.  Sing a Word Aware song including the word **quiet**.
2 **Teach** 	**Equipment: Concept Cat toy, china cups, a drum and a book.** Concept Cat is a clever, clever cat. He looks here, he looks there, learning as he goes and, when he comes home, he tells us a story. Concept Cat is a clever, clever cat. This story is all about **quiet**. Listen out for the word **quiet**. Concept Cat is awake. Mum is having a rest. She says, 'Concept Cat, please be **quiet**!' Concept Cat gets a drink. He bangs the cups. He is not being **quiet**. Mum says, 'Please be **quiet**!' Concept Cat bangs the drum. That is not **quiet**. Mum says, 'Please be **quiet**!' Concept Cat finds a book. Now Concept Cat is **quiet**. Then he has a sleep. He is **quiet**. Concept Cat was not **quiet** when he banged the cups. When he banged the drum, he was not **quiet**. When Concept Cat read the book, he was **quiet**. When Concept Cat fell asleep, he was **quiet**. Concept Cat, what a clever, clever cat. He knows all about **quiet**.
3 **Teach**	A Model to the children talking in a **quiet** voice and a not **quiet** voice. B Listen to **quiet** music and not **quiet** music.
4 **Activate**	A Practise being as **quiet** as possible when a group of children has to go somewhere, eg to wash hands. B Play 'The King's Keys' game. Sit a blindfolded child on a chair at one end of the room. All of the other children start walking quietly from the other end of the room. The aim is to pick up the keys without being heard. A child must sit down if they are pointed to by the 'King'. Emphasise that they all need to be **quiet** to play this game.
5 **Review**	 **Activity:** think of places that are **quiet** and not **quiet**, eg a playground, the park, your bedroom at night-time.  **Word Bag:** put in the bag a musical instrument that can be **quiet** or not **quiet**.  **Concept book:** see page 76 for details.  **Family:** challenge the family members to talk in **quiet** voices for a minute.

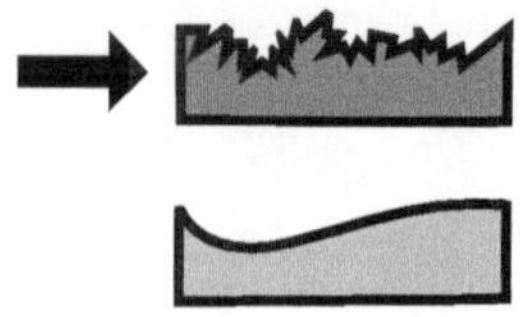

Rough

1 Teach

Use a sign or gesture for **rough**.

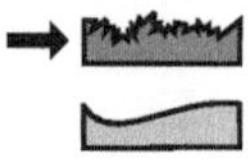

Look at the symbol together.

Say the word **rough** to your partner.

Sing a Word Aware song including the word **rough**.

2 Teach

Equipment: Concept Cat toy, some rough wood, some rough carpet, a T-shirt and a mirror.

Concept Cat is a clever, clever cat. He looks here, he looks there, learning as he goes and, when he comes home, he tells us a story. Concept Cat is a clever, clever cat. This story is all about **rough**. Listen out for the word **rough**.

One day, Concept Cat was told to be careful of something that was **rough**. But Concept Cat did not know what **rough** meant, so he set off to find out all about **rough**.

First, Concept Cat touched a mirror. That did not feel **rough**. Next, Concept Cat touched a T-shirt. That was not **rough**. Next, he found some wood. The wood was **rough**. Then he touched the carpet. The carpet was **rough** too.

The mirror was not **rough**. The T-shirt was not **rough**. The wood was **rough**. The carpet was **rough**. To learn about **rough**, you need to touch things with your hands.

Concept Cat, what a clever, clever cat. He knows all about **rough**.

3 Teach

Place **rough** and not **rough** objects in a feely bag. The children take turns selecting objects from the bag. Support the children to feel the objects, pass them around the group and sort into **rough** versus not **rough**.

4 Activate

A Place various textured items on the table. Take turns at describing whether the objects are **rough** or not **rough**.

B Walk around the playground searching for **rough** things.

5 Review

Activity: ask the children to remember all of the **rough** things they touched.

Word Bag: put a nail file or a piece of sandpaper in the bag. Talk about it being **rough**.

Concept book: see page 76 for details.

Family: spend a few minutes in the garden or in the park. Touch things and talk about whether they are **rough**.

Same

1 Teach

Use a sign or gesture for **same**.

Look at the symbol together.

Say the word **same** to your partner.

Sing a Word Aware song including the word **same**.

2 Teach

Equipment: Concept Cat toy, four socks and four shoes (two of each should be the same).

Concept Cat is a clever, clever cat. He looks here, he looks there, learning as he goes and, when he comes home, he tells us a story. Concept Cat is a clever, clever cat. This story is all about **same**. Listen out for the word **same**.

One morning, Concept Cat was getting dressed. He put on one sock. He needed to find a sock that was the **same**. He found another sock. No, that was not the **same**. He found another sock. No, that was not the **same**. Then he found another sock. That was the **same**. These two socks are the **same**.

Then Concept Cat put on his shoes. He put on one shoe. He needed to find a shoe that was the **same**. He found another shoe. That was not the **same**. He found another shoe. That was not the **same**. Then he found another shoe. That was the **same**. These two shoes are the **same**.

Concept Cat, what a clever, clever cat. He knows all about **same**.

3 Teach

A Look at the children's clothes and make comparisons. For example, 'All the people with the **same** jumper as Edi come and stand here. Look, these are the **same**. Now let's look at who has the **same** socks as Shania.'

B Using building bricks, say 'These two are not the **same**. Find two which are the **same**.'

4 Activate

A Go on a treasure hunt looking for things that are the **same**.

B Ask the children to find objects that are all the **same** colour.

5 Review

Activity: look around the room for items that are the **same**.

Word Bag: put any two identical objects in the bag. Talk about them being the **same**.

Concept book: see page 76 for details.

Family: ask the children to bring from home two things that are the **same**, eg pairs of toys or socks.

Note: children should have the concepts of **two** and **first** well established before **second** is introduced.

Second

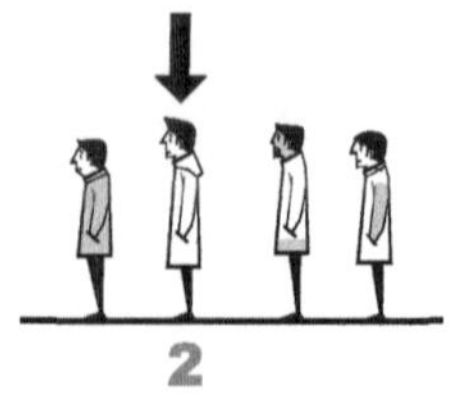

1 **Teach**	 Use a sign or gesture for **second**.  Look at the symbol together.  Say the word **second** to your partner.  Sing a Word Aware song including the word **second**.
2 **Teach** 	**Equipment: Concept Cat toy and several other soft toys (including an elephant).** Concept Cat is a clever, clever cat. He looks here, he looks there, learning as he goes and, when he comes home, he tells us a story. Concept Cat is a clever, clever cat. This story is all about **second**. Listen out for the word **second**. (Place one toy in a queue/line.) Concept Cat went to the summer fair. He went to get some food (pushing in). His friend said, 'Concept Cat, you can't push in. You can go **second**.' (Line up all of the toys with Elephant **second** in the queue.) Concept Cat saw his friend Elephant in a queue or line. Elephant was **second** in the queue or line. 'Hello Elephant.' (Place one toy in a queue or line.) Concept Cat wanted to go on the bouncy castle. Concept Cat saw the queue or line but he did not push in. He waited and went **second**. Concept Cat went **second** in the queue at the summer fair. Elephant was **second** in the queue. At the bouncy castle, Concept Cat went **second**. Concept Cat, what a clever, clever cat. He knows all about **second**.
3 **Teach**	Line up several children. Identify who is **second**. Change their order and repeat.
4 **Activate**	A Talk about who is **second** when the children line up to go down the slide. B Play buses and form queues or lines, identifying the order in which the children go on the bus, using the word **second**.
5 **Review**	 **Activity:** whenever small groups of children are asked to do a task, identify who is **second**.  **Word Bag:** put in the bag several play people and a toy bus which they queue for. Talk about which person is **second**.  **Concept book:** see page 76 for details.  **Family:** place small food items (grapes, berries, raisins and mini-biscuits) on the table. Talk about the order in which they will be eaten: 'This one first and this one **second**.'

Shiny

1 **Teach**	 Use a sign or gesture for **shiny**.  Look at the symbol together.  Say the word **shiny** to your partner.  Sing a Word Aware song including the word **shiny**.
2 **Teach** 	**Equipment: Concept Cat toy, a shiny ball, another ball which can be cleaned to be shiny, and equipment for cleaning and polishing.** Concept Cat is a clever, clever cat. He looks here, he looks there, learning as he goes and, when he comes home, he tells us a story. Concept Cat is a clever, clever cat. This story is all about **shiny**. Listen out for the word **shiny**. Concept Cat's friend had a new ball. The ball was **shiny**. Concept Cat wanted his Dad to buy a **shiny** ball. His Dad said, 'No. You can make your ball **shiny**.' Concept Cat looked at the ball. It was not **shiny**. He bounced the ball. It was not **shiny**. His Dad said, 'You need to clean it to make it **shiny**.' Concept Cat cleaned the ball until it was **shiny**. He liked the **shiny** ball. Concept Cat, what a clever, clever cat. He knows all about **shiny**.
3 **Teach**	A Give each child a **shiny** sticker. Talk about the sticker being **shiny**. B Collect various items and sort them into **shiny** and not **shiny**.
4 **Activate**	A Clean the bikes and make them **shiny**. B Give the children dirty objects that need polishing (such as mirrors) and clean them until they are **shiny**. C At snack time, make the apples **shiny**.
5 **Review**	 **Activity:** look around the room for **shiny** things.  **Word Bag:** put any **shiny** item in the bag. Talk about it being **shiny**.  **Concept book:** see page 76 for details.  **Family:** when out shopping, look at the window displays for **shiny** things.

Short

1 **Teach**	 Use a <u>sign</u> or <u>gesture</u> for **short**.  Look at the <u>symbol</u> together.  <u>Say</u> the word **short** to your partner.  <u>Sing</u> a Word Aware song including the word **short**.
2 **Teach** 	**Equipment: Concept Cat toy, a short and a long pencil, a short and a long ruler.** Concept Cat is a clever, clever cat. He looks here, he looks there, learning as he goes and, when he comes home, he tells us a story. Concept Cat is a clever, clever cat. This story is all about **short**. Listen out for the word **short**. Concept Cat likes **short** things. He wants to find some **short** things for his collection. 'I know. I will look for some **short** pencils.' Concept Cat finds a pencil. 'Oh no! That pencil is <u>not</u> **short**. I will look for some more.' Concept Cat finds another pencil. 'Oh great. This pencil is **short**. It will go with my **short** things.' Concept Cat goes looking for a **short** ruler. He finds a ruler but it is <u>not</u> **short**. Then he finds another one. This ruler is **short**. 'Great, this **short** ruler will go with my **short** things.' Concept Cat now needs to look for some friends who have **short** hair to help hold the **short** things. (Pick two children with **short** hair.) 'Great, you have **short** hair. You can help me hold the **short** things. Here is a **short** pencil and here is a **short** ruler.' Concept Cat, what a clever, clever cat. He knows all about **short**.
3 **Teach**	Cut various lengths of paper strips. Compare them and identify which ones are **short**.
4 **Activate**	A Collect **short** pencils and crayons and compare them with others which are <u>not</u> **short**. B In craft activities, cut out paper streamers of various lengths, including **short** ones.
5 **Review**	 **Activity:** line up streamers or pieces of string and identify which are **short** and <u>not</u> **short**.  **Word Bag:** put two play people in the bag, one of which is **short**. Talk about which one is **short**.  **Concept book:** see page 76 for details.  **Family:** sharpen some pencils and talk about which ones are **short** and <u>not</u> **short**.

Side

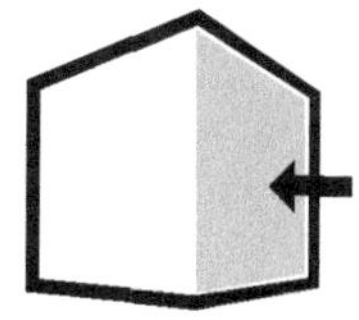

1 **Teach**	 Use a <u>sign</u> or <u>gesture</u> for **side**.  Look at the <u>symbol</u> together.  <u>Say</u> the word **side** to your partner.  <u>Sing</u> a Word Aware song including the word **side**.
2 **Teach** 	**Equipment: Concept Cat toy, another soft toy, a toy bed, a book and a toy box.** Concept Cat is a clever, clever cat. He looks here, he looks there, learning as he goes and, when he comes home, he tells us a story. Concept Cat is a clever, clever cat. This story is all about **side**. Listen out for the word **side**. Concept Cat and his sister, Alanna, are tidying their bedroom. Concept Cat needs to put the toy box somewhere. His sister says, 'Put the toy box at the **side** of the bed.' Concept Cat does <u>not</u> know what **side** means. He puts the toy box down. (Place it on the bed.) 'That is <u>not</u> **side**. Put it at the **side**.' Concept Cat places the toy box down again. (Place the toy box in front.) His sister says again, 'That is <u>not</u> the **side**. I said put it at the **side**. Like this.' (Place the toy box at the **side**.) 'But this is also the **side**.' (Place the box on the other **side**.) Concept Cat spends a few moments deciding which **side** he should put the toy box. He is happy now that the toy box is at the **side** of the bed. He puts a book on the **side** too. (Place the book on the other **side**.) Concept Cat, what a clever, clever cat. He knows all about **side**.
3 **Teach**	A Ask all of the children to stand up and rub their hands down each **side** of their body. Then ask them to point to another part of their body which is <u>not</u> their **side**. Now show them the **side** of their head and instruct them to touch it. B Give each child a soft toy. Place the toy at their **side** and <u>not</u> at their **side**.
4 **Activate**	A Pretend to be soldiers and stand with your arms at the **side**. B When sitting in small groups, talk about who is on one **side** and then who is on the other **side**.
5 **Review**	 **Activity:** look around the room and see what is at the **side** of the door or chair, etc.  **Word Bag:** put in the bag a lunch box with a sticker on each **side**.  **Concept book:** see page 76 for details.  **Family:** look around the living room or bedroom and talk about what is at the **side** of the sofa, bed or television.

Slow

<table>
<tr><td>1
Teach</td><td> Use a <u>sign</u> or <u>gesture</u> for slow.
 Look at the <u>symbol</u> together.
 <u>Say</u> the word slow to your partner.
 <u>Sing</u> a Word Aware song including the word slow.</td></tr>
<tr><td>2
Teach
</td><td>Equipment: Concept Cat toy, a toy slide, a toy roundabout and a toy seesaw.

Concept Cat is a clever, clever cat. He looks here, he looks there, learning as he goes and, when he comes home, he tells us a story. Concept Cat is a clever, clever cat. This story is all about slow. Listen out for the word slow.

Concept Cat went to the playground. He ran up the slide. ‘Concept Cat you need to go slow,’ said his teacher. Concept Cat did <u>not</u> go slow. He fell off the slide. Concept Cat went on the roundabout. His teacher said, ‘Go slow Concept Cat, go slow.’ Concept Cat did <u>not</u> go slow. Oh dear! Concept Cat fell over. Concept Cat went on the seesaw. He remembered to go slow. ‘Well done, Concept Cat, you remembered to go slow.’

Concept Cat went on the slide. He did <u>not</u> go slow. Concept Cat went on the roundabout. He did <u>not</u> go slow. Concept Cat went on the seesaw. He went slow.

Concept Cat, what a clever, clever cat. He knows all about slow.</td></tr>
<tr><td>3
Teach</td><td>A Ask the children to clap their hands slowly and <u>not</u> slowly.
B Ask all of the children to stand up and walk in a circle slowly and <u>not</u> slowly.</td></tr>
<tr><td>4
Activate</td><td>A Do an everyday activity such as snack time in a slow manner. The group can eat slow, drink slow and move slow.
B Pretend to be animals that move in a slow manner such as tortoises or seahorses. Cast a magic spell to make the animals go <u>not</u> slow before going back to slow again.</td></tr>
<tr><td>5
Review</td><td> Activity: read ‘The Tortoise and the Hare’. Listen out for slow.
 Word Bag: put any toy animal in the bag. When you take it out, make the animal move in a slow manner and <u>not</u> slow.
 Concept book: see page 76 for details.
 Family: run races with your child. Talk about who was slow and who was <u>not</u> slow. Occasionally wave your ‘magic wand’ and get everyone to move in a slow manner.</td></tr>
</table>

Small

1 **Teach**	Use a <u>sign</u> or <u>gesture</u> for **small**. Look at the <u>symbol</u> together. <u>Say</u> the word **small** to your partner. <u>Sing</u> a Word Aware song including the word **small**.
2 **Teach** 	**Equipment: Concept Cat toy, a small bag and items which are small enough to fit in the bag (eg a toy car, a doll and a ring). Also items which won't fit in the bag (eg a ruler, a ball and a bat).** Concept Cat is a clever, clever cat. He looks here, he looks there, learning as he goes and, when he comes home, he tells us a story. Concept Cat is a clever, clever cat. This story is all about **small**. Listen out for the word **small**. One day, Concept Cat found a **small** bag. He went looking for **small** things to go in the **small** bag. First, he found a ruler. The ruler was <u>not</u> **small**. Then he found a ball. That was <u>not</u> **small**. Then he found a bat. That was <u>not</u> **small**. But look, here is something **small**: a **small** toy car. Then he found a **small** doll too. This ring is **small** too. Concept Cat found lots of **small** things to go in the **small** bag. Concept Cat found a **small** bag. The ruler was <u>not</u> **small**. The ball was <u>not</u> **small**. The bat was <u>not</u> **small**. The toy car was **small**. The doll and the ring were **small**. Concept Cat, what a clever, clever cat. He knows all about **small**.
3 **Teach**	A Compare your hands with the children's hands. Talk about whose are **small**. B Give each child a **small** sticker or draw a **small** circle on each child's hand.
4 **Activate**	A Find matching pairs of items, one **small** and one <u>not</u> **small**. Sort them and talk about which ones are **small**. B Go on a treasure hunt and find **small** things. As a talking point, 'accidentally' include some items that are <u>not</u> **small**.
5 **Review**	**Activity:** hold up two items of different sizes and talk about which one is **small**. **Word Bag:** put (very) **small** items in a clear plastic bottle to go in the bag. **Concept book:** see page 76 for details. **Family:** cut a sandwich into **small** pieces and talk about **small**.

Smooth

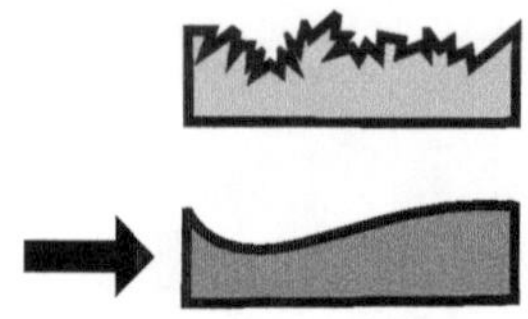

1 **Teach**	 Use a <u>sign</u> or <u>gesture</u> for **smooth**. 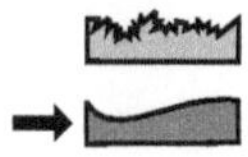 Look at the <u>symbol</u> together.  <u>Say</u> the word **smooth** to your partner.  <u>Sing</u> a Word Aware song including the word **smooth**.
2 **Teach** 	**Equipment: Concept Cat toy, a girl toy ('Alanna'), a toy slide, a rough stone, doll's clothes, a toy wash basin and a mirror.** Concept Cat is a clever, clever cat. He looks here, he looks there, learning as he goes and, when he comes home, he tells us a story. Concept Cat is a clever, clever cat. This story is all about **smooth**. Listen out for the word **smooth**. One day, Concept Cat's sister, Alanna, wanted to collect **smooth** things. The problem was that Concept Cat did not know what **smooth** meant. Alanna said, 'You have to touch them with your hands.' First, Concept Cat found a stone and touched it. Alanna said, 'This stone is <u>not</u> **smooth**.' Next, Concept Cat found some doll's clothes. He touched them to see if they were **smooth**. Alanna said, 'No, they are <u>not</u> **smooth**.' Then he went into the playground and sat on the slide. He touched the slide. Alanna said, 'Yes, it is **smooth**.' He went down the slide. It was **smooth**. Concept Cat knew some other things that are **smooth**. He went to the bathroom. The wash basin was **smooth** and the mirror was **smooth** too. The stone was <u>not</u> **smooth**. The doll's clothes were <u>not</u> **smooth**. The slide was **smooth**. The wash basin was **smooth**. The mirror was **smooth**. To learn about **smooth**, you need to touch things with your hands. Concept Cat, what a clever, clever cat. He knows all about **smooth**.
3 **Teach**	Pass round various objects and touch them to see whether they are **smooth**.
4 **Activate**	A Go on a treasure hunt around the setting, looking for things that are **smooth**. B Go down the playground slide and feel that it is **smooth**.
5 **Review**	 **Activity:** talk about whether an apple or a pineapple is **smooth**.  **Word Bag:** put a **smooth** stone in the bag.  **Concept book:** see page 76 for details.  **Family:** look around the house for as many **smooth** things as you can find.

Soft

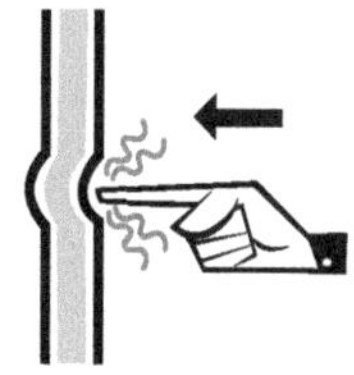

1
Teach

Use a sign or gesture for **soft**.

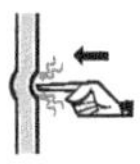
Look at the symbol together.

Say the word **soft** to your partner.

Sing a Word Aware song including the word **soft**.

2
Teach

Equipment: Concept Cat toy, one table, one hard chair and one soft chair, a soft cushion and a soft teddy bear.

Concept Cat is a clever, clever cat. He looks here, he looks there, learning as he goes and, when he comes home, he tells us a story. Concept Cat is a clever, clever cat. This story is all about **soft**. Listen out for the word **soft**.

One day, Concept Cat was feeling sleepy, so he went looking for somewhere **soft** to have a nap. He curled up on the table but, no, that was not **soft**. He curled up on the chair but, no, that was not **soft**. In the living room, he found another chair. That was **soft**. Then he found a **soft** cushion. His friend, Teddy, was also **soft**.

The table was not **soft**. One chair was not **soft**. The other chair was **soft**. The cushion was **soft**. Teddy was **soft** too.

Concept Cat, what a clever, clever cat. He knows all about **soft**.

3
Teach

A Ask the children to feel their own hair, clothing and shoes. Talk about which ones are **soft**.

B Pass around various items that are **soft** and not **soft**.

4
Activate

A Sort items into **soft** and not **soft**. Put the **soft** symbol next to the **soft** items.

B Make a **soft** corner with cushions, toys, blankets, etc.

5
Review

Activity: put out the **soft** and not **soft** items on the table with the symbol for **soft**. Ask the children to sort them.

Word Bag: put cotton wool balls in the bag. Talk about them being **soft**.

Concept book: see page 76 for details.

Family: make a play den with the help of your child. Find **soft** things to put in it. Touch the items and talk about which ones are **soft**.

Some

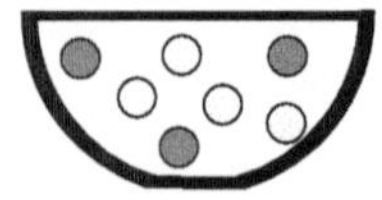

1 **Teach**	 Use a sign or gesture for **some**.  Look at the symbol together.  Say the word **some** to your partner.  Sing a Word Aware song including the word **some**.
2 **Teach** 	**Equipment: Concept Cat toy, sweets, grapes and raisins.** Concept Cat is a clever, clever cat. He looks here, he looks there, learning as he goes and, when he comes home, he tells us a story. Concept Cat is a clever, clever cat. This story is all about **some**. Listen out for the word **some**. Concept Cat likes sweets. Mum said he could have **some** sweets. (Concept Cat takes many sweets.) Mum says, 'That's not **some** sweets.' (Concept Cat puts all of the sweets back. Then he takes one sweet.) Mum says, 'That's not **some** sweets. You can have **some** sweets. I will give you **some** sweets.' (Adult gives **some**.) 'Now you have **some** sweets.' Now Concept Cat knows **some**. He can take **some** grapes. (Take **some** grapes.) Now he can take **some** raisins. (Take **some** raisins.) Concept Cat now has **some** sweets, **some** grapes and **some** raisins. Concept Cat, what a clever, clever cat. He knows all about **some**.
3 **Teach**	A Give each child a bowl. Before you give out counters, talk about who has **some**. Give **some** children **some** counters. Talk about who has **some**. Give counters to every child and talk about **some**. Repeat with dried pasta or rice. B Show a whole cake, **some** cake (different amounts) and an empty plate. Talk about which is **some** and not **some**.
4 **Activate**	A At snack time, talk about who has **some** drink or food and who does not have **some**. B When handing out pencils, paper or other materials, use the word **some**.
5 **Review**	 **Activity:** give one item to one child, **some** to another and none to the others. Talk about who has **some**.  **Word Bag:** put a bundle of pencils in the bag. Take out **some**.  **Concept book:** see page 76 for details.  **Family:** share a banana, a cake or a sandwich, having **some** each.

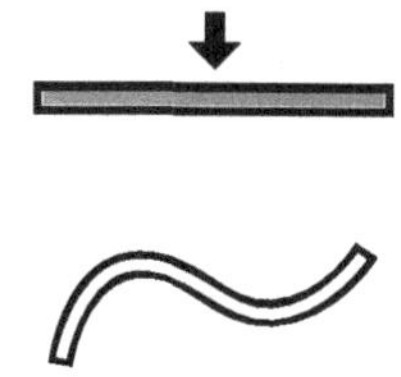

Straight

1 **Teach**	 Use a sign or gesture for **straight**. 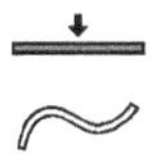 Look at the symbol together.  Say the word **straight** to your partner.  Sing a Word Aware song including the word **straight**.
2 **Teach** 	**Equipment: Concept Cat toy, a pen and paper.** Concept Cat is a clever, clever cat. He looks here, he looks there, learning as he goes and, when he comes home, he tells us a story. Concept Cat is a clever, clever cat. This story is all about **straight**. Listen out for the word **straight**. One day, Concept Cat's teacher asked him to draw some **straight** lines. Concept Cat did not know what **straight** meant. He needed to find out about **straight**. Concept Cat drew a circle. (Draw a circle.) Maybe this was **straight**. 'No!' said his teacher, 'That's not **straight**.' (Draw a zigzag line.) Maybe this line was **straight**. 'No!' said his teacher, 'That's not **straight**.' Concept Cat drew another line. (Draw a wavy line.) Maybe this was **straight**. 'No!' said his teacher, 'That's not **straight**.' Concept Cat drew another line. (Draw a **straight** horizontal line.) Maybe this was **straight**. 'Yes!' said his teacher, 'That is **straight**. And this one is **straight** too.' (Draw a **straight** vertical line.) The circle was not **straight**. This line was not **straight**. This line was not **straight**. This line was **straight**. This line was **straight** too. Concept Cat, what a clever, clever cat. He knows all about **straight**.
3 **Teach**	A Model to the children standing **straight** and not **straight**. Encourage them to copy your actions. B Give each child a pipe cleaner. Make them **straight** and not **straight**.
4 **Activate**	A Draw chalk lines. Make them **straight** and not **straight**. B When drawing and painting, talk about **straight** lines and not **straight** lines.
5 **Review**	 **Activity:** draw lines on the board and talk about **straight** and not **straight**.  **Word Bag:** put a ruler in the bag. Talk about it being **straight**.  **Concept book:** see page 76 for details.  **Family:** lie on the floor next to your child. Both lie **straight**. Then try to make yourselves not **straight**.

Note: avoid using **taller** and **tallest** until the concept of **tall** is secure. See pages 167 and 163 for **taller** and **tallest**.

Tall

1 Teach

Use a sign or gesture for **tall**.

Look at the symbol together.

Say the word **tall** to your partner.

Sing a Word Aware song including the word **tall**.

2 Teach

Equipment: Concept Cat toy, a small box, a tall cupboard (or a tall box representing the cupboard), a toy frog, lamb and giraffe.

Concept Cat is a clever, clever cat. He looks here, he looks there, learning as he goes and, when he comes home, he tells us a story. Concept Cat is a clever, clever cat. This story is all about **tall**. Listen out for the word **tall**.

One day, Concept Cat is at home. He wants to get a box which is on top of the **tall** cupboard. He tries to reach but he is not **tall**. His friend Frog comes over. He tries to reach but Frog is not **tall**. His friend Lamb comes over but she cannot reach because she is not **tall**. Then Giraffe comes over. She can reach because she is **tall**.

Concept Cat is not **tall**. Frog is not **tall**. Lamb is not **tall**. Giraffe is **tall**.

Concept Cat, what a clever, clever cat. He knows all about **tall**.

3 Teach

A Measure the children against the wall to see how **tall** they are.

B Give a few building bricks to two children and lots to one child. Ask the children to make towers. Compare the towers and identify which one is **tall**.

4 Activate

A Walk on stilts to become **tall**.

B Make a play den with a low door to keep out **tall** people (adults).

C Make **tall** trees or sunflowers out of paper.

5 Review

Activity: line up the children and talk about who is **tall**.

Word Bag: put a ruler and a doll in the bag. Use it to measure something that is **tall**.

Concept book: see page 76 for details.

Family: stand on tiptoes and chairs to see who can be **tall**. Line up the family in order of height and see who is **tall**.

Thick

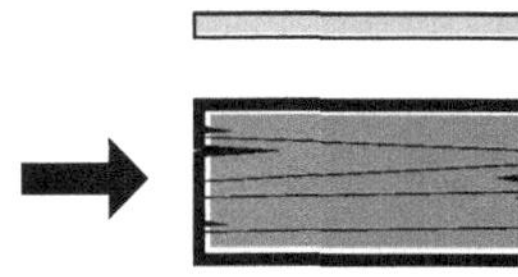

1
Teach

 Use a <u>sign</u> or <u>gesture</u> for **thick**.

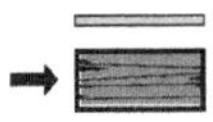 Look at the <u>symbol</u> together.

 <u>Say</u> the word **thick** to your partner.

 <u>Sing</u> a Word Aware song including the word **thick**.

2
Teach

Equipment: Concept Cat toy, pieces of bread, cheese, tomato and cucumber which are thick and ham (or beef) which is not thick.

Concept Cat is a clever, clever cat. He looks here, he looks there, learning as he goes and, when he comes home, he tells us a story. Concept Cat is a clever, clever cat. This story is all about **thick**. Listen out for the word **thick**.

One day, Concept Cat was hungry, so he made a **thick** sandwich. He cut two **thick** slices of bread. He cut some **thick** slices of cheese. He cut the tomato **thick**. Then he cut **thick** slices of cucumber. The ham (or beef) was <u>not</u> **thick** but he put that on anyway.

What a **thick** sandwich! The bread was **thick**. The cheese was **thick**. The tomato was **thick**. The cucumber was **thick**. The ham (or beef) was <u>not</u> **thick**. Concept Cat ate the **thick** sandwich.

Concept Cat, what a clever, clever cat. He knows all about **thick**.

3
Teach

A Look at a range of books. Lay them down and talk about books that are **thick**.

B Make a **thick** sandwich. This can be done with either real or toy food.

4
Activate

Make a **thick** bed in the home corner. Use lots of blankets to make the bed **thick**.

5
Review

 **Activity:** sort various items into **thick** and <u>not</u> **thick**. You could include rope, books, jumpers and sandwiches.*

Word Bag: put a piece of **thick** and <u>not</u> **thick** rope in the bag.

 **Concept book:** see page 76 for details.

 **Family:** look for **thick** books in the house or at the library. Alternatively, try to make a **thick** sandwich.

* Paper, hair and cloth can all be described as **thick** but the difference is very subtle, so it is best to use more obvious items at first.

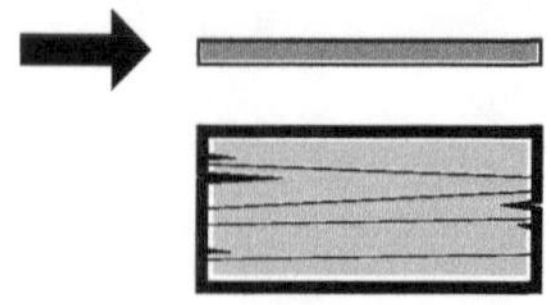

Thin

1 **Teach**	 Use a sign or gesture for **thin**. 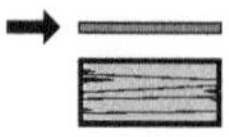 Look at the symbol together.  Say the word **thin** to your partner.  Sing a Word Aware song including the word **thin**.
2 **Teach** 	**Equipment: Concept Cat toy, a cushion, a toy car and train and a ruler.** Concept Cat is a clever, clever cat. He looks here, he looks there, learning as he goes and, when he comes home, he tells us a story. Concept Cat is a clever, clever cat. This story is all about **thin**. Listen out for the word **thin**. One day at home, Concept Cat dropped his toy car behind the sofa. His Dad said, 'You need something **thin** to get the car out.' Concept Cat nodded but he did not know what **thin** meant. He needed to find out about **thin**. First, Concept Cat put his paw in. 'No,' said his Dad, 'your paw is not **thin**. You need something **thin**.' Next, Concept Cat tried using a cushion. Maybe the cushion was **thin**. His Dad laughed, 'That is not **thin**. You need to find something that is **thin**.' Then Concept Cat tried using a toy train. The train was not **thin**. Concept Cat looked around and found a ruler. 'Yes,' said his Dad. 'The ruler is **thin** if you turn it this way.' Concept Cat could reach his car because he found something **thin**. Concept Cat's paw was not **thin**. The cushion was not **thin**. The train was not **thin**. The ruler was **thin**. Concept Cat, what a clever, clever cat. He knows all about **thin**.
3 **Teach**	A Compare rope and string, talking about which one is **thin** and not **thin**. B Compare pens, pencils and crayons, also using the terms **thin** and not **thin**.
4 **Activate**	A Look around the classroom and outside. Find objects that are **thin** and not **thin**. B Put cord of varying widths on the threading table. Talk about them, using the words **thin** and not **thin**.
5 **Review**	 **Activity:** place **thin** and not **thin** objects in a feely bag. Ask the children to take out items and discuss whether they are **thin**.  **Word Bag:** put a **thin** ruler in the bag.  **Concept book:** see page 76 for details.  **Family:** in the park or garden, find **thin** sticks.

Through

1 Teach

Use a sign or gesture for **through**.

Look at the symbol together.

Say the word **through** to your partner.

Sing a Word Aware song including the word **through**.

2 Teach

Equipment: Concept Cat toy, a toy lamb, card rolled into a tunnel, card folded to make a tent, a den structure and a toy door.

Concept Cat is a clever, clever cat. He looks here, he looks there, learning as he goes and, when he comes home, he tells us a story. Concept Cat is a clever, clever cat. This story is all about **through**. Listen out for the word **through**.

One day in the playground, Concept Cat chased Lamb. Concept Cat chased Lamb **through** the tunnel. Concept Cat chased Lamb **through** the tent. Concept Cat chased Lamb **through** the den. Concept Cat chased Lamb, but Lamb shut the door. Concept Cat could not chase Lamb **through** the door. Concept Cat bumped his head.

Concept Cat chased Lamb **through** the tunnel. Concept Cat chased Lamb **through** the tent. Concept Cat chased Lamb **through** the den. Concept Cat could not chase Lamb **through** the door.

Concept Cat, what a clever, clever cat. He knows all about **through**.

3 Teach

A Ask a few children to make an arch. Then ask another child to go **through** it.

B Place the children in a row and encourage them to pass a ball **through** their legs.

4 Activate

A Put the symbol **through** next to the threading activity.

B Place the tunnel outdoors and talk about going **through** the tunnel. What else is outdoors that the children can go **through**?

5 Review

Activity: read *We're Going on a Bear Hunt* (Rosen, 1995). Then pretend to go on a bear hunt yourselves. Think about all of the places you could go **through**.

Word Bag: put in the bag a string threaded **through** a bead.

Concept book: see page 76 for details.

Family: go for a walk around your house. Talk about the places you can get **through**.

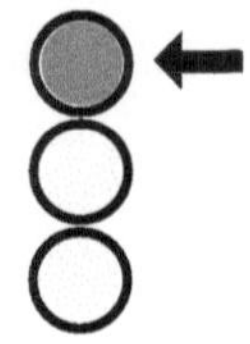

Top

1 **Teach**	 Use a <u>sign</u> or <u>gesture</u> for **top**. 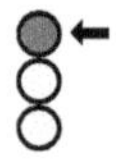 Look at the <u>symbol</u> together.  <u>Say</u> the word **top** to your partner.  <u>Sing</u> a Word Aware song including the word **top**.
2 **Teach** 	**Equipment: Concept Cat toy, toy stairs (or folded paper to represent stairs), a toy rabbit and a toy slide.** Concept Cat is a clever, clever cat. He looks here, he looks there, learning as he goes and, when he comes home, he tells us a story. Concept Cat is a clever, clever cat. This story is all about **top**. Listen out for the word **top**. One day, Concept Cat was helping to tidy the house. Mum asked him to put his toy rabbit at the **top** of the stairs. Concept Cat put the rabbit on the stairs. (Place it in the middle.) Mum said, 'No, I said at the **top** of the stairs. Put the rabbit at the **top**.' Concept Cat put the rabbit on the stairs. (Place it at the bottom.) Mum said, 'No, I said at the **top** of the stairs. Put the rabbit at the **top**.' Concept Cat climbed to the **top** of the stairs and put the rabbit at the **top**. 'Well done, you put it at the **top**.' Then Concept Cat went outside and climbed to the **top** of the slide. He could touch the **top** of his head too. Concept Cat put the rabbit at the **top**. He climbed to the **top** of the stairs and the slide. He touched the **top** of his head. Concept Cat, what a clever, clever cat. He knows all about **top**.
3 **Teach**	A Tell the children to touch the **top** of their head. Then ask them to balance a book on **top** of their head. B Gather a selection of small items. Instruct the children to place an item on **top** of the table, box or cupboard.
4 **Activate**	A Explore items that are jumbled up. Attach stickers to the **top** of the items, eg box, toy table, fridge, cooker, house, cupboard. B Find some stairs and climb to the **top**. Go to the slide and climb to the **top**.
5 **Review**	 **Activity:** place a few interesting items on **top** of a cupboard. Ask the children whether they can spot what is on **top** of the cupboard.  **Word Bag:** put a toy table in the bag. Take it out and place things on **top** of it.  **Concept book:** see page 76 for details.  **Family:** go on a treasure hunt around the house. Look at what is on **top** of the cupboards.

Under

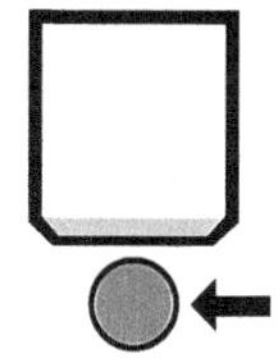

1 Teach

Use a <u>sign</u> or <u>gesture</u> for **under**.

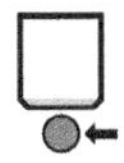

Look at the <u>symbol</u> together.

<u>Say</u> the word **under** to your partner.

<u>Sing</u> a Word Aware song including the word **under**.

2 Teach

Equipment: Concept Cat toy, a leaf, garden table, log, plant pot and toy frog.

Concept Cat is a clever, clever cat. He looks here, he looks there, learning as he goes and, when he comes home, he tells us a story. Concept Cat is a clever, clever cat. This story is all about **under**. Listen out for the word **under**.

One day, Concept Cat was outside. He could hear a frog croaking but he could not see it. He thought it must be **under** something. He looked **under** a leaf. The frog was <u>not</u> **under** there. He looked **under** the log. The frog was <u>not</u> **under** there. He looked **under** the garden table. The frog was <u>not</u> **under** there. He looked **under** the plant pot. 'Croak, croak!' The frog was **under** there. The frog was **under** the pot.

The frog was <u>not</u> **under** the leaf. The frog was <u>not</u> **under** the log. The frog was <u>not</u> **under** the garden table. The frog was **under** the plant pot.

Concept Cat, what a clever, clever cat. He knows all about **under**.

3 Teach

A Put out a selection of blank pieces of paper (or shapes). Hide some pictures **under** some of them. Look at and talk about what is **under** the pieces of paper.

B Hold a rope low and horizontally and encourage the children to go **under** it.

4 Activate

A Play hide-and-seek and hide **under** blankets or table cloths, etc.

B Make an obstacle course that requires children to go **under** things.

5 Review

Activity: place counters **under** objects and talk about where the counters are.

Word Bag: put a small object with a sticker on the bottom in the bag. Look to see what is **under** the object.

Concept book: see page 76 for details.

Family: at bedtime, get **under** the bed clothes.

Wet

1 Teach	Use a <u>sign</u> or <u>gesture</u> for **wet**. Look at the <u>symbol</u> together. <u>Say</u> the word **wet** to your partner. <u>Sing</u> a Word Aware song including the word **wet**.
2 Teach 	**Equipment: Concept Cat toy, a toy dog, coat, hat, boots, socks, trousers, plus additional clothes to change into, and water.** Concept Cat is a clever, clever cat. He looks here, he looks there, learning as he goes and, when he comes home, he tells us a story. Concept Cat is a clever, clever cat. This story is all about **wet**. Listen out for the word **wet**. One day, Concept Cat is out walking his dog. It starts to rain. Concept Cat gets **wet**. (Put clothes in front of cat and make them **wet**.) It rains some more. The dog gets **wet** too. They splash in the puddles and get **wet**. They get home. Dad says, 'You look very **wet**. Your coat is **wet**. Your boots are **wet**. Your hat is **wet**. Your trousers are **wet**. Go and get some clothes that are <u>not</u> **wet**.' Concept Cat takes off all of his **wet** clothes. He takes off his **wet** coat. He takes off his **wet** hat. He takes off his **wet** boots. He takes off his **wet** socks. He takes off his **wet** trousers. He puts on clothes that are <u>not</u> **wet**. Oh no! The dog shakes himself and Concept Cat is **wet** again. He will need to get some more clothes that are <u>not</u> **wet**. Concept Cat, what a clever, clever cat. He knows all about **wet**.
3 Teach	A Ask the children to dip their hands in water and **wet** them. Make them <u>not</u> **wet** and then repeat. B Take clothing that is <u>not</u> **wet** and dip it in water. Compare it with clothing that has not been dipped in water. Talk about **wet** and <u>not</u> **wet**.
4 Activate	A In the water play area, talk about getting **wet** and <u>not</u> **wet**. B Wash the table top and make it **wet**. Then get some towels and make the table top <u>not</u> **wet**. Feel the towels now.
5 Review	**Activity:** feel the clothes on a washing line. Talk about whether they are **wet** or <u>not</u> **wet**. **Word Bag:** put a face cloth in the bag. Dip a corner of it in water and make it **wet**. **Concept book:** see page 76 for details. **Family:** at bath-time, talk about **wet** and <u>not</u> **wet**. Talk about towels, face cloths, hair and bodies being **wet**.

Whole

1 Teach

 Use a <u>sign</u> or <u>gesture</u> for **whole**.

 Look at the <u>symbol</u> together.

 <u>Say</u> the word **whole** to your partner.

 <u>Sing</u> a Word Aware song including the word **whole**.

2 Teach

Equipment: Concept Cat toy, a toy or pretend sandwich, cake and chocolate.

Concept Cat is a clever, clever cat. He looks here, he looks there, learning as he goes and, when he comes home, he tells us a story. Concept Cat is a clever, clever cat. This story is all about **whole**. Listen out for the word **whole**.

Concept Cat was hungry. He wanted a sandwich. Mum said, 'Yes, you can eat a sandwich, but do <u>not</u> eat the **whole** sandwich.' Concept Cat then ate the **whole** sandwich.

Concept Cat was still hungry. He wanted some cake. Mum said, 'Yes, you can eat the cake but <u>not</u> the **whole** thing.' Concept Cat ate the **whole** cake.

Concept Cat was still hungry. He wanted some chocolate. Mum said, 'Yes, you can eat the chocolate but <u>not</u> the **whole** bar.' Concept Cat ate the **whole** chocolate bar.

Concept Cat then got a stomach ache. It was because he ate a **whole** sandwich, a **whole** cake and a **whole** chocolate bar. Concept Cat said, 'Next time, I will <u>not</u> eat a **whole** sandwich, a **whole** cake and a **whole** chocolate bar.'

Concept Cat, what a clever, clever cat. He knows all about **whole**.

3 Teach

A Give each child a small biscuit. Ask them to eat just a little bit, that is, <u>not</u> **whole**. Then eat the **whole** thing.

B Present a **whole** pretend pizza. Cut it up and feed the **whole** thing to a monster.

4 Activate

A Make play dough food and then cut it up so that it is <u>not</u> **whole**.

B Cut shapes (triangles, rectangles, etc) into parts and then ask the children to arrange them so they are **whole**.

5 Review

 **Activity:** talk about pizza and who can eat the **whole** thing.

Word Bag: in the bag put a shape with a piece cut out which can then be replaced to make it **whole** again.

 **Concept book:** see page 76 for details.

 **Family:** talk about eating a **whole** apple, orange or banana.

Wide

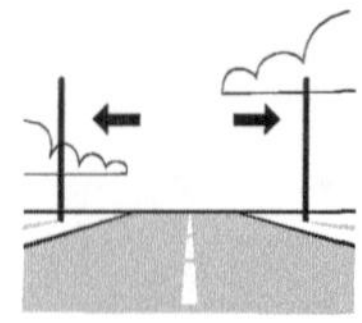

1 **Teach**	 Use a sign or gesture for **wide**.  Look at the symbol together.  Say the word **wide** to your partner.  Sing a Word Aware song including the word **wide**.
2 **Teach** 	**Equipment: Concept Cat toy, a large toy car, another soft toy ('Amina') and three roads drawn on a large piece of paper, two of which are not wide enough for the car and one that is.** Concept Cat is a clever, clever cat. He looks here, he looks there, learning as he goes and, when he comes home, he tells us a story. Concept Cat is a clever, clever cat. This story is all about **wide**. Listen out for the word **wide**. Concept Cat is driving his car to see his friend Amina. Mum asks him to drive on the **wide** roads. Concept Cat says, 'Yes, I know all the **wide** roads.' But Concept Cat does not know where the **wide** roads are. Concept Cat starts off looking for the **wide** roads. 'Oh no, this road is not **wide** and my car will not go on it.' Concept Cat tries another way. 'Oh no! This road is not **wide** and my car won't go on it. I need to look for a **wide** road.' Concept Cat tries again. 'Ah! Here is the **wide** road. My car can go on this road.' Concept Cat drives all the way to his friend Amina on the **wide** road. Concept Cat found it hard to get to see his friend Amina. This road was not **wide**. The car could not go on it. The next road was not **wide**. The car could not go on it. But this road was **wide** and the car went on it all the way to Amina's house. Concept Cat, what a clever, clever cat. He knows all about **wide**.
3 **Teach**	A Ask the children to make a **wide** gap with their hands and then to make them not **wide**. Next, ask them to do the same with their feet. B Open the door **wide** and not **wide**.
4 **Activate**	Create an obstacle course around the room. Make some places that are **wide** and easy to get through. Make some places that are not **wide**.
5 **Review**	 **Activity:** ask the children if they were carrying lots and lots of things, would they need the door to be **wide** or not **wide**?  **Word Bag:** put two small boxes and a toy train in the bag. Change the gap between the boxes to make it **wide** and not **wide**. Talk about the train getting through the **wide** and not **wide** gaps.  **Concept book:** see page 76 for details.  **Family:** play with toy cars. Using empty food boxes, make gaps that are **wide** and not **wide** for the cars to go through.

Comparatives and superlatives

By using the comparative (**–er**) and superlative (**–est**) forms of words, children can make comparisons and expand their understanding and ability to talk about the world. The main concept needs to be firmly established before developing the comparative or superlative form; for example, a child must consistently understand and use **big** before **bigger** or **biggest** is taught.

There is surprisingly little in the literature about the development of comparatives and superlatives, and what is written disagrees about which grammatical form, **–est** or **–er**, develops first. In our clinical judgement, **–est** is phonologically stronger (easier to hear) and its meaning is more distinctive: for example, having the **biggest** ice-cream is more exciting than having a **bigger** ice-cream. Therefore, we suggest working on superlatives first and getting them firmly established before moving on to work on comparatives.

There is a small selection of concept teaching sequences for superlatives and comparatives on the following pages. Practitioners may wish to write more but, once the principle is in place across several words, children will probably be able to generalise the skill.

Concept teaching sequences are provided for the following words.

Superlative	Comparative
biggest	bigger
heaviest	heavier
longest	longer
tallest	taller

Biggest

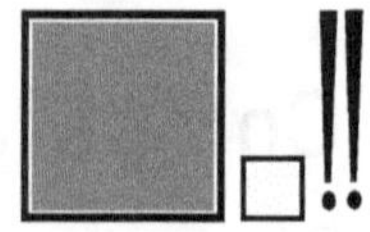

1 **Teach**	 Use a sign or gesture for **biggest**. 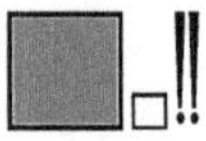 Look at the symbol together.  Say the word **biggest** to your partner.  Sing a Word Aware song including the word **biggest**.
2 **Teach** 	**Equipment: four boxes (optionally gift-wrapped) of various sizes, but one clearly the biggest. The biggest one should contain lots of building bricks.** Concept Cat is a clever, clever cat. He looks here, he looks there, learning as he goes and, when he comes home, he tells us a story. Concept Cat is a clever, clever cat. This story is all about **biggest**. Listen out for the word **biggest**. It was Concept Cat's birthday and he had lots of presents. His Dad said, 'Open the **biggest** one first.' Concept Cat went to open a present. 'That one is not the **biggest**,' said Dad. So Concept Cat went to open another present. 'No, that one is not the **biggest** either. Open the **biggest**,' said Dad. He put all of the presents in a row. 'Now see which one is the **biggest**,' said Dad. Concept Cat took the **biggest** present and opened it. It was the **biggest** box of bricks he had ever seen. This present was not the **biggest**. This present was not the **biggest**. This one was the **biggest**. Inside was the **biggest** box of bricks ever. Concept Cat, what a clever, clever cat. He knows all about **biggest**.
3 **Teach**	A Gather four or more jumpers (pullovers) of different sizes, one of which is clearly the **biggest**. Tell the children to try them on and see which one is the **biggest** and which ones are not the **biggest**. B Hang the clothes on a washing line and talk about which one is the **biggest** and which ones are not the **biggest**.
4 **Activate**	Collect groups of objects of different sizes together (at least three). Place them on a table and talk about which one is the **biggest** or not **biggest**.
5 **Review**	 **Activity:** talk about birthday cake and which piece you would like to eat. The **biggest**!  **Word Bag:** put a set of (at least three) objects of different sizes in the bag. Talk about which is the **biggest**.  **Concept book:** see page 76 for details.  **Family:** at home, go from room to room and see who has the **biggest** bed.

Heaviest

1 **Teach**	 Use a sign or gesture for **heaviest**.  Look at the symbol together.  Say the word **heaviest** to your partner.  Sing a Word Aware song including the word **heaviest**.
2 **Teach** 	**Equipment: Concept Cat toy, several grocery bags containing food items of different weights, including rice and tinned food.** Concept Cat is a clever, clever cat. He looks here, he looks there, learning as he goes and, when he comes home, he tells us a story. Concept Cat is a clever, clever cat. This story is all about **heaviest**. Listen out for the word **heaviest**. One day, Concept Cat went to the shops with his Mum. She said, 'Give me the **heaviest** bag.' Concept Cat gave Mum a bag. She said, 'That one is not the **heaviest**.' Concept Cat gave her another bag but that was not the **heaviest**. Mum said, 'Pick up all the bags, so you can see which one is the **heaviest**.' Concept Cat picked up all the bags one by one. He picked up the bag with rice and tins in it. It was the **heaviest** bag. He gave Mum the **heaviest** bag. This bag was not the **heaviest**. This bag was not the **heaviest**. This bag was the **heaviest**. Concept Cat, what a clever, clever cat. He knows all about **heaviest**.
3 **Teach**	Let the children pick up the bags used in the story. Talk about which one is the **heaviest** and not the **heaviest**. Move items around in the bags and decide again which one is the **heaviest** and not the **heaviest**.
4 **Activate**	Set up a weighing station with lots of items of different weights and talk about which one is the **heaviest** and not the **heaviest**. Change the items each day and repeat the activity.
5 **Review**	 **Activity:** talk about a time you went on holiday and who had the **heaviest** bag.  **Word Bag:** compare any two items in the bag to see which is the **heaviest**.  **Concept book:** see page 76 for details.  **Family:** pick up grocery items at home and see which ones are the **heaviest** and not the **heaviest**.

Longest

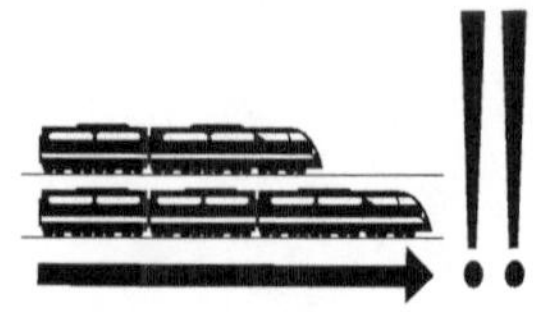

1 **Teach**	 Use a sign or gesture for **longest**.  Look at the symbol together.  Say the word **longest** to your partner.  Sing a Word Aware song including the word **longest**.
2 **Teach** 	**Equipment: Concept Cat toy (with a long tail) and a toy giraffe and elephant.** Concept Cat is a clever, clever cat. He looks here, he looks there, learning as he goes and, when he comes home, he tells us a story. Concept Cat is a clever, clever cat. This story is all about **longest**. Listen out for the word **longest**. One day, Concept Cat and his animal friends were all playing a game. First, who had the **longest** neck? Concept Cat did not have the **longest** neck. Giraffe had the **longest** neck. Who had the **longest** nose? Concept Cat did not have the **longest** nose. Elephant had the **longest** nose: his trunk. Who had the **longest** legs? Concept Cat's legs were not the **longest**. Elephant's legs were not the **longest**. Giraffe's legs were the **longest**. Who had the **longest** tail? Concept Cat had the **longest** tail. Concept Cat did not have the **longest** neck. Giraffe had the **longest** neck. Concept Cat did not have the **longest** nose. Elephant had the **longest** nose: his trunk. Concept Cat did not have the **longest** legs. Giraffe had the **longest** legs. Concept Cat's tail was the **longest**. Concept Cat, what a clever, clever cat. He knows all about **longest**.
3 **Teach**	A Ask the children to look at their hands and find their **longest** finger. B Give every child a piece of string of different lengths. Ask them to compare with each other to see who has the **longest**.
4 **Activate**	A Compare pencils and tie a ribbon (or other marker) to show which one is the **longest**. The others are all not the **longest**. B In the playground, draw chalk lines. Talk about which ones are the **longest** and not the **longest**.
5 **Review**	 **Activity:** look at each other's socks. Who has the **longest** socks?  **Word Bag:** put three or more rulers in the bag, one of which is the **longest**.  **Concept book:** see page 76 for details.  **Family:** find out who in your family has the **longest** arms.

Tallest

1 Teach

Use a sign or gesture for **tallest**.

Look at the symbol together.

Say the word **tallest** to your partner.

Sing a Word Aware song including the word **tallest**.

2 Teach

Equipment: Concept Cat toy, paper flowers of different heights: one red, one blue, one pink and one yellow, which is the tallest.

Concept Cat is a clever, clever cat. He looks here, he looks there, learning as he goes and, when he comes home, he tells us a story. Concept Cat is a clever, clever cat. This story is all about **tallest**. Listen out for the word **tallest**.

One day, Concept Cat found some flowers in the garden. He wanted to see which one was the **tallest**. Concept Cat saw a red flower. That was not the **tallest**. Then he saw a blue flower. That was not the **tallest**. Then he saw a pink flower. That was not the **tallest**. The yellow flower was the **tallest**.

The red flower was not the **tallest**. The blue flower was not the **tallest**. The pink flower was not the **tallest**. The yellow flower was the **tallest**.

Concept Cat, what a clever, clever cat. He knows all about **tallest**.

3 Teach

Compare heights to see who is **tallest**: the teacher or a child? Who is not the **tallest**?

4 Activate

A Go for a walk in the local neighbourhood and find the **tallest** building, the **tallest** tree and the **tallest** person.

B If you have grown plants, you can compare them and see which one is the **tallest** and which ones are not the **tallest**.

5 Review

Activity: talk about who is the **tallest** person in school.

Word Bag: put several play people in the bag, one of whom is the **tallest**.

Concept book: see page 76 for details.

Family: find out who in the family is the **tallest**.

Bigger

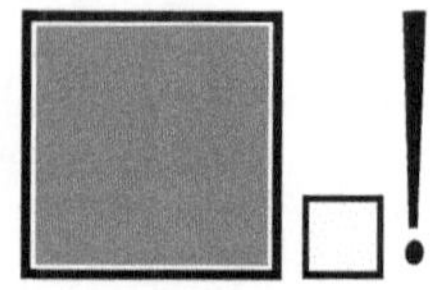

1 Teach

Use a sign or gesture for **bigger**.

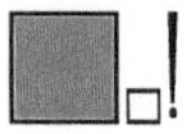
Look at the symbol together.

Say the word **bigger** to your partner.

Sing a Word Aware song including the word **bigger**.

2 Teach

Equipment: Concept Cat toy, another soft toy ('Tia') and five cakes, all clearly of different sizes (these may be cardboard, toy or real cakes).

Concept Cat is a clever, clever cat. He looks here, he looks there, learning as he goes and, when he comes home, he tells us a story. Concept Cat is a clever, clever cat. This story is all about **bigger**. Listen out for the word **bigger**.

One day, Concept Cat is with his friend Tia. He gives Tia a cake. (Give the middle-sized cake.) Tia says, 'I don't want that one. I want a **bigger** cake.' Concept Cat gives her another cake. (Give the second smallest cake.) Tia says, 'That cake is not **bigger**. I want one that is **bigger**.' Concept Cat gives her another cake. (Give the smallest cake.) Tia says, 'That cake is not **bigger**. I want one that is **bigger**.' Concept Cat gives her another cake. (Give the second biggest cake.) Tia says, 'Thank you Concept Cat. That cake is **bigger**.' She eats the **bigger** cake.

Concept Cat goes into the kitchen and finds a cake that is **bigger** than Tia's. He eats the cake that is **bigger** than Tia's cake.

Concept Cat, what a clever, clever cat. He knows all about **bigger**.

3 Teach

A Gather together pairs of familiar objects, ensuring that one of each pair is **bigger** than the other. Compare them side by side, labelling the one that is **bigger**.

B Play with modelling clay, making some balls **bigger** than others.

4 Activate

A At snack time, cut fruit into various sizes. Talk about the pieces which are **bigger** and not **bigger**.

B Using Russian dolls (or similar sequentially sized toys), encourage the children to place them in order. Then talk about which one is **bigger**.

5 Review

Activity: give the children forced choices about familiar objects, for example: 'Which one is **bigger** – a mouse or an elephant?'

Word Bag: put two objects in the bag, one of which is **bigger** than the other.

Concept book: see page 76 for details.

Family: give each child a balloon which they can blow up and make **bigger**.

Heavier

1 **Teach**	 Use a <u>sign</u> or <u>gesture</u> for **heavier**.  Look at the <u>symbol</u> together.  <u>Say</u> the word **heavier** to your partner.  <u>Sing</u> a Word Aware song including the word **heavier**.
2 **Teach** 	**Equipment: Concept Cat toy, another soft toy ('Alfie'), a shopping bag, an apple, a stone and a filled water bottle.** Concept Cat is a clever, clever cat. He looks here, he looks there, learning as he goes and, when he comes home, he tells us a story. Concept Cat is a clever, clever cat. This story is all about **heavier**. Listen out for the word **heavier**. One day, Concept Cat and his friend Alfie were looking around to find things that were **heavier** than Concept Cat. First, they found a shopping bag. The shopping bag was <u>not</u> **heavier** than Concept Cat. Then they found an apple. That was <u>not</u> **heavier** than Concept Cat. Next they found a stone. The stone was **heavier** than Concept Cat. Then they found a water bottle. That was **heavier** than Concept Cat too. Alfie picked up the water bottle and the stone. He said, 'The water bottle is **heavier** than the stone.' The shopping bag was <u>not</u> **heavier** than Concept Cat. The apple was <u>not</u> **heavier** than Concept Cat. The stone was **heavier** than Concept Cat. The water bottle was **heavier** than Concept Cat. The water bottle was **heavier** than the stone. Concept Cat, what a clever, clever cat. He knows all about **heavier**.
3 **Teach**	Place objects in several rucksacks so that they weigh different amounts. The children take it in turns to put them on and compare which ones are **heavier** than others.
4 **Activate**	Place the Concept Cat toy and a range of objects on a table. Encourage the children to pick up two objects at a time to investigate which one is **heavier**.
5 **Review**	 **Activity:** talk about a time when they carried a bag that was **heavier** than someone else's.  **Word Bag:** put two objects of similar size in the bag, one of which is **heavier** than the other.  **Concept book:** see page 76 for details.  **Family:** give the child two shopping bags containing groceries and talk about which one is **heavier**.

Longer

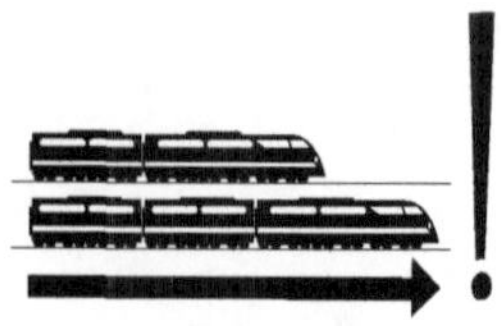

1 Teach

Use a <u>sign</u> or <u>gesture</u> for **longer**.

Look at the <u>symbol</u> together.

<u>Say</u> the word **longer** to your partner.

<u>Sing</u> a Word Aware song including the word **longer**.

2 Teach

Equipment: Concept Cat toy, clothes to hang up and five pieces of string of various lengths (two should be long enough to make into a washing line).

Concept Cat is a clever, clever cat. He looks here, he looks there, learning as he goes and, when he comes home, he tells us a story. Concept Cat is a clever, clever cat. This story is all about **longer**. Listen out for the word **longer**.

One day, Concept Cat has some washing to dry. He needs some string to make a washing line. He finds some string but he needs something **longer**. He finds another piece of string but that is <u>not</u> **longer**. And the next piece of string is <u>not</u> **longer**. He goes looking again and finds string that is **longer** and another piece that is even **longer**. Now he can tie up his washing line.

This string needed to be **longer**. This piece was <u>not</u> **longer**. This one was <u>not</u> **longer**. This one was **longer** and this one was even **longer**.

Concept Cat, what a clever, clever cat. He knows all about **longer**.

3 Teach

A Give pieces of string to pairs of children. Talk about whose string is **longer** and whose is <u>not</u> **longer**.

B Talk about whose hair is **longer** than the teacher's hair.

4 Activate

A Cut tape into various lengths and talk about **longer** and <u>not</u> **longer**.

B Hang up streamers of various lengths. Ensure that one is a different colour and of intermediate length. Talk about which ones are **longer** and <u>not</u> **longer** than the middle-sized streamer.

5 Review

Activity: make a string of beads. Let the children help to make it **longer**.

Word Bag: put a piece of elastic in the bag. Stretch it so that it is **longer**.

Concept book: see page 76 for details.

Family: give everyone an elastic band each so they can talk about making it **longer**.

Taller

1 Teach

Use a sign or gesture for **taller**.

Look at the symbol together.

Say the word **taller** to your partner.

Sing a Word Aware song including the word **taller**.

2 Teach

Equipment: Concept Cat toy, a soft toy ('Mia') and several building bricks.

Concept Cat is a clever, clever cat. He looks here, he looks there, learning as he goes and, when he comes home, he tells us a story. Concept Cat is a clever, clever cat. This story is all about **taller**. Listen out for the word **taller**.

One day, Concept Cat and Mia are building towers. Concept Cat wants to build his tower so that it is **taller** than Mia's. Concept Cat builds his tower. It is not **taller** than Mia's. He builds some more. It is still not **taller**. He adds some more bricks. Still it is not **taller**. Then he adds a few more bricks. Now Concept Cat's tower is **taller**. Concept Cat makes it even **taller**. But look out! (The tower falls down.) Now Concept Cat's tower is not **taller** than Mia's.

Concept Cat built a tower. It was not **taller** than Mia's tower. Then he added more bricks but still it was not **taller**. He added more until his tower was **taller**. Then he added more bricks and it fell down, so Concept Cat's tower was not **taller** again.

Concept Cat, what a clever, clever cat. He knows all about **taller**.

3 Teach

A Ask the children to start in a crouching position and make themselves **taller** and **taller** and **taller** until they are on tiptoes.

B Compare various children against a point on the door frame. Who is **taller** and who is not **taller**?

4 Activate

Draw or make flowers of various lengths and talk about them being **taller** and not **taller**.

5 Review

Activity: look for trees. Find one and then see if you can find a **taller** one.

Word Bag: put a stretchy toy figure in the bag. Stretch it to make it **taller**.

Concept book: see page 76 for details.

Family: on the way home, talk about who is **taller** and not **taller** than the child and who is **taller** and not **taller** than the parent.

Chapter 5
Fun with Words

Chapter 5
Fun with Words

Introduction

This chapter is all about playing with words, enjoying words and simply having fun with words. Some serious-minded souls may dismiss this as a waste of time but we advocate play with a purpose, as outlined below.

Enjoying words

Classroom observation suggests that children who play with words become more interested in words and, subsequently, develop as word learners. We can never teach children all of the words they need to know so, instead, we need to promote their interest in words. This can be achieved by playing word games as part of a general culture of appreciating vocabulary.

Reviewing words that have been taught

REVIEW GAME

Once words have been introduced, children need to hear them again. By incorporating taught words into games, children can review the new vocabulary and slowly build up their own understanding. Word games help children to think of the words in different ways and thus establish the word fully.

Building up word-learning skills

Many word games use skills that involve exploring speech sounds and/or the meaning of a word. So, by playing word games, children are also developing their word-learning skills.

To learn words effectively, children need to be able to both identify and remember the speech sound components of words as well as be able to talk about their meaning. Children in the Early Years are just starting this learning but, over time, they should be introduced to the following word-learning skills.

Speech sounds		Meaning	
	Clap the syllables of a word		Say what we could do with it
b, c, t	Identify the first sound		Say where we could find it
	Make up a rhyming word		Say which category it is in
			Describe it

Sounds in words

The games described in this chapter give children the opportunity to develop phonological (speech sound) awareness skills. These are important factors in their ability to learn and recall words as well as important foundation skills for literacy.

Syllable games

Clapping syllables

Select a topic (eg animals, children's names, mini-beasts, colours, things at the seaside). The first child names an item connected with the chosen topic and claps out the syllables as he says the word. Everyone then says the word together and claps out the syllables. The next child then thinks of a different word from the same topic, and so on.

Bippity Boppity Bumble Bee

Members of the group sit in a circle. The adult holds a toy bee and begins the chant and walks round the circle to a child.

Adult: 'Bippity Boppity Bumble Bee, will you say your name for me?'

Child: 'Ricardo.'

Adult: 'Let's all say it.' (The class says his name out loud, while clapping once for each syllable.)

Adult: 'Let's all whisper it.' (The class whispers his name, while quiet clapping the syllables again, once per syllable.)

Everyone: 'Bippity Boppity Bumble Bee, thank you for saying your name for me!'

Repeat with another child and his name. As the children become familiar with the game, you can allow them to take on the adult role. You could also include other categories for example, 'Bippity Boppity Bumble Bee, say an animal name for me.' Then 'Bippity Boppity Bumble Bee, thanks for saying [an animal's name] for me.'

(Source: www.earlychildhoodteacher.org/blog/5-quick-easy-and-fun-phonemic-awareness-activities)

Syllable divide

Draw a picture of an object on a piece of card and then cut up the word into the corresponding number of syllables. For instance, a picture of an **el–e–phant** would be cut into three. Say the word as you point to each cut-out segment, emphasising the syllables.

Syllable rhythm

Give every child a percussion instrument. Present pictures of multisyllabic words, saying them slowly with spaces between the syllables. The children take turns at tapping the number of syllables.

Robot words

Start off with all of the children pretending to be robots, including moving their arms robotically. Put a selection of objects in a bag. Each child is required to take out an object and say the word in a robot voice.

The robot says one syllable at a time and moves his robot hands for each syllable. Make sure that the objects have a variety of syllable lengths.

Talking twins

Introduce two dolls or puppets to the children. The 'talking twins' finish off each other's words. One starts the word and the other finishes it. Have a few objects out to label, eg twin one says 'ta' and twin two says 'ble'.

Use a variety of lengths of word, eg **cater … pillar**, **sau … sage**, **pota … to**. Avoid one-syllable words because the aim is to use whole syllables. Initially, the adult takes the role of twin one and the children take the role of twin two. But once the children have the idea of the game, they can be assigned to both roles.

Rhyme games

Willoughby, wallaby

Hold a soft toy (eg an elephant) above the children's heads and say 'Willoughby, wallaby' followed by a nonsense word that rhymes with one child's name, and finishing with 'the elephant fell on ...' At this point, the children name who the soft toy should fall on. Repeat in a random order for all of the group members.

Start with multisyllabic names as they are easier to hear, eg 'Willoughby, wallaby, tenjamin, the elephant fell on ... Benjamin!'

Caterpillar or zaterpillar

Draw a picture of a familiar word (such as **caterpillar**) and then draw a crazy looking counterpart. Label the second picture with a rhyming word (eg **zaterpillar**). Introduce the pictures to the children. Ask them to point to the one you say. Make it harder by adding a third picture (eg **raterplilar**). Continue with other word combinations.

Rhyme rounds

Make up a rhyming string to go with the children's names. Start off with one child's name and add a word that rhymes with it. Often the rhyming words are nonsense words but sometimes they can be real words. The next person then adds another word that rhymes.

See how many rhyming words the group can make. For example, 'Philippa, tilippa, shilippa, bilippa, kilippa, milippa ...' This can also be done with any topic or new word. For instance, when learning about shapes, think of words that rhyme with **triangle**, eg 'triangle, miangle, siangle, liangle.'

I know a word that rhymes

Present a series of pictures or one busy picture to the children. Make sure that they know the names of the objects in the pictures. Chant to the children, 'What's a word that rhymes with (eg please)?' Encourage the children to look at the pictures and choose the rhyming word.

Once the correct word has been chosen, all chant together, for example, 'What's the word that rhymes with "please"? The word that rhymes with "please" is cheese!' Repeat the last line and encourage the children to repeat too.

Rhyme and sound games

b, c, t

Phoneme feely bag

Put some objects in a feely bag. Without showing the children, give an initial phoneme and a word that rhymes with it. For example, 'This object starts with a "c" and rhymes with "tup".'

Broken words

Cut pictures of common one-syllable nouns in two. Show one 'broken picture' (eg **shoe**) to the children and explain that the word is broken. Divide the word into onset (initial consonant or consonant blend) and rime (remainder of the word) and tell the children to listen to how the word has been broken (eg **sh-oe**).

Now it needs to be fixed. They can fix the word by putting the two parts together (eg **sh-oe** = **shoe**). This only works for words that start with a consonant.

Sound games

b, c, t

Run to the sound

Put pictures representing a speech sound (phoneme) around the classroom (or outside), such as a snake for 's'. Say the sound and encourage the children to run to the right picture.

'I Spy'

Play the traditional 'I Spy' game: 'I spy with my little eye something beginning with …' Just make sure that you say the phoneme (speech sound) and not the letter.

Forgetful teacher

At various times during the day, 'forget' the name of a common item and only remember its initial phoneme (speech sound). For instance: 'I've forgotten what it is but I need some sss … that's it, scissors.'

Word jump

The whole class starts in a squatting position. The children start by repeating the target word quietly. They continue repeating the word, getting louder as they move slowly to a standing position. Everyone finishes by shouting the word as they jump. A song to accompany this action is free to download or on the 'Word Aware' Youtube channel.

Word meaning

These games give children the opportunity to explore the meanings of words and how they are related. So, as well as having fun, the children will be strengthening their word-learning system.

Describing games

Pass the object

Find an interesting object which has many features, for example, a toy elephant or train. Pass the object round the group. Each person says something to describe it. For example, for **train**: 'It has wheels, it has windows, it goes fast, it goes "choo choo", it runs on a track and people ride in it.'

What did you see in the picture?

Present a busy picture with lots happening in it. Encourage the children to look at it closely. After a few moments, hide it and then ask the children to recall what they saw in as much detail as possible.

If they cannot remember all of the items, give useful clues, such as what the object can do or its category, rather than what it looks like.

'I Spy' adjectives

You can adapt the traditional 'I Spy' game by using adjectives instead, eg 'I spy something coloured **red/blue** …' or 'something **round/spiky/shiny** …', 'something that is **big/beautiful/smelly/ growing /hot/noisy** …'

I give you this gift

Place a range of interesting objects in a bag. Tell the group that they will be choosing a 'gift' from the bag to give to someone else in the group. They will need to describe their gift using an adjective. To get the children thinking about adjectives, talk about words that can be used to describe objects. Then take one object out of the bag and use it as an example.

Prompt the children to think about colour, size, texture or specific attributes. Start the activity by choosing the first object and giving it to one of the children. Use the sentence, 'I give you this gift because …', and add a suitable adjective. For example, 'I give you this gift because it is sparkly.' This child then chooses a gift to give to the next child.

(Source: Nash, 2013)

Comparing items

Start with real objects so that the children can use their senses. Show two familiar items and talk about how they are the same and different. Make the differences very obvious, eg 'This car is green and this car is blue. They both have four wheels. This one is dirty, but this one is clean.'

Scavenger hunt

Ask the children to look around and find anything that has a particular attribute, eg has wheels, is shiny, has a tail, is soft, is bendy or is small. Bring the children back to one place and compare the objects they have found.

What do you see?

This game works particularly well if you use a pair of large glasses (spectacles), or your hands, to make imaginary ones. Give one child a pair of glasses. Then describe an imaginary trip in some detail. When you reach your destination, ask the chid with the glasses to describe what they see. If they need prompting, give clues. Other children can then join in and ask questions before the glasses are passed to the next child.

For example, 'Today we are going on a trip to the farm. We take our packed lunches and get on the bus. It's a long way all the way to the countryside. It's a bit bumpy. But look, I can see the farm now. Dylan, look through the special glasses so you can see the farm too. What do you see?' (Add prompts if needed. 'There might be some animals' or 'Look out where you step because …').

Teach a new word to Teddy

Introduce a soft toy or puppet and tell the children that Teddy needs help learning a new word. Ask the children to tell Teddy what they know about the word.

When the children have made their contribution, Teddy then summarises it back to them, thus providing a solid definition.

What's in the bag?

Place a selection of interesting objects in a bag. Then everyone sings and claps to:

> What's in the bag?
>
> What's in the bag?
>
> E-I-ADIO
>
> What's in the bag?'

(sung to the tune of 'The Farmer's in His Den').

Then one child takes an object out of the bag. He says one thing about the object before passing it on to the next child to add his contribution.

This is a great game with children of varying abilities because you can encourage a range of naming, associated verbs or descriptive vocabulary.

Mystery box

Make a box with a hole cut out of the side. Cover the hole with a piece of fabric. Place various items in the box. One child then puts his hand in the box, selects an item and describes it.

There is a great free song you can play between turns which is available at:

> supersimplelearning.com/songs/original-series/two/mystery-box

For more information and pictures, go to: uk.pinterest.com/pin/520799144386205744

Five things REVIEW GAME

Show the children an object or a picture. Discuss what you all know about it. When five suitable suggestions have been made, say and act them out all together.

For example, for **astronaut**: '**Astronauts** can go in a rocket. **Astronauts** can walk on the Moon. **Astronauts** can explore outer space. **Astronauts** can land the spaceship. **Astronauts** are really smart.' Accompany each sentence with an action.

Alien definition

Gather a few interesting objects and an 'alien' puppet. Introduce the activity by saying that 'the alien' is learning all about things on Earth and the children's job is to help him. To do this, they must describe to him what things are.

Pass each object round the group, one at a time, and encourage the children to talk about each one in turn using sentences, prompting as necessary. For example, for **pebble**: 'A **pebble** is round. A **pebble** is heavy. A **pebble** comes from the beach.' Once several children have contributed, 'the alien' summarises what he heard.

Category games

Draw items in a category

Draw a big circle on a large piece of paper. Explain that you are going to be drawing items in a particular category (eg fruit). Encourage the children to think of other items.

Draw items that belong in the category in the circle. If items that do not belong in the category are suggested, draw them outside the circle. Talk about why objects are in or not in the category.

Beanbag categories

Name a familiar category such as 'animals'. Name one item from that category and pass on the beanbag to a child. Encourage him to name another word from that category before passing it on to the next child. Continue going round the group. Finish when the children have run out of words to add.

(Source: Nash, 2013)

Odd one out

Once the children have got the idea of categorisation, you can extend their knowledge with this activity.

Present three or four familiar pictures or objects, one of which is not related to the others. Ask the children to work out which is the 'odd one out'. This can be done with simple categories (eg cat, cow, frog, jumper or pullover), by function (eg scissors, knife, saw, table) or with topic-based vocabulary (eg astronaut, moon, Earth, tree).

'Odd one out' picture cards are available from **www.routledge.com/cw/speechmark.** You can also use items from the Early Years setting or your own pictures.

Tidy up time!

Before putting toys away, talk about where they need to go. Encourage the children to also explain where toys are stored and why. For example, 'The pig is a farm animal, so it goes in this drawer with the farm toys. The toy chair belongs in the playhouse because the doll needs to sit on it.'

Sort it out

Place two hoops on the floor. Gather a selection of objects that belong to two different categories. Ask the children to sort the objects into categories. Start by categorising by action (eg things that you drive) rather than by semantic (meaning) category (eg transport). Talk about why objects go together, using simple repetitive language. For example, if talking about food items: 'Bread is food because you eat it. Bananas are food because you eat them.'

Verb games

What can it do?

Take an object out of a bag. The first child names its function before passing it to the next child who adds his contribution. Encourage the children to use sentences. For example, for **apple**: 'You can eat an **apple**. You can cut an **apple**. You can bite an **apple**.'

Let's all do it (REVIEW GAME)

This game is best if it compares the verb to a similar but familiar verb. Encourage all of the children to copy the action and then to choose which action to do. For example, 'Let's start walking and now let's **stomp**. **Stomp**, **stomp**, **stomp**. Shahad, shall we **stomp** or walk?'

Act it out (REVIEW GAME)

This is an extension of the previous game. Make up a short story including a verb that has previously been taught. Act it out. Ask the children to copy the actions and then encourage them to retell the story. For example, 'We built a very, very big tower but when Florence put on one more brick, the tower came **crashing** down.'

Action 'Advent' calendar (REVIEW GAME)

Make an 'Advent' calendar. Place a picture of a verb behind each door. When the picture is revealed, the whole group does the action.

It can be useful to choose action words that have already been taught. Interesting and useful actions could include: **creep**, **gobble**, **leap**, **march**, **peep**, **plod**, **race**, **scream**, **search**, **shout**, **shuffle**, **snatch**, **squeeze**, **stare**, **stomp**, **stroll**, **tiptoe**, **trip**, **whine**, **whisper**, **wipe**, **wobble**, **yell** and **zoom**.

(Source: adapted from an idea by Julie Sanders from Pershore High School, UK)

Ready, steady, everybody move!

Gather a selection of verb pictures. One child chooses a picture and then tells everyone to do the action on it, starting with **ready**, **steady**, **everybody** ...

For example, 'Ready, steady, everybody **search**!' To make it more lively, play some music to accompany the action so that, when the music stops, all movement needs to stop too.

Ways of talking

Practise using a range of ways of talking, eg Let's all **yell** 'We love books!' or '**Whisper** your favourite colour to the person sitting next to you.'

Use a range of words, including: **giggle**, **moan**, **mumble**, **repeat**, **roar**, **scream**, **shout**, **whisper** and **yell**.

Action Alice

Introduce a doll as 'Action Alice' (or another alliteration you prefer). Tell the children that she goes to lots of places and does lots of things, but she does the right things in the right places.

Start the game by giving Alice to one child and whispering in his ear a location the doll has been to (eg the swimming pool). The child then says, 'Alice went to the swimming pool.' The other children then suggest what Alice did at the swimming pool. The child holding Alice then decides whether that is what Alice did. Encourage this child to use complete sentences, eg 'Alice **splashed** in the water at the swimming pool.'

Then pass Alice to another child and repeat the activity for another location.

Ways of walking REVIEW GAME

Practise using different ways of walking when you need to move around the classroom, nursery or kindergarten, eg 'Let's all **march** to the door', or 'Everyone **tiptoe** when you go towards the toilet.'

Use a range of words, including: **creep**, **march**, **plod**, **race**, **shuffle**, **stomp**, **stroll**, **tiptoe** and **zoom**.

General games

'Snap!' REVIEW GAME

Make up four sets of identical pictures, each representing a word from the topic, eg **hatch**, **chick**, **tadpoles** and **bud**. They do not all need to be nouns.

Deal out all of the cards to two or three children. Each child turns over the card and names the picture. If there are two the same, the child has to shout 'Snap!' This will need adult support to encourage the children to label the pictures.

Objects from home REVIEW GAME

Ask the children to bring in an object from home that exemplifies a chosen adjective. For instance, **furry** might be represented by a teddy bear or a toy mouse. Once you have several objects, encourage the children to talk about their object, prompting them to use the adjective.

Compare objects, again encouraging the use of the adjective. Add in one or two 'mistake' items which do not belong, to help define the concept.

Kim's Game REVIEW GAME

This memory game is useful for reviewing the concrete nouns that the children have learned. Place the objects on a tray and then name them all.

Next, out of view, remove one object. Encourage the children to inspect the tray and name which object is missing. If they cannot remember the missing item, give them clues about its function or features.

(Source: Kipling, 1901)

Picture dictionary

Take lots of photographs of the children with objects showing the new words they have learned. Or take pictures of children doing the action. Make these into a book. This can be reviewed as a group or left in the book corner for children to review as they wish.

Topic picture

Look at a busy picture that relates to a previous topic. Take turns at giving clues about what you see. For example, for **seagull**: 'At the seaside I might see something that flies around and makes a loud noise. I might see a … Now it's your turn.'

Mystery paper bag

Make a 'mystery paper bag' by decorating a paper bag (or box) with question marks, ensuring that it folds down to protect from prying eyes. Ask one child to bring in an object and, without the other children seeing, put it in the bag. Encourage the children to ask questions, providing prompts and summarising key information.

Once it has been correctly guessed, remove the item from the bag and the owner can talk about and show it some more.

A similar activity can be used to review words that have been previously taught.

(Source: inspired by http://joyfullearninginkc.blogspot.co.uk/2012/07/science-journals-and-science-ideas.html#.VynzJNQrKXa (accessed May 2016))

Puzzle pictures

Find pictures of nouns or verbs that have recently been introduced. Stick them on card. Cut each picture card into three or four segments. Mix up the pieces. Look at each piece with the children and encourage them to talk about what they see. Guess what it might be before finding the other pieces to make the whole picture.

Help me find it

This game is suitable for nouns. Pretend to have lost one of the objects you want to review and that you cannot remember what it is called. Describe the object until the children guess. Find the object, name it and, as a class, describe it together. Jointly decide a way in which you will remember it for next time.

What am I?

To be accessible to very young children, riddles need to be straightforward, rather than the conundrums that older children enjoy so much. Three to four simple clues are usually adequate, for example:

- You find me … (place)
- I can … (action)
- An important thing about me is … (particular attribute)
- I look … (physical descriptor).

Reveal the object once it is guessed and repeat the clues to reinforce the learning.

For example: 'You find me in the kitchen. I can cook food. I have a handle and lid. I am a …'

Secret word

Before a break, tell the children a secret word. Talk about what it means, what sound it starts with, and then discuss how they might remember the word. Tell the children they need to remember this word as it will be needed to gain access to the classroom or the next activity.

When it is time to start the next activity, ask the children individually to whisper the word to you. If a child cannot remember it, give him a clue about its meaning or first sound.

Imagination station

Create topic-related play areas with dressing-up items, objects and pictures, all based on a theme. Ensure that you include written vocabulary to remind the adults to use key words also. Themed areas will give children the opportunities to explore the relationships between words.

Introduce children to the role play area, specifically by having an 'unveiling', ensuring that all items are labelled and discussed. This will provide the children with language models which they can later include in their free play.

Experience books

Take photographs of events and make them into a book. They do not need to be of exciting visits. Instead they might be about 'messy play' or 'what we do outdoors'. Label key vocabulary on some pages to remind the adults to talk about the events. Talk about the pictures with the children, using the key vocabulary in a natural manner.

Remember that the emphasis is on the adult using the word again, rather than testing the children.

Word bottles

Fill transparent juice bottles with coloured water, pom-poms, rice or pasta. Collect small interesting objects on a theme and, together with colourful, sparkly objects, put them in the bottles. This obviously suits an 'under the sea' topic but it can be adapted to any topic. The purpose is to make engaging items, which will attract the children's attention, and to talk about what they see.

(Source: inspired by www.pinterest.com/pin/453526624949548976)

Noun spinner REVIEW GAME

Make the spinner in the Appendix (page 257). Present an object or a picture that was introduced previously. The children take turns with the spinner and answer the corresponding question. Encourage full sentence responses.

For example, for **tadpoles**:

'The **tadpoles** wiggled in the water. The **tadpoles** were in our pond. **Tadpoles** are special because they grow into frogs. **Tadpoles** are wiggly and wriggly.'

I think she is ...

This game requires transitive verbs which need an object, such as **squeeze**, **fetch** and **search**. (You have to **squeeze** something, **fetch** something and **search** for something.)

Introduce one verb and act it out together. Brainstorm together lots of different nouns that go with that verb. Then ask one child to act it out again, thinking of a specific example. Encourage the other children to guess but using full sentences. For example, for **squeeze**: 'I think Reuben is **squeezing** some play dough. I think he is **squeezing** his toothpaste.'

Other good transitive verbs are: **build**, **buy**, **catch**, **climb**, **collect**, **cook**, **crush**, **eat**, **kick**, **look**, **make**, **munch**, **play**, **remove**, **ride**, **search**, **stir** and **throw**.

Word rounds

Choose one of the following:

- a noun category, eg animals
- an attribute, eg shiny things
- an action, eg something you can cut
- a place, eg a beach.

Go round the circle asking for items which fit that description. Encourage complete answers such as 'I can cut paper. I can cut my hair.'

For example, for 'things that we **find at the beach**': sand, pebbles, sea, ice-cream and towels.

Story telling with objects

Allow the children to explore stories by providing structured play opportunities. In a play area, place a book that has been read to the class, together with key characters and objects from the story. Encourage the children to act out the story.

Adult interaction will be instrumental in this activity to promote narrative in connected sentences and the use of vocabulary. If key words from the book are visible to the adults, they will be reminded to use them also.

Noun–verb connections

Select a common noun. The children are then required to think of verbs associated with that noun. For instance, if the selected noun is **dog**, the verbs could be **bark**, **bite**, **chew**, **growl**, **leap**, **lick**, **snarl**, **wag** or **yap**. Ask the children to act out the verbs as they are identified and say the verb in a phrase, eg 'The **dog** is **barking**.'

The opposite process can also be done. Select a verb such as **ride** and think of as many nouns as possible that can be associated with it. For **ride**, the selected nouns could be **horse**, **donkey**, **camel** or **bike**.

- Nouns for children to link with verbs: **cat**, **chicken**, **farmer**, **grandad**, **lion**, **monkey** or **mouse**.
- Verbs for children to link with nouns: **bend**, **eat**, **grow**, **make**, **sit**, **stretch** or **wash**.

A word I like

Read out a few interesting words that you come across in a story. Ask the children which word they liked the best and why.

Wordless picture books

Wordless picture books are an excellent resource for pre-readers. Before you share it with the children, look through the wordless picture book and think about any key vocabulary that might be relevant.

When you talk through the book, emphasise the key vocabulary as part of the story, repeating the word several times. Add a sticker to the inside cover so that other adults can also highlight the same word when they share the book.

Talking tins

Talking tins are robust, easy-to-use, recording devices. They are available at www.talkingproducts.com or search online for 'talking tins'. They can be used in different ways, including attaching a picture to the talking tin and leaving it in play areas. Children can then record what is on the label and play it back, so that they hear the word again.

Analogies

To complete an analogy, children must have sophisticated language. So, start simple and provide supportive language and more examples before asking the child to respond. Here are some examples to get you going.

- A fish swims, a dog runs, a rabbit ...
- Pens are for drawing with, pencils are for colouring with and paint brushes are for ...
- You put a hat on your head, you put gloves on your hands, you put shoes on your ...
- If you are hungry, you need to eat. If you are thirsty, you need to drink. If you are tired, you need to ...
- A sheep has a lamb, a dog has a puppy, a cat has a ...

Make this game harder by either reducing the examples to one or making the vocabulary more challenging, for example:

- A mouse is very small, a giraffe is very ...
- A caterpillar grows up to be a butterfly, a tadpole grows up to be a ...

Things we like to play with

Ask the children to collect one toy which they like to play with and bring it back to the group. In turns, encourage the children to talk about their toy. Write down on small pieces of card any adjectives that they use. Add a few more applicable adjectives.

Now place all of the toys in the middle of the group and mix up the adjective cards. Take turns picking an adjective card (for the adult to read). Ask the children to identify objects that the adjective describes. One adjective could be used to describe more than one object, so use this as a discussion point. Encourage the children to use the words in phrases such as 'the **shiny** car, the **sparkly** ball and the **big** crocodile.'

My Granny went to the …

This familiar game is particularly useful for auditory memory but also for reinforcing vocabulary. The traditional way is to start with 'My Granny went to the market and bought …' (add a food item). The first child names one item. The second child repeats the first child's item before adding his own, and so on. This does get hard, so aim for three or four items to start with.

Variations could be 'My Granny went to a (name a place) and saw …' Begin with familiar places, such as the home corner or the garden, before introducing less familiar places, such as a farm and the seaside.

Magic carpet ride

This activity can be embellished in many ways, so let your imagination take over! Gather the children on a 'magic carpet'. They are going on a journey so they may like to dress up for the part, taking binoculars as well. Take them on an imaginary journey across the roof tops to a place such as a farm, beach or jungle, the North Pole or outer space.

Create the atmosphere by providing relevant objects that children discover, as well as an exciting activity such as being chased by a polar bear. Talk about what you see, hear and smell. Let the children take a souvenir of their trip on the return journey. When you all return from your adventure, encourage the children to tell another adult about their trip. Photographs of the trip will aid retelling.

(Source: based on an original idea from www.teachingideas.co.uk)

Before you play

Free play is crucial to children's development and should be given priority within any Early Years curriculum. However, by taking small groups of children to one play area and spending a few minutes in discussion, it is possible to model some more advanced vocabulary as well as add new play elements.

For instance, introducing a bike repair garage (as well as the tools) to an outdoor bike-riding area will extend vocabulary and play. Similarly, talking about **emergencies** and **accidents** that superheroes can help with will extend both play and vocabulary.

Word Wizard

Dress up in a wizard costume (or a hat at least) and explain to the children that today the Word Wizard will be visiting and casting spells, so she will hear some wonderful words. The Word Wizard will be moving about the nursery collecting wonderful words as well as suggesting even more wonderful words.

At the end of the session, the Word Wizard unrolls her scroll and talks about all of the wonderful words that she has heard.

Word album

Whenever you hear a child using great vocabulary, take a photograph of them doing what they were doing when they said the word. Then, at group time, encourage the child to share this with the whole group. Label the picture with the word before adding it to an album to be reviewed at any time.

Words we like

This activity can be extended to involve parents and can be done in any language. Ask the children to collect words that they like. These can be from home, books or other media sources. Once they have decided on a word, the children draw a picture of it. Make these pictures into a display, adding optional photographs of the children.

What would make you feel ...?

Put pictures of two emotions on the whiteboard. Use emotions such as **angry**, **bored**, **cross**, **disgusted**, **excited**, **frustrated**, **happy**, **proud**, **sad**, **scared**, **tired** or **worried**. Describe a scenario and ask the children to think which emotion it might provoke.

For example, if **tired** and **proud** are on the board, the adult asks 'Imagine you have stayed up very late. Would you be **tired** or **proud**?' The adult points to the corresponding picture as they say the word.

Expand the discussion by talking about times when the children may have experienced those emotions.

Gobbledygook

Read a sentence but miss out a word and instead say 'gobbledygook'. Encourage the children to guess the word. There may be several possible answers.

For example:

- 'The boy gobbledygooked down the road.'
- 'The girl ate a big gobbledygook.'

Video story

Once a story has been read to the children, dress up and act it out, or use small world toys to act it out. Ensure that key vocabulary is included in the story. Video the story and play it back to the class.

Non-fiction books alive

Non-fiction books often include topic-specific vocabulary and so should not be neglected. Make engaging hands-on learning stations by displaying the book together with items from it. Encourage the children to find the pictures in the book and compare the real-life objects with them.

A special word box

Make an attractive word box out of an old shoe box or something similar. Encourage the children to collect interesting objects and place them in the box. At opportune times, encourage the child who placed the item in the box to talk about it.

Extend this activity by adding other verbs and adjectives and by talking about what the item does and describing it.

Find your partner: pairs

Gather pairs of pictures or objects. Give each child a random picture or object. On the count of three, they need to find their matching pair. When they have found their partner, they can talk about what the object can do and then feed back to the whole class.

Love glove

Find an interesting glove. Explain that it is a 'love glove' and that it helps you to think of things that you love (or really like). Start by giving the group an example, such as 'I love to eat chocolate cake.' Pass the glove round with each child putting it on in turn and saying one thing they love.

The first time around, let the children say the name of any item they love. After everyone has had a turn, choose a specific category for the group, eg television shows, food, toys or games. Pass the glove round and encourage the children to name their favourite item in that category.

(Source: Nash, 2013)

Talking books

Talking books are recording devices in book form, allowing a photograph to be inserted and an accompanying soundtrack to be recorded. For example, take photos of the children acting out particular verbs and then get them to record what they were doing.

Talking books are available from www.smartkids.co.uk.

Rolling adjectives

Find a clear plastic container such as an old sweet jar. Put some cut-up sparkly paper in it to act as a reminder that this activity is about describing. Place one interesting item in the jar (eg a soft toy lion).

Explain that the aim of the activity is to describe the object in sentences. The adult starts, using the format 'The noun is (adjective)', eg 'The lion is **fierce**.' The sweet jar is then rolled to a child who adds his contribution. Stop occasionally to repeat what has been said.

Busy pictures REVIEW GAME

If your aim is general language enrichment then any detailed picture may be used. If your aim is to review a topic then find a related busy picture. Follow the children's lead, encouraging them to talk about what they see.

Make comments ('I like the sound of that') and open questions ('I wonder why that happened?'). These should invite longer responses, rather than closed questions such as 'What's that?' or 'Are there any blue cars?' which require limited answers. Where possible, try to use a range of nouns, verbs and adjectives in your interactions.

Bookmarks

Give the children a bookmark which has a range of vocabulary-related tasks on it. This can be sent home as a task for parents to do with their children after they have read a story to their child.

There are sample bookmarks on the next page which can be either copied and cut out or downloaded from the website.

Word Aware
Different Words

When you have finished reading do one of these challenges.

Find a word that your child likes. Why do they like it?

Find an action word and act it out together.

Find a describing word. Think of something else you could describe using this word, eg:

blue freezing glowing

Find a word your child hasn't seen or heard before. Talk about what it means.

Find words for different ways of talking. Have fun by saying the same sentence in different ways.

Word Aware
Different Words

When you have finished reading do one of these challenges.

Find a word that your child likes. Why do they like it?

Find an action word and act it out together.

Find a describing word. Think of something else you could describe using this word, eg:

blue freezing glowing

Find a word your child hasn't seen or heard before. Talk about what it means.

Find words for different ways of talking. Have fun by saying the same sentence in different ways.

Word Aware
Different Words

When you have finished reading do one of these challenges.

Find a word that your child likes. Why do they like it?

Find an action word and act it out together.

Find a describing word. Think of something else you could describe using this word, eg:

blue freezing glowing

Find a word your child hasn't seen or heard before. Talk about what it means.

Find words for different ways of talking. Have fun by saying the same sentence in different ways.

Chapter 6
Supporting Children with Higher Needs

Chapter 6
Supporting Children with Higher Needs

Introduction

Most children will make progress with whole class teaching but some children will need more support to develop their vocabulary. This chapter will help you to identify which children need that support and how to provide it. Enjoyment is a crucial component of vocabulary learning, so ensure that activities are fun and rewarding as well as precisely targeted.

Identifying children who need support with basic nouns, verbs and concepts

Nurseries, kindergartens and schools are usually very good at spotting children who are not using many spoken words. Some of these children may have very few words at all, while others use lots of words at home but just lack confidence in their educational setting. Other children may understand words but find them harder to say. It can be trickier to work out a child's needs if she or he speaks English as an additional language (English language learners). So this group requires careful detective work.

If you identify a child who is not speaking very much in your setting, use one of the questionnaires on pages 192–3 to find out more about what they say at home and assess early developing concepts (see page 194). Then use the flow chart on page 195 or page 196 to work out how best to support the child.

The intervention described in this chapter aims to develop children's understanding and use of basic nouns, verbs and concepts but not to replace specialist advice. Discuss any doubt or significant concerns with your SENCO or special education teacher and/or the speech and language therapist/pathologist. The aim of this programme is to develop vocabulary. Children may have broader difficulties with speech, language or communication and require more specialist assessment and intervention.

Investigating how children are talking at home

There are many reasons children do not speak in Early Years settings such as nurseries, schools and kindergartens. Before action can be taken, a careful assessment is needed. To kick-start this process, use the questionnaires on the following pages. The questionnaire for children who speak English only at home is on page 192. The questionnaire on page 193 is for families who speak languages other than English and is appropriate to use in monolingual and multilingual home environments.

Sit with the parents while they fill in the questionnaire. Prompts or examples may help but reassure parents that an accurate picture is important. If they are not fluent in English then an interpreter will be necessary.

A general guide is that by three years old a child should be able to use a range of words linked to their everyday environment. The table below shows an approximate developmental profile for a three-year-old child, which can be adapted for children of different ages. Further information is available from:

- American Speech–Language–Hearing Association (www.asha.org/public/speech/development/chart.htm)
- Talking Point (www.talkingpoint.co.uk).

Questions	By three years old a child should be able to do the following, in their first language
• Do they say people's names? • Which ones?	Name all familiar adults and children
• Do they ask for things to eat or drink by name? • What do they say?	Use the names of all familiar food items
• When looking at a book, do they name the pictures? • Do they talk about what is happening in the pictures? • What do they say?	Have an interest in books and be able to name a range of common items and actions. Eg in a seaside book, can name 'bucket', 'swimming', 'splash' and 'bird'
• Do they talk about what they have been doing? • What do they say?	Use a range of actions in short phrases. Eg 'I do painting' or 'Mummy go shopping'
• Do they say the names of objects in the house? (eg toothbrush, coat, table, fridge, clock, bathroom, stairs, door)	Know the names of the household items they use
• Which body parts can they label?	Know a range of the main body parts
• How many words can they put together in a sentence?	Use at least three words per sentence on average as well as some longer sentences

Understanding how your child is talking at home

Does your child say people's names? Which ones?
Do they ask for things to eat or drink by name? What do they say?
When looking at a book, do they name the pictures? Do they talk about what is happening in the pictures? What do they say?
Do they talk about what they have been doing? What do they say?
Do they say the names of objects in the house like toothbrush, coat, table, fridge, clock, bathroom, stairs, door?
Which body parts can they say?
How many words can they put together in a sentence?
What is the most advanced or surprising word your child has used?

Understanding how your child is talking at home

Which languages do you speak at home? ____________________________

Who uses which language? ____________________________

<table>
<tr><td>Does your child say people's names?
Which ones?</td><td colspan="2"></td></tr>
<tr><th>Questions</th><th>In English</th><th>In other language(s)</th></tr>
<tr><td>Do they ask for things to eat or drink by name?
What do they say?</td><td></td><td></td></tr>
<tr><td>When looking at a book, do they name the pictures?
Do they talk about what is happening in the pictures?
What do they say?</td><td></td><td></td></tr>
<tr><td>Do they talk about what they have been doing?
What do they say?</td><td></td><td></td></tr>
<tr><td>Do they say the names of objects in the house like toothbrush, coat, table, fridge, clock, bathroom, stairs, door?</td><td></td><td></td></tr>
<tr><td>Which body parts can they say?</td><td></td><td></td></tr>
<tr><td>How many words can they put together in a sentence?</td><td></td><td></td></tr>
<tr><td>What is the most advanced or surprising word your child has used?</td><td></td><td></td></tr>
</table>

Assessing early developing concepts

If a child is using very little language in nursery, school or kindergarten, it is useful to check whether they understand these early developing concepts. This assessment should be one-to-one with the child. They do not need to say anything, and should not feel pressured to speak. Use an interpreter if the child speaks a language other than English at home.

Use simple language and interact with the child in an engaging, encouraging manner.

Child's name:	**Age:**
Language used for assessment:	**Date:**

Concept	Equipment	Instructions	Achieved
more	Teddy bear and some building bricks	Give Teddy a few bricks. Say, 'Teddy wants **more**. Give Teddy **more**.'	
empty	Three cups and some water	Pour water into two of the cups. Ask, 'Which cup is **empty**?'	
under	Chair and a toy (small enough to fit under the chair).	Ask the child to 'put the toy **under** the chair.'	
fast	Three toy horses	One at a time, make the horses move. Make one go fast. Ask 'Which one went **fast**?'	
big	Three different-sized dolls, one clearly bigger than the others	Present the dolls and ask the child to 'find the **big** doll.'	
wet	Three socks, one of which is wet	Present the socks and say, 'Show me which one is **wet**.'	

Notes

If you cannot easily find the objects in the examples above, use substitutes.
Repeating the tasks will increase reliability and reduce the chance of 'lucky guesses'.

Children who speak English at home

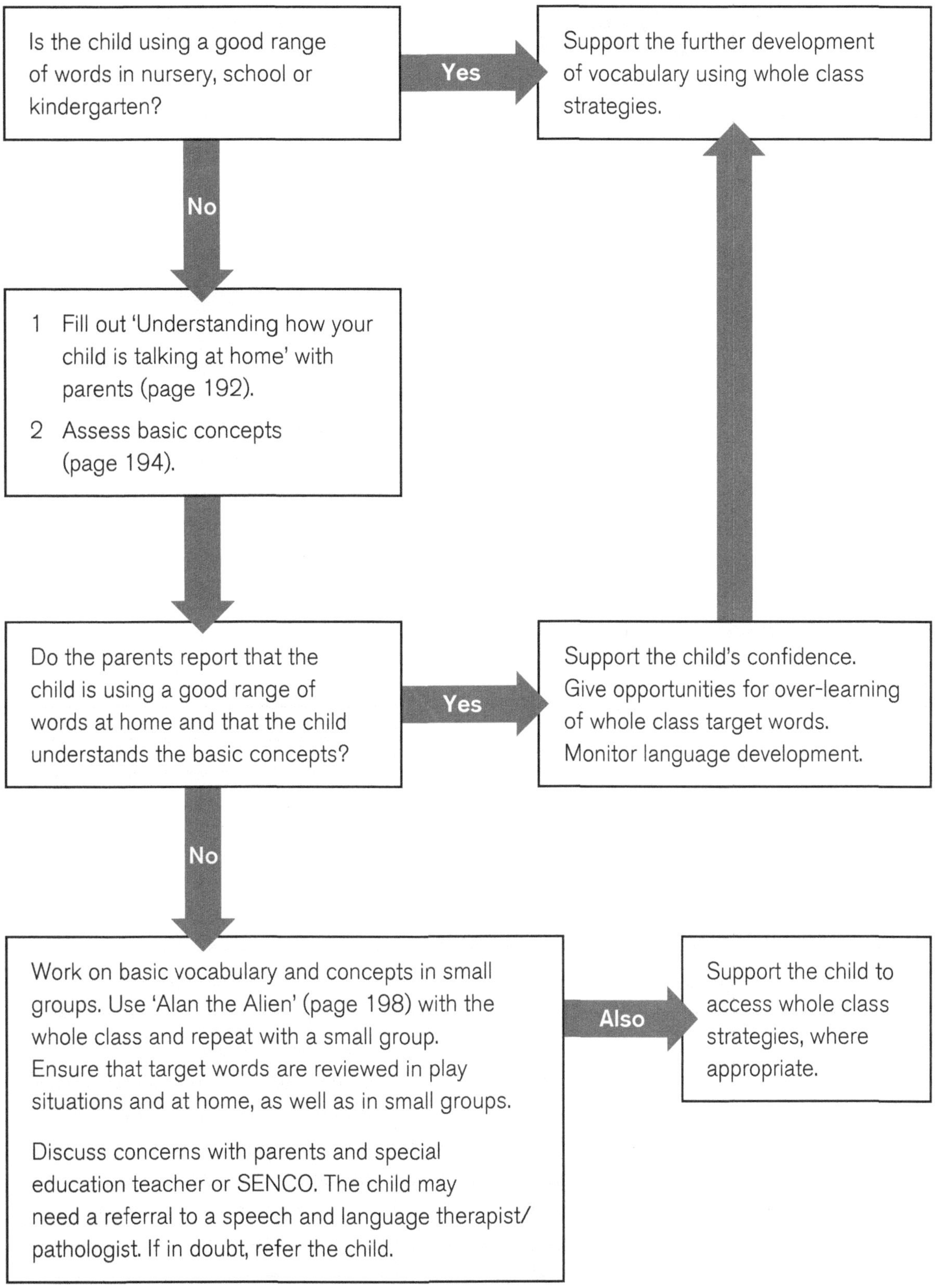

Children who speak English as an additional language (English language learners)

Is the child using a good range of words in nursery, school or kindergarten?

Yes → Support the further development of vocabulary using whole class strategies.

No ↓

1 Fill out 'Understanding how your child is talking at home' with parents (page 193).

2 Assess basic concepts (page 194).

↓

Do the parents report that the child is using a good range of English words at home and understands the basic concepts in English?

Yes → Support the child's confidence. Give opportunities for over-learning of whole class target words. Monitor language development. → Support the further development of vocabulary using whole class strategies.

No ↓

Do the parents report that the child is using a good range of words at home and assessment shows that the child understands the basic concepts in his or her own language?

Yes → Work on basic vocabulary and concepts in small groups. Use 'Alan the Alien' (page 198) with the whole class and repeat with a small group. Ensure that target words are reviewed in play situations and at home, as well as in small groups. Support parents to review the target words in the home language. → Support the child to access whole class strategies, where appropriate.

No ↓

Discuss concerns with parents and special education teacher or SENCO. The child may need referral to a speech and language therapist/pathologist. If in doubt, refer. → Work on basic vocabulary and concepts in small groups.

How to support children with higher needs

Completing the parental questionnaire and the assessment of early developing concepts may highlight areas of difficulty. If so, you may need to provide additional support in your setting and/or to refer the child to speech and language therapy/pathology.

The vocabulary group outlined on the following pages will get you started as well as enable you to understand the children's needs better, although onward referral may still be warranted.

Intervention principles of small group work

- **Plan the group well.** This increases the chances that the group runs smoothly, is fun for the children and they make progress.
- Use **objects** rather than pictures wherever you can. Children in Early Years learn best with things they can touch and hear (as well as smell and taste).
- Make sure you build in lots of **repetition** within the small group and in free play. All children need to hear the same words over and over again, and this need increases for children with higher needs.
- Make sure that you spend lots of time **reviewing** words that the children have learned. This increases the likelihood that the children will retain the words you have taught.
- Give the children lots of **different examples** of the word so that they get a full understanding of it.
- Use **families** to reinforce the words learned. Give the families specific tasks to reinforce new words. If English is not spoken at home, show the parents how to do the activities in their own language. Remember, a strong home language will support the development of English.
- Make the activities **fun** so that they have **a high impact**. Children learn best when they enjoy themselves.
- **Run the group regularly**: ideally, every day, even if only for 10 minutes. Also make sure that the words are reinforced in context throughout the day.
- **Access support** from your special education teacher or SENCO. You may also need support from an outside professional such as a speech and language therapist/pathologist.

In each group session:

- Look in the 'Alan the Alien' box (see page 198) and name the objects.
- Work on the understanding of one noun, one verb and one concept.
- Review words using the Word Bag. Add new objects for any new words.
- Write the target words on a sticker to remind all adults to use the words in context.
- Give ideas to parents for activities they can do at home.

All of these activities are included on the group plan on page 205, with a completed example on page 204. They are described further in the next section.

Early words group structure

Alan the Alien

You will need an 'alien' puppet or soft toy and a box. Introduce 'the alien' to the children. Tell the children that Alan the Alien does not speak the same language as us and he is just learning the English words for things. Put some items in the box and then encourage the children to tell Alan what the objects are called. Then say that the children can put things in the box so that we can tell Alan what the things are called.

The idea is to encourage children to put in items they do not know the name of. Adults can also put in items they think will be useful. Naming the items can be done with all of the children but repeated with children who have identified needs.

A noun, a verb and a concept

Select the noun, verb and concept you aim to teach. Remember to teach the words that are at the right level and will be most useful for the children. We advise that the selected words are linked to the curriculum so that children will naturally encounter them throughout the day. Some groups will need very early developing words while other groups may be able to access the whole group teaching if they are pre-taught the words. The word lists on pages 199–200 will provide additional guidance.

Choose an activity for each noun, verb and concept. There are suggestions for nouns and verbs on pages 199–200 and for concepts on page 201. Repeat the same words for several sessions. Vary the activities where you can but repeating activities occasionally will also help to embed learning.

Word Bag

Have a special Word Bag for children in the 'Early Word Group'. This is used for reviewing words, to ensure they are not forgotten. When you have finished teaching a new word, put an object inside the bag to represent that word. There are suggested objects for all concepts in Chapter 4. For verbs, a picture may be needed, but it may be possible to find objects to represent some verbs. Photographs of the children doing the action can also be engaging.

In each session, take out of the bag an object or a picture that you have previously introduced. Encourage the children to name it or act it out in some way. Use the activities for nouns and verbs on pages 202–3 for inspiration. Try to be as creative as possible.

Stickers

Print out a set of stickers with 'Words I need to hear today …' (see below), plus the target words written on them. Stick them on the children to prompt all adults to use the words with the right children. This gives the children opportunities to hear the words more and learn about them in their natural context. Encourage all adults to use sign and gesture to support the children's understanding.

Words I need to hear today …

Families

It is really important to involve families in word learning. Give specific ideas to families for activities they can do at home. Invite them to the nursery, school or kindergarten to learn signs and get them involved in supporting their children's development.

Try to be creative with suggestions: aim to make them easy, have high impact and fit into daily routines. It is also good to suggest some activities that can be done in 'dead' time (on a bus or in a car, on the walk home, waiting in the doctor's surgery). For example, look for something **big** on the way home.

Useful basic nouns

Here are some examples to get you thinking about basic nouns. This is a starting point to help you generate your own lists.

Everyday objects: chair, cup, apple, toilet, dog, phone, computer.

Less common everyday objects: scissors, cooker, sofa, beanbag, dinosaur.

Body parts: eyes, hair, legs, elbow.

Clothing: trousers, skirt, scarf.

Places: park, school/nursery/kindergarten, bedroom, shop, garden, doctor's.

Transport: bike, fire engine, ambulance.

People: family members, police officer, teacher.

Topic-based words: use the anchor words from the topic word list (see Chapter 3).

Useful basic verbs

This is a rough guide to some common basic verbs. Add your own words and pick your own priorities. You might like to pick verbs that are either associated with your topic or used in story books.

break	build	feel
cry	buy	hear
cut	colour	smell
dance	draw	squeeze
drink	listen	taste
eat	make	touch
jump	paint	
laugh	read	
play	ride	
run	see	
shout	stick	
sing	write	
sleep		
swim		
wake up		
walk		

early to later developing verbs →

(Source: http://education.yourdictionary.com/for-teachers/simple-action-words-for-pre-k-children.html)

Useful basic concepts

The concepts in **bold** are the ones you will have assessed (see page 194). The teaching sequence for all of these concepts are on the pages indicated.

Topic	Concept	Suggested teaching sequence on page ...
Size	**big**	91
	little	120
	fat	104
Touch/look	**dry**	99
	wet	156
Sound	noisy	132
	quiet	137
	loud	123
Movement	**fast**	103
	slow	144
Space	in	113
	out	134
	under	155
	behind	87
	top	154
	bottom	94
Quantity	**empty**	101
	full	109
	more	124
	lots	122

Activities for nouns

Activity	What to do
What's in the bag or box?	Children take an object out of the bag or box and are given time to label it. If they cannot, gently provide the label.
Find it	Hide the object and ask the child to find it. This can be as simple as placing it under a chair or on a shelf in clear view. Label the object when it is found.
Teddy play	Say the word over and over in a play scene with Teddy. Engage children in the play with the soft toy and an object. Example for **chair**: 'Teddy sits on the **chair**. Uh oh, Teddy fell off the **chair**. Teddy gets back on the **chair**.'
Make the scene	Use objects to create a scene to talk about, eg the **park**, a **bedroom**, the **doctor's** (surgery). Talk about what you see in that location.
Focused play	Once you have introduced the words, include them in structured play using a few specific objects which the group is learning, eg washing clothes, getting dressed, cooking, washing dishes and shopping. Use the words many times.

Activities for verbs

Activity	What to do
Move your body	Model the action for the children and encourage them to copy you. Take it in turns to watch each other. Example: 'Now it's Elliot's turn to **wake up**. Let's all watch Elliot **wake up**.'
Teddy does it	Act out the verb with Teddy. Take turns at acting out the action and repeat several times. Example: 'Teddy is **building**.'
Link it to objects	Find objects that can do this particular action. Use the object and the verb in simple sentences. Examples: 'I am **drinking** from the **cup**.' 'Olivia is **throwing** the **ball**.'
Small world scene	Gather small world objects and explore the verb through play. Each child takes a turn at moving their toy to show the verb. Example: 'The man is **running**. The mummy is **running**. The child is **running** too.'
Videos	Make a short video of the children or Teddy acting out the word. Play it back and describe what you see.
I got it wrong!	Intentionally act out the incorrect use of the verb in very obvious scenarios. Example: 'Oh no! Dolly is **drinking** the table! Dolly can't **drink** a table. Quick, give her a cup so that she can **drink**.'
Link places to actions	Go to the place where you are likely to use the words. Use the words in context many times. Example for **climbing**: 'Let's go **climbing** on the **climbing** frame.'
Conga	Line up the children, one behind another. Everyone does the action and says the word. Example: 'We are **painting**, we are **painting**.'
Take photos	Take photographs of the children doing the action. Make the photos into books or displays. Send the photos home and encourage parents to talk about them at home.

Early Words Group Plan

Group members: ______________________ **Date:** ____________

Alan the Alien's box		Look in Alan the Alien's box. Talk about what is in the box. Pass round the objects, saying the words. Make sure that you name each object several times. Only take out a maximum of three objects in any one group session.	
Type of word	**Target**	**Activity**	**Ideas for families. These activities can be done in any language. Ask families to:**
Noun	*scissors*	*Find it*	*Do some cutting at home and use the word* ***scissors****.*
Verb	*dance*	*Move your body*	*Find some music and* ***dance****. Use the word dance many times.*
Concept	*big*	*Activities on page 91*	*Look for something* ***big*** *on the way home.*
Objects for Word Bag		Put items in the Word Bag that relate to the items from today's session. Talk about an object that you have worked on before.	Objects: *scissors, a toy ballerina, a little sock and a big sock.*
Stickers		Write the noun, verb and concept on a sticker for each child so that adults use the words in context.	Words I need to hear today … *scissors, dance, big*

EXAMPLE

Early Words Group Plan

Group members: ______________________ **Date:** __________

Alan the Alien's box		Look in Alan the Alien's box. Talk about what is in the box. Pass round the objects, saying the words. Make sure that you name each object several times. Only take out a maximum of three objects in any one group session.	
Type of word	**Target**	**Activity**	**Ideas for families. These activities can be done in any language. Ask families to:**
Noun			
Verb			
Concept			
Objects for Word Bag		Put items in the Word Bag that relate to the items from today's session. Talk about an object that you have worked on before.	Objects:
Stickers		Write the noun, verb and concept on a sticker for each child so that adults use the words in context.	Words I need to hear today …

Chapter 7

Word Detective: Developing Word Learning Strategies

Chapter 7
Word Detective: Developing Word Learning Strategies

Introduction

There are literally thousands of words to learn which means that they cannot all be taught, no matter how much time is devoted to vocabulary teaching. If children are going to learn at the required rate, they need to learn words independently. Therefore, the aim is to build on their innate word-learning skills by ensuring that they are aware of words, interested in words and become autonomous 'word detectives'.

In the Early Years, the two main features of this are:

(a) identifying unknown words

(b) asking what unknown words mean.

Identifying unknown words

Start off by building in opportunities throughout the day to identify words that are not known and wonder about what they might mean. Build on this further by doing the following activities.

Modelling

Be a model to young children. When reading or talking, identify words that the children may not know. 'Think aloud' about these words, commenting, 'I don't know what that word means. I wonder what that word means?'

Alan the Alien and his box

For this, you will need an 'alien' puppet or soft toy and a box. Introduce 'the alien' to the children. Tell the children that Alan the Alien does not speak the same language as us and he is just starting to learn the English words for things. Put some items in the box and ask the children to tell Alan what the objects are called. Then encourage the children to put items in the box so that they can tell Alan what they are called. Also encourage the children to put in items which they do not know the name of, so that they can learn the names together with Alan.

Adults may also add items that they think will be useful for children to know. Naming the items may be done with all of the children but repeated with children who have identified needs.

(Source: based on an idea developed by Caroline McCallum, Speech and Language Therapist in Hackney, London, UK)

Alien words

Use Alan the Alien again. This time, explain that Alan sometimes uses 'alien' words. Encourage the children to spot the 'alien words', eg 'I wanted a drink, so I went and got a tibblygot. Did Alan use any alien words?'

Once the children have spotted the 'alien' word, encourage them to think what it might mean, eg cup, milk, juice. Try this with lots of made-up 'alien words' and then start introducing real words that the children are unlikely to have heard of. Can they hear the 'alien words' and try to predict what the words might mean? Encourage the children to spot other people using 'alien words' at any time.

Asking what unknown words mean

Once unknown words have been identified, the next step is to ask what they mean.

Classroom observation indicates that children who are able word learners are much more likely to ask about the meaning of words than their peers who know fewer words. To promote the word learning of all children, it is therefore important to develop a culture where asking about the meaning of words is accepted, encouraged and celebrated.

Adults can start this process by modelling how to ask about word meanings. When words that the children may not know are encountered, make a comment such as, 'I don't know what that word means. I'll need to ask someone.' Then take the children with you when you ask another adult, so that the children see the process at first hand.

Encourage the children to use these strategies. You can directly model the words by making comments such as, 'You could say "I don't know what that word means. I need to ask someone".' Whenever a child does ask about word meanings, praise him and discuss the word's meaning using simple language.

Display the poster on page 212 to remind all members of staff to encourage the children to ask. Encourage families to facilitate their children to ask at home. Home is a great place to ask about new words because there is a more favourable adult-to-child ratio. There is a poster for families on page 213.

To encourage children to identify and ask about new words, send home the bookmark overleaf with the children's reading books. There is also an explanatory sheet on page 211 which you can send home.

Reading with families bookmark

Word Aware
New Words

These ideas can be used when you are reading and talking about books with your child.

Before you read the book, say, 'Let's look out for new words that you've never heard before.'

Once in a while, stop and ask, 'Did you hear any new words?'

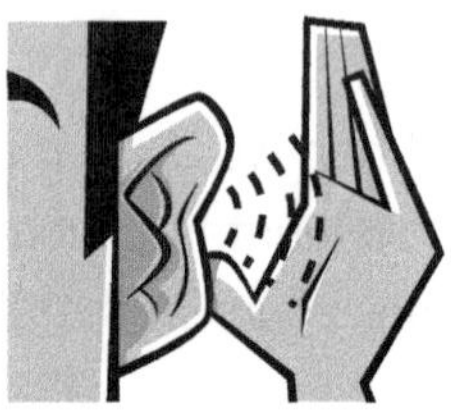

If your child says 'Yes', talk about that word's meaning.

If your child says 'No', identify a word you think might be tricky. Talk about what the word means.

Word Aware
New Words

These ideas can be used when you are reading and talking about books with your child.

Before you read the book, say, 'Let's look out for new words that you've never heard before.'

Once in a while, stop and ask, 'Did you hear any new words?'

If your child says 'Yes', talk about that word's meaning.

If your child says 'No', identify a word you think might be tricky. Talk about what the word means.

Word Aware
New Words

These ideas can be used when you are reading and talking about books with your child.

Before you read the book, say, 'Let's look out for new words that you've never heard before.'

Once in a while, stop and ask, 'Did you hear any new words?'

If your child says 'Yes', talk about that word's meaning.

If your child says 'No', identify a word you think might be tricky. Talk about what the word means.

Information sheet for families

Learning new words as you read

Helping your child learn the meaning of new words

Enjoying books is a good first step in learning to read.

To become good readers, children need to know letters and sounds but they also need to know what the words mean.

You can help your child to learn new words by using this bookmark and talking about new words as you read with your child.

Remember:

- Have fun with words.
- It is about talking as much as reading.
- When talking about words, use comments rather than questions.

Word Aware New Words

These ideas can be used when you are reading and talking about books with your child.

Before you read the book, say, 'Let's look out for new words that you've never heard before.'

Once in a while, stop and ask, 'Did you hear any new words?'

If your child says 'Yes', talk about that word's meaning.

If your child says 'No', identify a word you think might be tricky. Talk about what the word means.

Learning new words

If a child doesn't know a word, encourage them to ask.

* An 'alien' word is any unknown word.

Encourage your child to ask what new words mean

To get on well in school and in life, children need to know lots of words. One of the best ways of learning what new words mean is to ask.

- **Praise** your child when they ask about the meaning of words.
- **Show** your child how to ask, eg 'Let's go and ask Grandad what that word means.'

Chapter 8
Involving Families

Chapter 8
Involving Families

Introduction

The interaction that children have with their families from a very early age forms the foundation for later vocabulary learning. So, before a child starts in an Early Years setting, families will have played an important role. Families also have a crucial role in the ongoing support of word learning and should be viewed as an integral part of vocabulary instruction, rather than an optional 'add-on'. Obviously, the more that families are involved the better but participation can be at a variety of levels.

Children need to hear all new words many times in order to learn them. Each time they hear a new word, they will learn a little more about it. So, by working together with families and including them, the number of exposures children have to new words can be greatly increased. Parents can also play simple word games, showing their children that word learning is fun, as well as providing opportunities to develop their child's skills.

At home, children have more chances for extended one-to-one conversations that follow their own interests. This allows them to link vocabulary to their own knowledge, thus developing their own personal understanding.

Families who have English as an additional language (English language learners) benefit from the same approaches as their monolingual peers, but they just need a little extra support. A strong basis in the home language will enhance the learning of English, so the use of the home language should be promoted. Families should be encouraged to play the games in their home language, thus supporting children to develop their vocabulary in both the home and the school language.

This chapter provides starter ideas for engaging with families about vocabulary. You can add many more activities to raise interest and motivation in your whole school community by building vocabulary into existing methods, or adapting the ideas provided, so that they work for both your school and families. Whatever you choose to do, make sure that families are involved.

Getting started

Begin by telling families about the Word Aware approach and inform them about the key principles (using page 219 and/or 220-221 to give the information to families). Build their interest by holding a launch event such as a 'Word Workshop for Families' (see the next section). Keep families updated as you progress by involving them in as many vocabulary-related activities as possible, whether this is further information sessions, easy-to-do homework or ideas in newsletters.

Word Workshop for Families

Word workshops are a valuable way to inform families about, and get them involved with, vocabulary. The content and structure will need to be tailored to suit different-aged children, so only a brief outline of the content to convey is provided here.

Information to convey to families

Vocabulary is important because it is closely connected with reading and writing. Children need to be able to understand words if they are to develop their understanding of what they read: 'Literacy floats on a sea of talk' (based on Britton, 1970). Children learn many important concepts in the Early Years, such as **different**, **before** and **many**, which form the basis of later learning in subjects such as history, mathematics and science.

In the Early Years, children learn the meaning of words by hearing them in sentences. The more times they hear them used by different people at different times, the more children can learn. School and families working together gives children the best chance to learn words.

Children are good at learning words but they need a little extra help. In the Early Years setting, there will be lots happening to develop children's vocabulary. You may then outline specifically the elements of Word Aware that you are implementing. At home, families can actively support this work by understanding six principles:

1 Words are important.

2 Home support for vocabulary makes a difference.

3 Have fun with words.

4 It is about talking as much as reading and writing.

5 When talking about words, use comments rather than ask questions.

6 Do a little every day.

This information is available as handouts and three posters on pages 220–7. They are also downloadable from the website.

Families of children with English as an additional language (English language learners)

The Word Aware approach will do much to support children with English as an additional language (English language learners) but by engaging with families, this can be enhanced. Where at all possible a workshop should be held for families in their most proficient language, which may not be English. The key principle to convey is that a strong home language supports English language learning.

Families are encouraged to use their strongest language to play the word games in this chapter, as well as other language activities such as telling traditional tales. Many families have a strong focus on literacy skills, so it is important to stress the role of speaking and listening. These activities can all be played in any language because having a good understanding of a word in one language will aid word learning in another.

When a specific target word is sent home, encourage parents to translate the word and discuss its meaning in their home language. It is straightforward for children to learn an English label for a concept they have a thorough understanding of in their home language. For instance, if a child learns what **rough** means in Somali, he understands the meaning and its application. Therefore, it is much easier for him to learn the English word **rough** than if he had no understanding of it in his first language.

Books expose children to a rich range of words and so, where possible, children should have books read to them in their first language. Traditional tales and songs will also give children important vocabulary learning opportunities.

- Children need to hear a good language model.
- Adults need to speak to children in the language they are truly fluent in.
- A strong home language supports English language learning.

Information sheet for families

Key principles to help your child learn words

- **Words are important**
  To learn well at school, children need to understand and speak many words. In particular: to progress with reading, children need to understand the words they read; to write well, they need a wide and varied use of words; in subjects such as maths and science, they need to understand the specific terms used.

- **Home support for vocabulary makes a difference**
  Children will learn words in their Early Years setting, but if they also come across these words at home, they will learn them faster and better. Home and school working together gets to a place neither can alone.

- **Have fun with words**
  By playing word games, children are also learning about words. We all know that children learn best when they are enjoying themselves. You do not need fancy games or gadgets to develop vocabulary; you just need a little conversation. Anyone can do that.

- **It is about talking as much as reading and writing**
  Speaking and listening are the foundation skills for reading and writing. If your child has the word in their spoken vocabulary, it is much easier to understand when they come across it in reading. When reading with your child, talk about the words in the book.

- **When talking about words, use comments rather than questions**
  Your child will come home with some activities to help learn new words, or specific words to talk about. To learn a word, your child needs to hear it lots of times first. Use the new word in the activities and in conversation, so that your child hears you use it. If they use the new word, notice and say, 'Well done'. Avoid just asking, 'What does that mean?' because if he or she is still learning the word, this will put them under pressure and may put them off.

- **Do a little every day**
  Word learning can happen everywhere, so build it into your routine, whenever and wherever it works for you. There will be times in the street, in the car and at bus stops when you can play a little word game. Stick the words your child is learning on your fridge, so that you remember to use them from time to time. Do whatever works for you, but do it every day.

Information sheet for families

How to help your child learn words

Things to remember

1 Words are important.
2 Home support for vocabulary makes a difference.
3 Have fun with words.
4 It is about talking as much as reading and writing.
5 When talking about words, use comments rather than ask questions.
6 Do a little every day.

Everyday things you can do to support vocabulary

You do not need expensive toys or gadgets to develop your child's vocabulary. You are the best word-learning toy there is!

Reading and talking

Books are an excellent source of interesting vocabulary. Reading to your child from an early age, and continuing to support their reading, is an effective way in which you can support vocabulary development.

Build on this by talking about word meanings.

- Are there any words that are new to your child?
- Are there any interesting words that your child likes?
- Are there good describing or action words?

Find words that sound funny. Find words that mean … By building this into your reading routine, you are developing your child's vocabulary.

New words from school

The words your child is learning about at school will be displayed somewhere so that you can see them. This might be on the window, door or board as you come in. Ask a staff member if you cannot see them. As your child is still just learning these words, it is best if you use the word in sentences and talk about them, rather than ask 'What does that mean?' If you want your child to use a word in a sentence, he or she must hear the word in sentences many times.

Listen, praise and add an extra word

Listen carefully to the words your child is using and look for opportunities to praise and add words. When he or she uses a new word, let them know by commenting on their word choice: 'What a great word!' If your child plays it safe and uses the same words repeatedly, give them alternatives. For instance: if the child says, 'I made a **big** tower', the parent says, 'Let me see your tower. It is **big** and it is **tall**.'

Learn a few simple word games

There might be times in the day when you do not have anything to play with, eg on journeys or when waiting. Use this 'dead time' to play word games. They will keep little minds occupied as well as being fun.

Information sheet for families

Daily activities to support word learning

- **You don't need anything special to develop your child's vocabulary.**
- **It's how you talk that makes the difference.**
- **Children need to hear a word many times before they use it, so do a little every day and you will notice change.**

Top tips for developing vocabulary

- **Follow your child's lead**: talk about what your child is focused on.
- **Take turns talking with your child**: a conversation should be balanced with both you and your child taking turns. Don't use too many words. Stopping and listening to your child is equally as important as talking.
- **Use a range of words**: introduce new words to your child, but make sure they are still at the right level. Vocabulary learning is a step-by-step process.
- **Explain what new words mean**: if you use a word your child does not know, explain it in simple terms he or she does know. Relate your explanations to experiences and knowledge your child has.

Things to do every day

Talk about where you are going

On the way somewhere, talk about where you are going and what you will see. Let your child join in as well. In this way, your child hears lots of new vocabulary. On the way home, or another time, talk about what you saw.

Touch, taste and smell

When your child tastes or smells something, use words to describe it other than **nice** or **bad**, eg **creamy** or **bitter**. As they touch interesting things, describe how it feels, using more precise words such as **rough** or **cosy**.

Cooking

Cook with your child and talk about what you are doing. Use interesting words such as **blending**, **rising** and **sprinkle**. It doesn't have to be special biscuits or cakes: get them to help with preparing meals.

Stories

Stories come from books, but they also come from people! Read stories, retell stories you know and make up stories. Talk about past events and let your child join in. Highlight interesting words in books or add your own to your stories.

Play

Play takes children to imaginary places, so join in the journey. Listen to your child and add some talk as you are playing. From time to time, include a new word. You don't have to play for a long time: a few minutes is fine.

(Source: www.hanen.org)

Word games to play at home

These word games can be played anywhere by all family members. As well as being fun, they also help to develop vocabulary.

Word rounds

Choose **one** of the following:

- a noun category – for example, **animals**
- an attribute – for example, things that are **shiny**
- an action – for example, something you can **cut**
- a place – for example, a **beach**.

Go round the circle, asking each person for items that fit the description. Encourage complete answers, such as 'I can cut paper', 'I can cut my hair.' An example for 'things that we find at the beach' might be: 'At the beach I found … **sand**, **pebbles**, **sea**, **ice-cream** and **towels**.'

What did you see in the picture?

Present a busy picture with lots happening in it. Everyone should look at it closely. After a few moments, remove it from view and then take it in turns to recall what they saw in as much detail as possible. If they cannot remember all of the items, give useful clues such as what the object can do or its category, rather than what it looks like.

'I Spy' variation

This is a variation on the traditional 'I Spy' game. You can adapt it by using adjectives (describing words) instead, such as, 'I spy something coloured **red / blue** …' or 'something **round / spiky/ shiny** …' or 'I spy something that is **big / beautiful / smelly / growing / hot / noisy** …'

Category call-out

On the bus or in the car, think of a category. You can choose any topic but here are some ideas for inspiration: 'living things', 'things with wheels', 'things with circles' or 'things made of metal'. Work as a team to see how many things you can see in a set time, such as two minutes. Next time, see if you can beat your previous total.

I went shopping

This game is good for developing memory, so it is good for adults too. One person starts by saying, 'I went shopping and I bought …' (names a food item). The second player says, 'I went shopping and I bought …' and repeats the first player's item before adding their own. The third player continues saying the first two items before adding their own. And so on. See how many items you can remember. A variation of this game is 'I went on holiday and I packed …'

Information sheet for families

Vocabulary homework

Your child's vocabulary will develop faster if you get involved. Homework will be simple things that do not require too much effort.

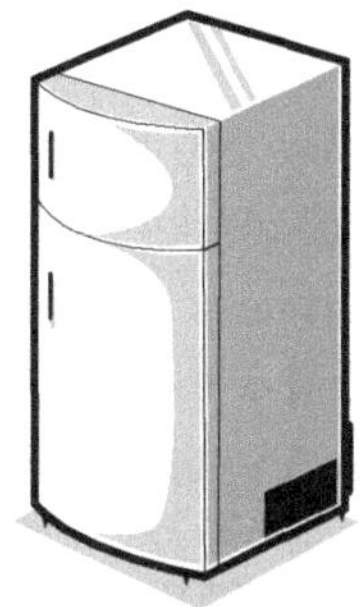

Fridge words

Your child will come home with words they are learning. Stick these on the fridge or somewhere you all see every day. Use the words in sentences when you can. Your child needs to hear new words lots of times before they start using them. Asking 'What does this word mean?' is not helpful.

Objects from home

Sometimes you may be asked to send an object from home which shows a word that is being learned at school. These will often be describing words such as **furry**, **flat**, **spiky** or **tiny**. Encourage your child to join in the search at home looking for suitable objects.

Photographs

We may ask you to take a photo of your child or their toys, showing what a new word means, and send the photo to school. This could be your child **escaping** out of the front door, holding their most **precious** teddy bear or being all **cosy**, wrapped up in a blanket.

On-the-way-home challenges

Some of the suggestions we will send you ask you to look out for things on the way home. For example, 'On the journey home, talk about things you see that there are **lots** of. It might be **lots of** cars, **lots of** people or **lots of** dogs.'

Special challenges

From time to time, we will also send home special activities to do. As with all of these activities, the aim is to have fun as well as learn. Do the activities for a few minutes once or twice.

General pointers

When introducing your child to new words, make sure that you use the words lots of times as this will help your child. Avoid asking lots of questions. Also avoid using opposites at the same time.

For instance, when introducing **behind**, instead of using **behind** and **in front**, use **behind** and not **behind** until your child has got a really good understanding of **behind**.

Information sheet for families

Reading and vocabulary

Children who read well and read for pleasure develop the biggest vocabularies. Set up your child for life by reading to him or her every day. Focus on vocabulary by following the prompts set out on the bookmarks we will send home from school.

There are two different bookmarks that you can use with your child. Both can be used with any book you are reading with your child.

The first bookmark (left) involves looking for different types of words.

The second bookmark (right) focuses on looking out for new words.

Word Aware Different Words

When you have finished reading, do one of these challenges.

Find a word that your child likes. Why do they like it?

Find an action word and act it out together.

Find a describing word. Think of something else you could describe using this word, eg:

blue freezing glowing

Find a word your child hasn't seen or heard before. Talk about what it means.

Find words for different ways of talking. Have fun by saying the same sentence in different ways.

Word Aware New Words

These ideas can be used when you are reading and talking about books with your child.

Before you read the book, say, 'Let's look out for new words that you've never heard before.'

Once in a while, stop and ask, 'Did you hear any new words?'

If your child says 'Yes', talk about that word's meaning.

If your child says 'No', identify a word you think might be tricky. Talk about what the word means.

(Source: based on Britton, 1970)

Learning words together

It is about talking as much as reading and writing.

Talk about what you are doing.

Talk about what you read.

Have fun with words.

Play word games.

When talking about words, adults should use comments rather than ask questions.

What does 'cosy' mean? ✗

That bed looks 'cosy'. I bet it's nice and warm. ✓

Children need to understand words to understand what they are reading.

Children will also need words to understand science, maths and other subjects.

Children learn best if teachers and families work together.

If you speak other languages at home, talk about words in your own language. Play games, or translate English words into your own language.

Learning words together

At school we will be working hard to learn more words.

We will be letting you know about which words we will be learning in school. Try not to ask, 'What does it mean?' Instead use these words in sentences.

Have fun with words. Play the games that we send home, but also play any word games that you know. You can play word games in any language.

Words are for speaking as well as reading. Talk about words as well as reading and writing them.

If you want to know more about supporting your child to learn words, speak to your child's teacher.

Chapter 9
Visual Summary of Word Aware

Chapter 9
Visual Summary of Word Aware

To implement Word Aware in an Early Years setting effectively, all team members need to share a common understanding of the approach.

Ideally, everyone would read this book from cover to cover. However, with all of the competing pressures that Early Years practitioners face on a daily basis, this is highly unlikely. An alternative is for an individual or a small group of 'experts' who have developed a more in-depth knowledge to share their expertise with other people.

To help with this process, there is a series of visual summaries on the following pages. These summaries are not a substitute for reading the earlier chapters in full but they are a prompt and a useful format for sharing with colleagues.

All of the visual summaries on pages 231–9 are also available on the website at **www.routledge.com/cw/speechmark.**

Training from the authors or other accredited trainers is also available. There is information about training courses at

Website: www.thinkingtalking.co.uk

Email: thinkingtalking@yahoo.co.uk

Make words count

Develop a language-enriched environment.

Concepts

Develop the understanding of concepts such as **quiet**, **soft**, **between**, **narrow**.

Word detective

Encourage the children to ask about words they do not know.

Involving families

Key messages to convey to parents are:

- Vocabulary is important.
- Home support for vocabulary makes a difference.
- Have fun with words.
- It is about talking as much as reading and writing.
- When talking about words, use comments rather than ask questions.

Fun with words

Play word games, any word games. This will engage children in word learning, can be used to review words and builds up word-learning skills.

Direct teaching (STAR)

- **Select** really useful words that will be encountered again.
- **Teach** the word using a multisensory approach, making it fun and interactive.
- **Activate** the word by using the word in context, in play.
- **Review** the word to make sure the child remembers it.

Supporting children with higher needs

Identify children who may need additional support in understanding and using words. Provide additional small group interventions to develop word learning.

Introduction

Chapter 1

Why use Word Aware?

- Why is vocabulary important?
- How can we make a difference with vocabulary?
- How can we support word learning for children with EAL (ELL)?

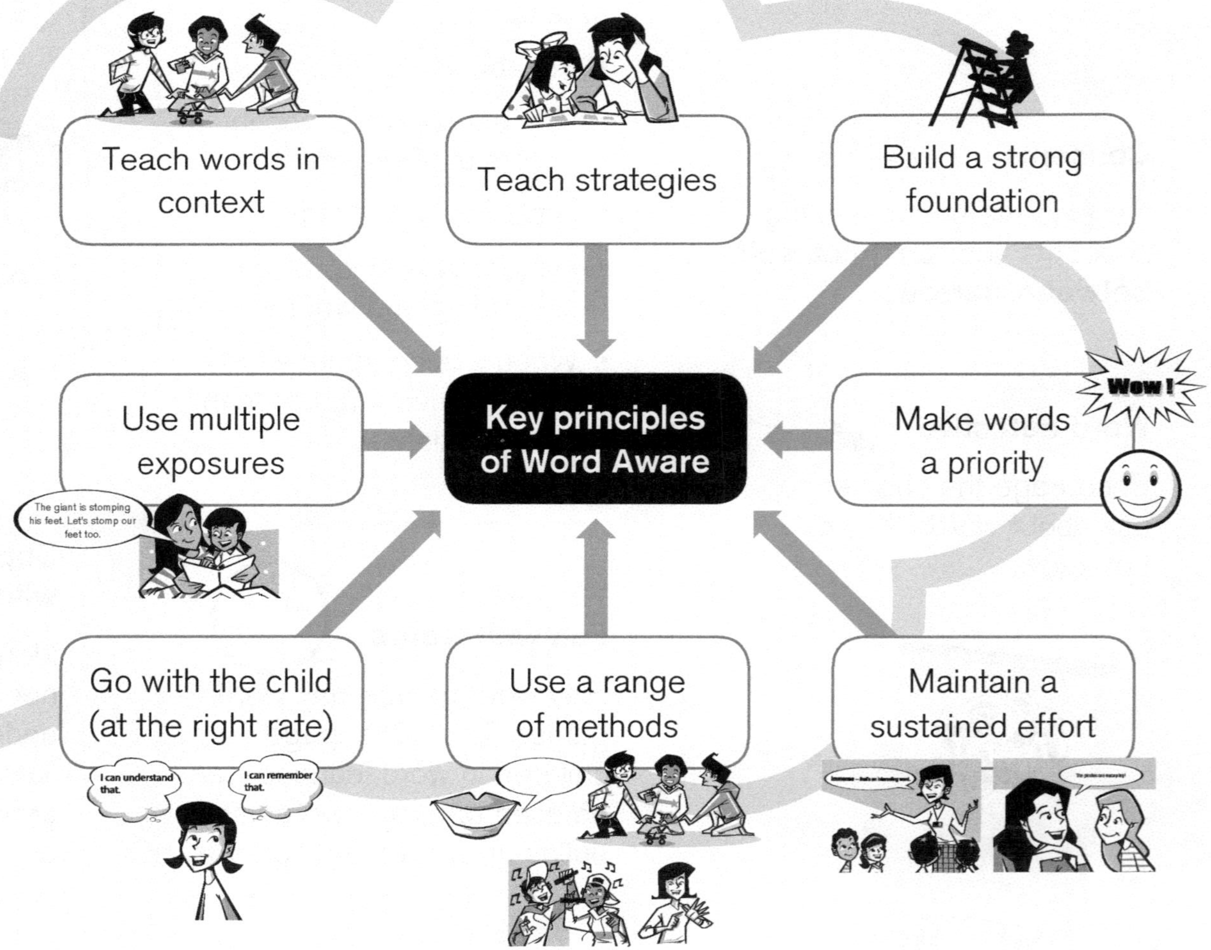

Make Words Count

Chapter 2

Promote language

- Adapt the environment
- Develop adult–child interaction
- Promote peer interaction
- Support language use in play
- Read and act out stories
- Use open questions
- Target children who have limited language
- Provide a clear structure to the day

Make sure children know that both spoken and written words are important

- Appreciate authors' use of vocabulary
- Highlight interesting words in books
- Prominently label vocabulary
- Use symbols
- Reinforce interesting words
- Highlight key words before doing a task
- Hold events to promote words

Facilitate word learning beyond the classroom

- Involve parents and carers
- Think about vocabulary on school outings or when walking or travelling somewhere

Expose children to a rich, wide and appropriately demanding vocabulary

- Adults use vocabulary at the right level
- Engage in extended conversations with children
- Expose children to a range of books, including audio books

Make word learning fun

- Play games
- Enjoy words!

Direct Teaching (STAR)

Chapter 3

SELECT

Pick a Goldilocks word:

- 'Not too easy and not too hard, but just right.'
- A word that is really useful and will be encountered again.
- Pick words from the topic or from a shared book.

TEACH

Teach the word using a multisensory approach:

Use a symbol

Do an action

Clap the syllables

Sing a song or rap

Say it to your partner

Display the word on a Word Wall to remind adults to use it

Expand the meaning by experiencing the word giving a simple definition, telling a story and relating the word to what children already know

ACTIVATE

Use the word in context in the classroom to help the children learn more about the meaning of the word, eg adults use the words in play, do sorting activities or go on treasure hunts.

REVIEW

Make sure the word is heard again so that its meaning grows and it's not forgotten by using a range of methods:

Word Bag Games Parents

Concepts (STAR)

Chapter 4

SELECT

Select concepts that are Goldilocks words from the topic, a literacy book or the concept list.

Make sure you don't teach opposites at the same time. Eg: teach **behind** and not **behind** rather than **behind** and **in front**.

TEACH

Teach the word using a multisensory approach:

Use a sign or a gesture

Say it to your partner

Use a symbol

Act out the Concept Cat story

Sing a song or rap

An activity that uses objects to experience the concept

An activity that allows children to physically experience the word but does not use objects (where possible)

ACTIVATE

Set up activities within the classroom or outdoors so that children can get hands-on experience and link new learning to what they know.

REVIEW

Build simple ways to review words into the class routine so they are not forgotten. For each new word, place a related object in the Word Bag, make a concept book and send an activity home for families.

Fun with Words

Chapter 5

Word games help build up speech sound and meaning skills

Eg for speech sound: **caterpillar** or **zaterpillar**

Draw a picture of a familiar word (such as caterpillar) and then draw a crazy looking counterpart. Label the second picture with a rhyming word (eg zaterpillar). Ask children to point to the word you say.

For meaning: **scavenger hunt**

Encourage children to look around and find anything that has a particular attribute, eg has **wheels**, is **shiny**, has a **tail**, is **soft**, is **bendy** or is **small**. Bring them back to one place and compare the objects that children have found.

Use games to review words you have already taught

Eg **Five things**

Show children an object or a picture. Discuss what you all know about it. Once five suitable suggestions have been made, say and act them out all together.

Eg for **astronaut**: '**Astronauts** can go in a rocket. **Astronauts** can walk on the Moon. **Astronauts** can explore outer space. **Astronauts** can land the spaceship. **Astronauts** are really smart.' Accompany each sentence with an action.

Children who enjoy words are better word learners

Eg **'I Spy' variation**

A variation on the traditional 'I Spy' game. Adapt it by using adjectives instead, such as: 'I spy something coloured **red / blue** …' or 'something **round/ spiky/ shiny** …', or 'something that is **big/ beautiful/ smelly/ growing/ hot/ noisy** …'

Supporting Children with Higher Needs

Chapter 6

Spot children who aren't using many words

- Parent questionnaire
- Concept assessment
- Use the flow charts in the book to work out what intervention children need
- Additional charts and formats for children who speak English as an additional language (English language learners)

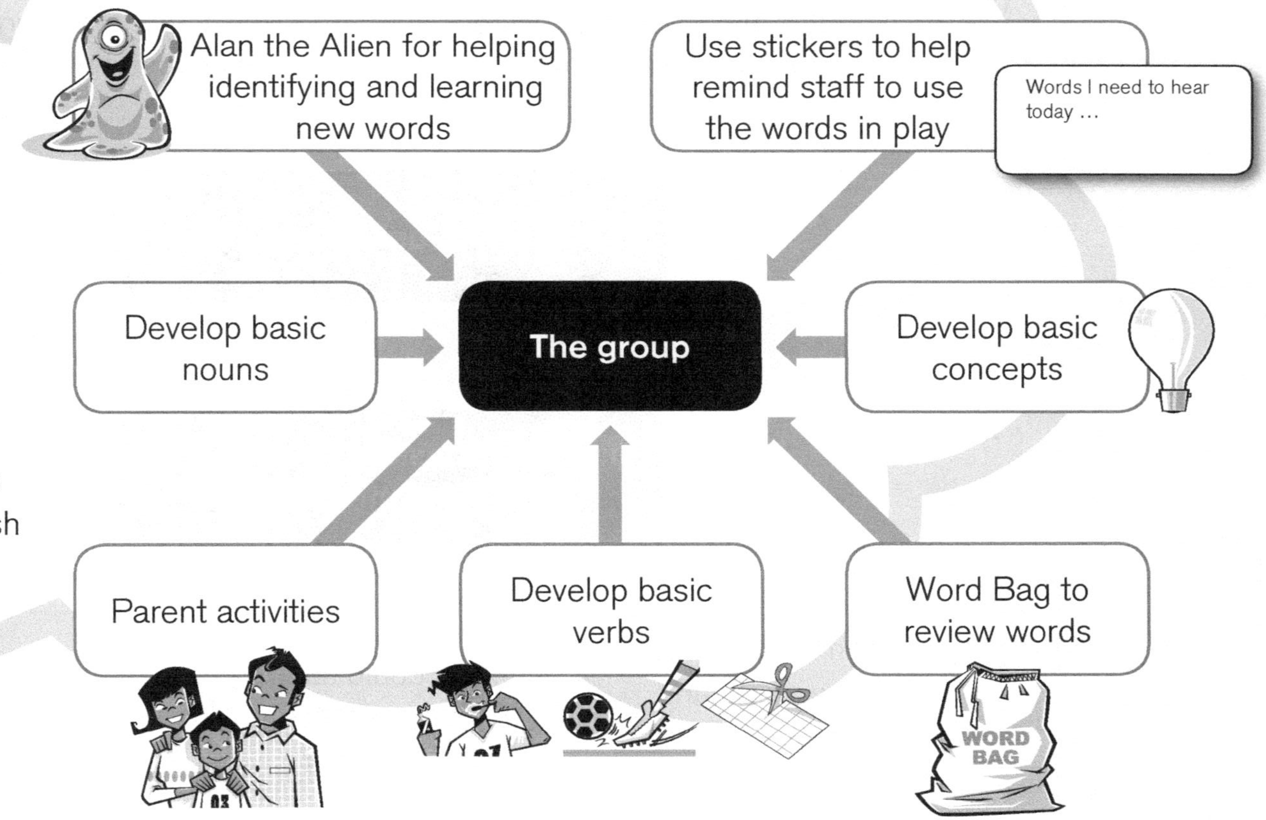

Word Detective

Chapter 7

Alan the Alien: helping children identify 'alien' words.

'That's an interesting word'. 'I wonder what it means'.

'Did you hear any new words'?

Identifying unknown words

'Let's look out for new words'.

If a child doesn't know a word: encourage them to ask.

'I don't know what that word means. Let's go and ask someone'.

You could say 'What does that word mean'?

Involve families in encouraging children to ask about new words

Involving Families

Chapter 8

Information to convey to parents

- Words are important.
- Home support for vocabulary makes a difference.
- Have fun with words.
- It is about talking as much as reading and writing.
- When talking about words, use comments rather than questions
- Do a little every day.

Support parents with

- Developing vocabulary while reading.
- Reinforcing vocabulary at home.
- Playing word games at home.
- Carrying out daily activities to support word learning.

Emphasise to parents that 'literacy floats on a sea of talk' (based on Britton, 1970).

Appendix

Appendix

Contents

STAR Select Vocabulary Planning

Topic:			
	 **Anchor words**	 **Goldilocks words** 'Not too easy and not too hard, but just right'	 **Step on words**
	Children have a thorough understanding of these words. Everyday spoken language for a child of this age. Used at home and in daily interactions.	**Really useful words** Likely to be encountered again. Average **older child*** has a **good** level of knowledge of the word. Words that are very topic-specific but core to the topic.	Less likely to be encountered again. Average **older child*** does **not have much** knowledge of the word. Words that are particularly topic-specific and not core to the topic.
Nouns			
Verbs			
Adjectives			
Other			

* An older child is defined as a child 2–3 years older than the children are currently.

(Source: adapted from Stahl & Nagy, 2005; Beck *et al*, 2002)

Fridge words

These are words that your child has been learning. Stick them on the fridge or somewhere you can see them every day. Your child needs to **hear** new words lots of times before they start to use them. Asking, 'What does this word mean?' is not helpful. **Use these words** whenever you can.

Word Aware songs

All of these songs can be used with any word. Just put your target word in the blanks.

Most of the songs have just one version. However, 'Clap the Word' has different versions depending on the number of syllables in the word.

There are two songs that are solely for verbs ('This Is the Way We' and 'We Are') and one song to introduce Concept Cat.

The songs can also be downloaded from **www.routledge.com/cw/speechmark** or Word Aware on Youtube. Blank songs and example songs are provided.

Clap That Word!

Hey hey ____________

Clap that word

____

Clap that word

____

Clap that word

____

That's it ____________

Jump Up High

Start down low ______________,

____

Move up more ______________,

____

A little bit more ______________,

____

Standing straight ______________,

____

Jump up high ______________,

____

Aaaaaahhhhhh!

What's the Word Today?

1 2 3 4 One, two, three, four.

What's the word today?

________________________________,

____

What's the word today?

________________________________,

____

What's the word today?

________________________________,

____

The Word for Today

The word for today is

______________ , ______________ ,

____

The word for today is

______________ , ______________ ,

____

Word Rap

Oh ah, say the word

____

Oh ah, clap the word

____

Oh ah, act the word

____

Oh ah, shout the word

____

Oh ah, whisper the word

____

Yes!

The Word to Learn Today

The word to learn today is

____

The word to learn today is

____

The word to learn today,
is what you want to say

The word to learn today is

____

Concept Cat

Meow! Concept Cat is a clever, clever cat.

He looks here, he looks there, learning as he goes. Meow!

And, when he comes home, he tells us a story.

Concept Cat is a clever, clever cat.

(This is a sung version of the introduction to Concept Cat.)

This Is the Way We

This song is only for verbs that are used with objects (transitive verbs).

  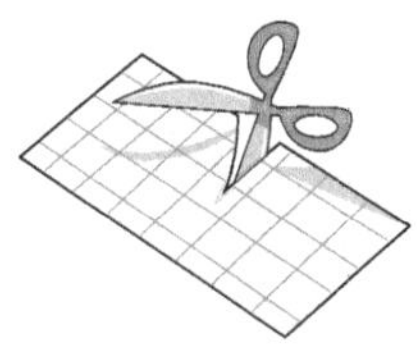

This is the way we ________ a ________ , we

________ a ________ , ________ a ________ .

This is the way we ________ a ________

we ________ , we ________ , we ________ ,

we ________ , we ________ , we ________

a ________ .

Variations could include: brush our teeth, sweep the floor, kick a ball, eat an apple, play a game, throw a ball, bake a cake, ride a bike, build a tower, make a picture, climb a hill, munch a biscuit, stir the soup, buy a drink, catch a ball.

We Are Looking, Listening, Learning

We are looking, listening, learning

________ we are ________, ________, ________

We are looking, listening, learning

________ we are ________, ________, ________

That's it!

This song is for verbs.

Blank concept planning sheet

Symbol

Concept ______________

1 **Teach**	 Use a sign or gesture.  Look at the symbol together.  Say the word to your partner.  Sing a Word Aware song including the word.
2 **Teach** 	**Equipment:** Concept Cat is a clever, clever cat. He looks here, he looks there, learning as he goes and, when he comes home, he tells us a story. Concept Cat is a clever, clever cat. This story is all about ____________ . Listen out for the word ____________ . Concept Cat, what a clever, clever cat. He knows all about ____________ .
3 **Teach**	
4 **Activate**	
5 **Review**	 **Activity:**  **Word Bag:**  **Concept book:**  **Family:**

Early Years concepts

	Level 1	Page	Level 2	Page	Level 3	Page
Size	big little fat	91 120 104	long short tall small large	121 142 150 145 114	thick thin wide narrow	151 152 158 126
Touch/look	dry wet	99 156	hard soft	111 147	shiny rough smooth	141 138 146
Sound	noisy quiet loud	132 137 123				
Movement	fast slow	103 144	quick	136		
Space	in out under behind top bottom	113 134 155 87 154 94	through near between side front back over around next to	153 127 90 143 108 84 135 83 130	above below forwards backwards	80 88 107 85
Quantity	empty full more lots	101 109 124 122	some less (a) bit all most	148 117 92 82 125	both few enough half whole	93 105 102 110 157
Order			first last	106 115	second next	140 129
Time			after before day night	81 86 97 131	early later	100 116
Comparison			old new same different	133 128 139 98		
Weight			heavy	112	light	118
Light					dark light	96 119
Shape					corner straight bendy	95 149 89
Superlatives and comparatives					bigger heavier taller longer biggest heaviest tallest longest	164 165 167 166 160 161 163 162

Note: this suggested developmental sequence should be used at the practitioner's discretion.

Noun spinner

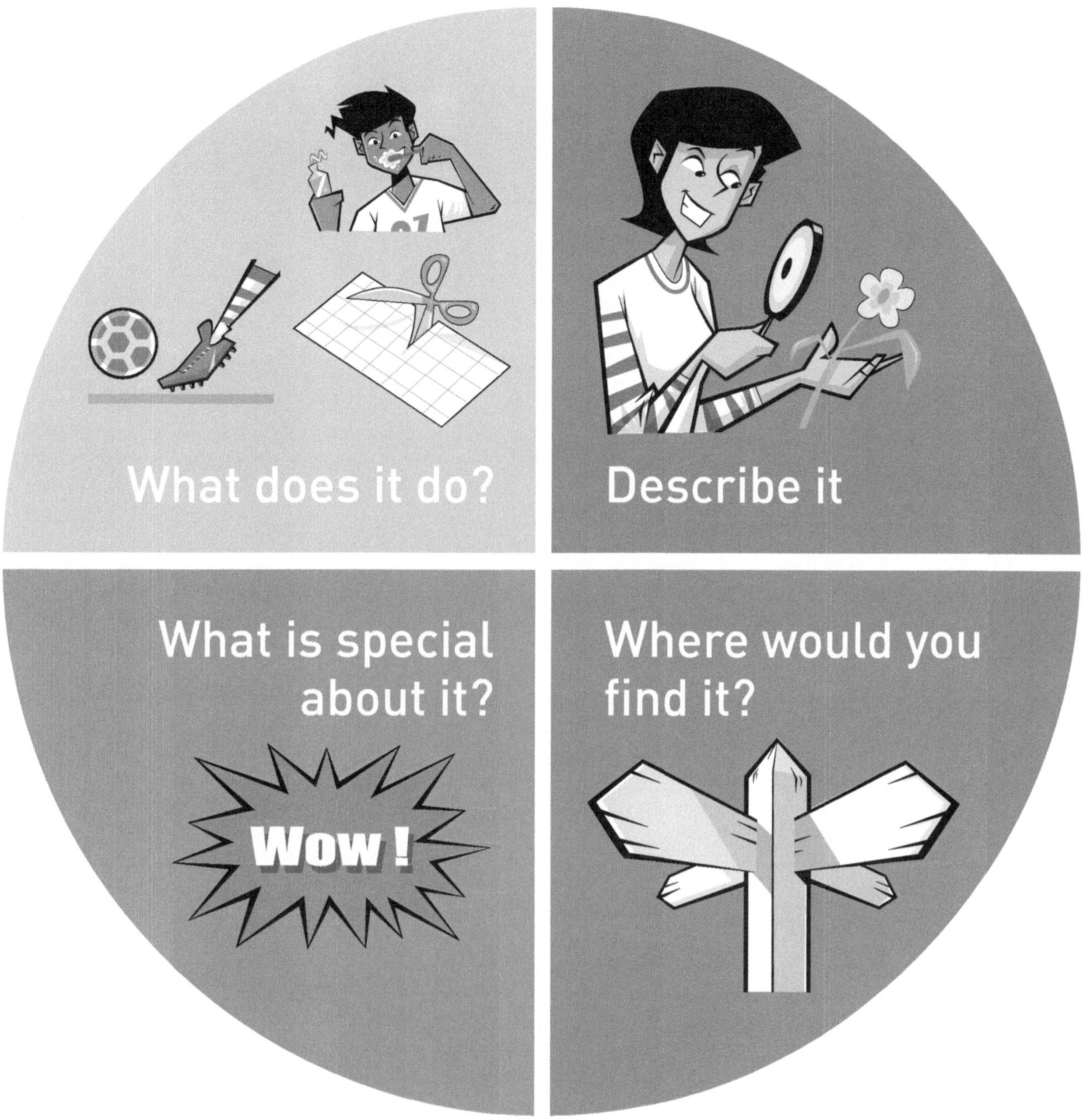

References

Andreae G (2010) *Commotion in the Ocean*, Orchard Books, London.

Antony S (2014) *The Queen's Hat*, Hodder, London.

Australian Government (2016) *Belonging, Being & Becoming – The Early Years Learning Framework for Australia*, online, www.dss.gov.au/our-responsibilities/families-and-children/publications-articles/belonging-being-becoming-the-early-years-learning-framework-for-australia (accessed January 2016).

Beck I, McKeown M & Kucan L (2002) *Bringing Words to Life: Robust Vocabulary Instruction*, Guilford Press, New York.

Beck I, McKeown M & Kucan L (2008) *Creating Robust Vocabulary*, Guilford Press, New York.

Biemiller A (2004) 'Teaching vocabulary in the primary grades: vocabulary instruction needed', Baumann JF & Kame'enui EJ (eds), *Vocabulary Instruction: Research into Practice*, Guilford Press, New York.

Blachowicz C & Fisher P (2010) *Teaching Vocabulary in All Classrooms*, 4th edn, Allyn and Bacon, Boston, MA.

Block C & Mangieri J (2006) *The Vocabulary Enriched Classroom*, Scholastic, New York.

Britton J (1970) *Language and Learning*, University of Miami Press, Coral Gables, Florida, FL.

Brown R (2012) *A Dark, Dark Tale*, Andersen Press, London.

Browne E (1995) *Handa's Surprise*, Walker Books Ltd, London.

Burningham J (2001) *Mr Gumpy's Outing*, Red Fox, London.

Burrows B (2006) *Developing Language Concepts*, Speechmark Publishing, Milton Keynes.

Chiat S (2000) *Understanding Children with Language Problems*, Cambridge University Press, Cambridge.

Clark E (1993) *The Lexicon in Acquisition*, Cambridge University Press, Cambridge.

Collins (2006) *Collins Cobuild English Dictionary*, HarperCollins, London.

Common Core (2016) *Kindergarten. Measurement & Data*, online, www.corestandards.org/Math/Content/K/MD (accessed January 2016).

Cunningham A & Stanovich K (1997) 'Early reading acquisition and its relation to reading experience and ability 10 years later', *Developmental Psychology*, 33, 934–45.

Dodd L (2002) *Hairy Maclary from Donaldson's Dairy*, Puffin, London.

Donaldson J & Scheffler A (1999) *The Gruffalo*, Macmillan Children's Books, London.

Donaldson J & Scheffler A (2001) *A Room on the Broom*, Macmillan Children's Books, London.

Edwards S, Letts C & Sinka I (2011) *New Reynell Developmental Language Scales*, GL Assessment, London.

Fearley J (2002) *A Perfect Day for It*, Egmont Books, London.

Foundation Years (2016) *Early Years Foundation Stage Statutory Framework*, online, www.foundationyears.org.uk/eyfs-statutory-framework (accessed January 2016).

Fox M (1991) *Possum Magic*, Thomson Learning, London.

Freeman D (2014) *Corduroy*, Viking Juvenile, New York.

French J & Whatley B (2006) *Diary of a Wombat*, HarperCollins, London.

Gleeson L (2006) *Amy and Louis*, Scholastic, Lindfield, Australia.

Gross J (2013) *Time to Talk*, Routledge, London.

Hart B & Risley T (1995) *Meaningful Differences in the Everyday Experience of Young American Children*, Paul H Brookes Publishing, Baltimore, MD.

Jarman E (2013) *The Communication Friendly Spaces Approach*, Elizabeth Jarman, Bethersden, Kent.

Kerr J (1968) *The Tiger Who Came to Tea*, Harper Collins, London.

Kipling R (1901) *Kim*, Macmillan & Co. Ltd, London.

Locke A (1985) *Living Language*, NFER-Nelson, Windsor.

Marulis L & Neuman (2010) 'The effects of vocabulary intervention on young children's word learning: a meta-analysis, *Review of Educational Research*, 80, 300–35.

Murphy J (2007) *Peace at Last*, Macmillan, London.

Nash S (ed) (2013) *Communication and Language Activities*, Hinton House Publishers, Buckingham.

Ormerod J & Gardiner L (2007) *Whoosh Around the Mulberry Bush*, Oxford University Press, Oxford.

Parsons S & Branagan A (2014) *Word Aware: Teaching Vocabulary Across the Day, Across the Curriculum*, Speechmark Publishing, London.

Penn A (1993) *The Kissing Hand*, Scholastic, New York.

Rice M, Buhr J & Nemeth M (1990) 'Fast mapping word-learning abilities of language delayed pre-schooler', *Journal of Speech and Hearing Research*, 55, 33–42.

Robson S (2006) *Developing Thinking and Understanding in Young Children: An Introduction for Students*, Routledge, Abingdon, Oxon.

Rosen M (1995) *We're Going on a Bear Hunt*, Walker Books, London.

Silverstein S (2010) *The Giving Tree*, Particular Books, London.

Stahl S & Nagy W (2005) *Teaching Word Meanings*, Lawrence Erlbaum Associates, Mahwah, NJ.

Waddell M & Benson P (1994) *Owl Babies*, Walker Books Limited, London.

Waddell M & Oxenbury H (1995) *Farmer Duck*, Walker Books Limited, London.

Wasik B & Bond M (2001) 'Beyond the pages of a book: interactive book reading and language development in pre-school classrooms', *Journal of Educational Psychology*, 93, 243–50.

Wiig E & Semel E (2006) *Pre-school Clinical Evaluation of Language Fundamentals*, Pearson, London.

Zimmerman I, Evatt Pond R & Steiner V (2014) *Pre-school Language Scales*, Pearson, London.